Sam

Galaxy Note5

&

S6 edge+:

The 100% Unofficial User Guide

By Aaron J. Halbert

Version 1.0

Foreword

Thank you very much for purchasing *Samsung Galaxy Note 5 & S6 Edge+: The 100% Unofficial User Guide.* I have worked hard to compile the most relevant and useful information for you, and I firmly believe that you will get your money's worth. Better yet, when you're finished with this book, your skills and knowledge will put you among the top 1% of power users.

If you have any feedback on this book, please email me at AJH@AaronHalbert.com or post a review on Amazon. By doing so, you will help all users get the information they need, and you will also have my gratitude. I carefully read and consider all the comments I receive, because I believe in listening to my customers.

A few things before we begin:

- This book covers both the Note 5 and the S6 Edge+. The two models have almost completely identical hardware and software, except for the Note 5's exclusive S Pen features and the S6 Edge+'s exclusive Edge Screen features. All S Pen-specific information is consolidated in Chapter 6 (p. 188), "The S Pen," and all Edge-screen-specific information is consolidated in Chapter 7 (p. 213), "The Edge Screen." The remainder of the book applies equally to both models.
- Throughout this book I sometimes suggest you purchase apps or accessories to improve your Galaxy experience. I am not affiliated with any of these companies, nor do I receive any sort of compensation from them. All of my recommendations are based on my own experience and research and are completely independent. My opinion is not for sale.
- The best way to learn from this book is to follow along on your own device. You'll learn much faster if you go through the motions yourself. Reading from start to finish is not mandatory, but active participation is extremely important if you want to remember what you read.
- This book is structured very logically and sequentially. I suggest you skim the Detailed Table of Contents (p. 5) right now to get a better idea of how the book will progress.

Contents at a Glance

Detailed Contents

Chapter 1: Introduction

Thank you for purchasing *Samsung Galaxy Note 5 & S6 Edge+: The 100% Unofficial User Guide*! This book is designed to help you unlock the potential of your Galaxy regardless of your previous Android experience. If you're brand new to Android, I'll explain everything from the ground up. If you already know your way around an Android device and are looking for device-specific information, you can easily skip straight to the intermediate and advanced chapters.

> ***TIP:*** *Click any underlined text to jump to another section of this book.*
>
> *External URLs (starting with http://) are links to websites, not locations in this book. If you are reading this book on a tablet, phone, or computer, you can click http:// links to open them in your web browser. However, if you're using an e-ink Kindle device like the Paperwhite, your web browser won't be capable of opening most external links and you'll need to manually type the URL into your computer's web browser.*
>
> *To make this easier, I provide short links (e.g., http://goo.gl/8Z3Uww) for long or complicated external URLs. These are much quicker to type and take you to the same place.*

Structure of This Book

Chapter 2, About the Note 5 and S6 (p. 21) Edge+, briefly recounts the history of the Galaxy Note and Galaxy S series. In this chapter, I explain what's new and exciting with the Note 5 and S6 Edge+.

Chapter 3, Getting Started (p. 25), guides you through initial setup to get your Galaxy up and running fast.

Chapter 4, Fundamentals for New Users (p. 50), is a crash course for first-time Android users. It covers topics such as the home screen, the lock screen, and the notification panel.

Chapter 5, Basic Functions (p. 84), teaches you how to perform everyday tasks on your Galaxy such as making calls, sending emails, sending text messages, taking photos, navigating using the GPS, installing apps, and more.

Chapter 6, The S Pen (p. 188), is a special chapter dedicated to the Note 5's stylus. There are numerous S Pen-related features built into the Note 5, and this chapter explains them all.

Chapter 7, The Edge Screen (p. 213), is a special chapter dedicated to the S6 Edge+. It provides an overview of the S6 Edge+'s unique Edge Screen features and includes detailed usage instructions.

Chapter 8, Intermediate Tips & Tricks (p. 221), helps you take your Galaxy to the next level with customizations and tweaks. For example, you'll learn how to encrypt your data, how to pair Bluetooth devices, how to block unwanted calls, how to print documents, and much more.

Chapter 9, Advanced Functions (p. 278), covers power-user topics such as rooting your Galaxy, programming and using NFC tags, and connecting USB devices such as flash drives and mice.

Chapter 10, Preloaded Apps (p. 295), provides brief summaries and reviews of apps that come pre-loaded on the Note 5 and S6 Edge+. In some cases, I point you toward better alternatives.

In Chapter 11, The 50 All-Time Best Android Apps (p. 306), I recommend my 50 most-used third-party apps (i.e., apps that do *not* come pre-loaded, but are available from the Google Play Store and other sources). This chapter contains something for everyone. It's a book-within-a-book; this information is normally sold separately on Amazon as the book *The 50 All-Time Best Android Apps*, but I've included it all here in Chapter 11, 100% free, as a way of saying "thanks" for your purchase.

Finally, in Chapter 12, Accessory Shopping Guide (p. 322), I discuss the types of accessories available for the Note 5 and S6 Edge+, provide examples, and make some recommendations.

Why Buy This Book?

Although it's possible to learn your Galaxy's features through online research and experimentation, it's a lot easier and faster to use this book. It consolidates everything you need to know in one place and presents the information in a logical and sequential fashion that you won't find anywhere else.

In this book, I will tell you how each and every app and feature works, but I won't stop there. I will also tell you which are worthwhile and which are gimmicks. I will suggest third-party alternatives that I trust. You will benefit from my years of experience with Android and other mobile platforms.

Other authors might assume that you already understand core concepts, which leads to confusion and frustration. On the other hand, I make as few assumptions as possible and explain everything from the ground up. But, I believe all of my readers are smart and capable. I won't baby you; I will teach you.

I have organized this book so that you can read it cover-to-cover, or just open it to the page you need. Use the Detailed Table of Contents (p. 5) to quickly find what you're looking for. Electronic editions of this book contain hundreds of clickable bookmarks (underlined text) so you can easily jump around and read more about topics of interest. Paper editions contain references to page numbers in place of clickable bookmarks.

Simply put, if you are a brand new Android user and you don't know the Play Store from the App Drawer, this book will teach you from first principles. If you already know and love Android, this book will teach you all the particular ins and outs of your new Note 5 or S6 Edge+.

Who Am I?

Who am I, and what are my qualifications?

First, I am a bestselling tech author. Some of my previous books include:

- *Samsung Galaxy S6 and S6 Edge: The 100% Unofficial User Guide*
- *Samsung Galaxy S5: The 100% Unofficial User Guide*
- *Samsung Galaxy Note 4: The 100% Unofficial User Guide*
- *Samsung Galaxy Note 3: The 100% Unofficial User Guide*, and
- *Unlock the Power of Your Chromecast.*

Check them out on my Amazon author page:

> http://www.amazon.com/Aaron-Halbert/e/B00H20GKF0/
>
> (Short link: http://goo.gl/D7fdlb)

But more importantly, I am an Android enthusiast just like you. I have owned and used more than 10 different Android devices since Android first hit the market in 2008 on the T-Mobile G1. I have pushed each one to its limits, both in stock and rooted configurations, and I have taught countless others to do the same. In the decade before Android hit the market, I used numerous Windows Mobile and Palm OS phones and

PDAs. In fact, I got my first one in 2002. I have written for several enthusiast websites, including one popular one that I started, owned, and ran in the early 2000s. This ain't my first rodeo.

The possibilities offered by devices like the Note 5 and S6 Edge+ are amazing. The first smartphones were little more than glorified day planners; today, your Galaxy can do nearly any task that your desktop computer can do—if you know how to use it.

If you want to make the most of your new phone, read this book.

Chapter 2: About the Note 5 & S6 Edge+

Summary

A New Generation of Galaxy

Samsung is a powerful force in today's smartphone world. In fact, it's *the* biggest manufacturer of Android smartphones, and the second biggest manufacturer of smartphones overall. The only company that sells more smartphones than Samsung is—you guessed it—Apple. To provide some perspective, the market research firm comScore reported in August 2015 that Apple controlled 44% of the smartphone market, with Samsung at 28% and the distant-third-place LG at just 8%.

Both the Galaxy Note and Galaxy S series have been crucial to Samsung's market growth over the last few years. However, the simultaneous release of the Note 5 and S6 Edge+ in August 2015 represents a new direction for the company. In past years, there was always a clear distinction between the Galaxy Note and Galaxy S lines. Each year's Note model had a bigger screen and more processing power than the same year's Galaxy S model. The Note was for power users and people who needed a stylus, while the Galaxy S was for the mass market.

But this year, Samsung's blurring the lines. The Note 5 and the S6 Edge+ have almost exactly the same features, specs, screen size, and price point. The main differentiator is no longer power, but rather, the subjective choice of the Note 5's S Pen vs. the S6 Edge+'s Edge Screen. In this way, the Galaxy Note and Galaxy S lines are on equal footing for the first time. Each device brings something different to the table, but neither one objectively outclasses the other.

Here's a quick summary of what's new and exciting in the Note 5 and S6 Edge+:

- **Build Quality:** Unlike Samsung's earlier phones, there's no plastic whatsoever on the Note 5 or S6 Edge+. The phones' fronts and backs are made of durable Corning Gorilla Glass 4 and their bezels are aluminum alloy. Samsung first introduced this design with the original S6 and S6 Edge, and has now made it standard across both the Galaxy Note and Galaxy S lines. There's no doubt that the Note 5 and S6 Edge+ are the best looking and sturdiest Samsung smartphones to date.

- **Improved Fingerprint Scanner:** The Note 4 and Galaxy S5 featured a fingerprint scanner built into the button, but it was difficult to use and required an awkward finger swipe. The Note 5 and S6 Edge+'s fingerprint scanner, on the other hand, requires a simple touch and is much faster and more accurate. You can use it to unlock your phone (p. 226), automatically log into websites (p. 273), and more. This is another feature that debuted on the original S6 and S6 Edge.
- **Premium Specs:** The Note 5 and S6 Edge+ are the most powerful Samsung smartphones yet. Samsung has increased total RAM to 4 GB on both phones and packed in a super-powerful 64-bit Exynos 7420 octa-core processor.
- **Insane Screen:** The Note 5 and S6 Edge+ both feature a 5.7" screen with 2560 x 1440 QHD Super AMOLED (2K) resolution. The Note 4's screen had the same resolution, but the panels in the Note 5 and S6 Edge+ have been qualitatively improved for even brighter colors and better contrast.
- **The Best Smartphone Camera Ever**: The rear camera on the Note 5 and S6 Edge+ is identical to that on the S6 and S6 Edge. It has been lauded as one of the best smartphone cameras ever and features a premium sensor, optical image stabilization (OIS), and a large f/1.9 aperture for low-light photography. Moreover, OIS now works for video as well as stills, and you can also capture images in RAW format for advanced post processing. The front camera has the same upgraded 5MP sensor found on the S6 and S6 Edge.
- **Powered-Up Battery Charging**: The Note 5 and S6 Edge+ innovate on battery charging in several ways. First, they feature Adaptive Fast Charging, which, according to Samsung, provides four hours of juice in 10 minutes of wired charging. Second, they have built-in compatibility with all industry-standard Qi and PMA wireless charging pads (p. 328), which can be purchased for about $20. Third, and even better, both phones are also compatible with Samsung's new Fast Charge wireless pad (p. 328) (~$70), which can wirelessly charge a completely dead battery in just two hours—significantly faster than Qi or PMA.
- **Improved S Pen (Note 5 Only):** The Note 5's S Pen is better than ever before. Most notably, it has a new "Screen Off Memo" mode that's activated just by removing the S Pen, even while the device is off—just pop out the S Pen and start to take notes—no need to wake or unlock the device first. Additionally, there's a new full-length screenshot mode to take screenshots of webpages and other screens that are longer than a single screen length, and new PDF editing capabilities. And on the hardware side, Samsung has tweaked its materials to minimize friction between S Pen and screen.
- **Samsung Pay:** This might be one of my favorite features. Not only can you use your Note 5 or S6 Edge+ to pay at tap-to-pay terminals, you can also use it to wirelessly trigger magnetic swipe terminals. Yes, that means that anywhere you can

swipe a credit card, you can use your phone—wirelessly. There's no catch; just wireless magnetic wizardry. It's pretty amazing technology.

Of course, the Note 5 and S6 Edge+ also carry over plenty of other classic Samsung features, like S Health (p. 258), Download Booster (p. 249), a heart rate sensor (p. 261), ultra power saving mode (p. 254), and more. Samsung has also further slimmed down and sped up TouchWiz (p. 50), the custom interface it layers atop the core Android OS.

What's Missing

There is a price for all of these improvements. Namely, neither the Note 5 nor S6 Edge+ have Micro SD memory card slots or removable batteries, features that have long been offered on Samsung smartphones. Fortunately, I'll give you tips & tricks to work around these limitations, like using Adaptive Fast Charging (p. 268) and USB power bricks (p. 327) to mitigate the need for swappable batteries, and using USB flash drives for data storage via USB OTG (p. 291).

Also, note that neither the Note 5 nor the S6 Edge+ has the IP67 waterproofing certification found on some earlier Galaxy models, nor IR blaster functionality to let you use your phone as a remote control, nor support for MHL-to-HDMI video adapters.

The S Pen

The Note 5's distinguishing feature vis-à-vis the S6 Edge+ is its S Pen. The concept of pen input is nothing new, but the Note series revived it after a period of dormancy. In the era of Palm OS devices, nearly every PDA and smartphone came with a stylus—a plastic pen that clipped into a slot on the device and was used to interact with the monochrome or crude color LCD touchscreen. These touchscreens used resistive technology; they sensed input by measuring pressure on the screen. Although it was possible to operate these touchscreens using your thumbnail, it was much easier to use a pointy object like a stylus.

With the invention of the capacitive touchscreen—the type on all modern smartphones that senses skin contact rather than pressure—it became possible to effectively use fingertips instead of styli. The concept of pen input was abandoned and even mocked. When Steve Jobs presented the first iPhone at Macworld 2007, he remarked, "Who wants a stylus? … [Yeechhhh!] Nobody wants a stylus [anymore]."

In many ways, Jobs was right. Styli can be clumsy and easy to lose. Capacitive touchscreens improve the user experience in many ways. For example, they make thumb-based virtual keyboards possible. There is no doubt it is easier and faster to thumb-type than to peck on a virtual keyboard with a stylus, or to write one character at a time as with Graffiti in Palm OS.

At the same time, Jobs vastly oversimplified the issue. While capacitive touchscreens increase the convenience of the user experience, they also decrease input precision. The tip of your index finger is hundreds of times larger than the tip of a stylus. Jotting a quick note or sketching a diagram using a finger on a smartphone is clumsy and impractical. Human beings invented writing implements for a reason.

In this way, stylus technology in mobile devices fell by the wayside—until Samsung revived it with the Galaxy Note series. The Note 5 combines the benefits of the finger-controlled capacitive touchscreen with the benefits of a precision input device—the S Pen. The Note 5's S Pen is more powerful and refined than on any previous Galaxy Note device. See Chapter 6 (p. 188) for a comprehensive discussion of the Note 5's S Pen.

The Edge Screen

The S6 Edge+ eschews an S Pen, instead featuring a curved screen that Samsung calls the Edge Screen. The Edge Screen is about both design and functionality. Aesthetically, it breaks out of the same old boring look of modern smartphones. Functionally, it offers some new features like Night Clock (displays the time along the edge of the screen), Information Stream (displays news, weather, etc. along the edge of the screen) and more. See Chapter 7 (p. 213) for a comprehensive discussion of the S6 Edge+'s Edge Screen.

Specifications

	Note 5/ S6 Edge+	**Note 4**	**S6/S6 Edge**
Size	153.2 x 76.1 x 7.6 mm / 154.4 x 75.8 x 6.9 mm	153.5 x 78.6 x 8.5 mm	143.4 x 70.5 x 6.8 mm / 142.1 x 70.1 x 7 mm
Weight	171g / 153g	176g	138g / 132g
Screen	5.7" Quad HD Super AMOLED (2,560 x 1,440)	5.7" Quad HD Super AMOLED (2,560 x 1,440)	5.1" Quad HD Super AMOLED (2,560 x 1,440)
Storage	32/64 GB (no microSD)	32/64 GB	32/64/128 GB (no microSD)
Processor	Exynos 7420 Octa-Core	2.7 GHz Quad-Core	1.5 GHz Cortex-A53 & 2.1 GHz Cortex-A57
RAM	4GB	3GB	3 GB
Camera	16MP + OIS, 5MP Front	16MP + OIS, 3.7MP Front	16 MP+OIS, 5 MP Front
Battery	3,000 mAh (fixed)	3,220 mAh	2,550 mAh (fixed); 2,600 mAh in Edge

Chapter 3: Getting Started

Device Anatomy

Noise-Canceling
Mic
Rear
Camera
Flash
Heart
Rate
Sensor
SAMSUNG
S Pen
(N5 Only)
Microphone
Speaker
USB/Charging Port

Initial Hardware Setup

What's a SIM Card?

Before using your new Galaxy, you'll need to install a SIM card. What is a SIM card? It's a small, removable chip that contains your cell account information and lets your Galaxy connect to your carrier's network.

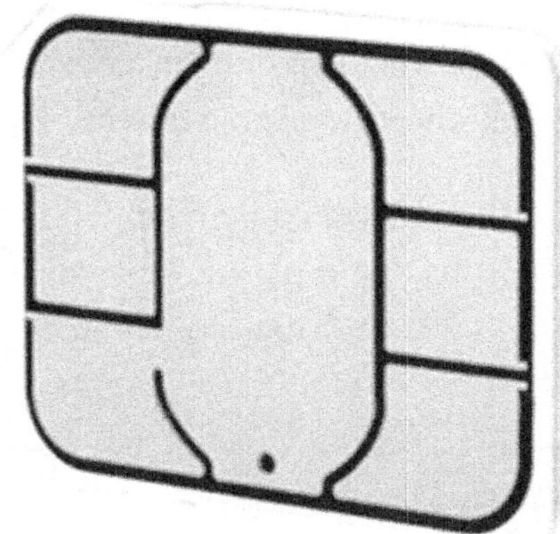

If you purchased your Galaxy brand new in a store, the salesperson most likely installed and activated your SIM for you. If your Galaxy is able to make and receive calls, then your SIM is already installed and you can skip this section.

> *TIP: A few years ago, CDMA networks like Sprint and Verizon didn't require SIM cards. However, this has changed with the introduction of 4G LTE. Your Galaxy requires a SIM card regardless of which carrier you have.*

The Note 5 and S6 Edge+ use nano-SIM cards, which are smaller than older mini-SIM and micro-SIM cards. If your previous phone used a nano-SIM card, you're in luck because you can simply swap your old card into your new Galaxy using the instructions below and it'll start working immediately. If you're not sure, just remove your SIM from your old phone (consult its instruction manual) and see if it fits your Galaxy's SIM tray. If yes, it's a nano SIM, and you're good to go. But if not, you'll need to get a nano SIM from a carrier store and call customer service to request a "new SIM activation." Note that many carriers include a free nano-SIM card with new phones, so check your Galaxy's box before going to a carrier store to purchase one.

It's also possible to convert a mini-SIM or micro-SIM card to nano SIM with a SIM cutting tool and sandpaper (really, no joke!)—but not necessarily cheaper or easier than getting a new nano SIM. I don't really recommend this method unless you know what you're doing and you have a reason not to simply get a new nano SIM. Proceed with caution if you choose to cut down your old SIM card! Search Google for instructions if you want to try this method.

Nano SIM Installation Instructions

Follow these steps to install your nano-SIM card. See below for helpful photographs of this process. You don't need to power off your Galaxy when installing a nano SIM, but you may be prompted to restart it once the nano-SIM card has been inserted.

1. If purchased new, your Galaxy will come wrapped in protective plastic. Don't peel it off yet; leave it on to protect your phone while you install the nano-SIM card.
2. Locate the SIM card removal tool that comes in the box. It's a small metal tool with a protruding pin.
3. Insert the pin into the SIM card slot's release mechanism, and gently push until the SIM card tray pops out.
4. Place your nano-SIM card into the tray, and re-insert the tray into your Galaxy. Make sure the orientation of the nano-SIM card matches the tray. The metal pins on the nano-SIM card should face down, and the flat corner should match the contour of the tray. If you have trouble re-inserting the SIM tray, stop and double check the orientation of both parts. Don't force the tray or you may damage your Galaxy.

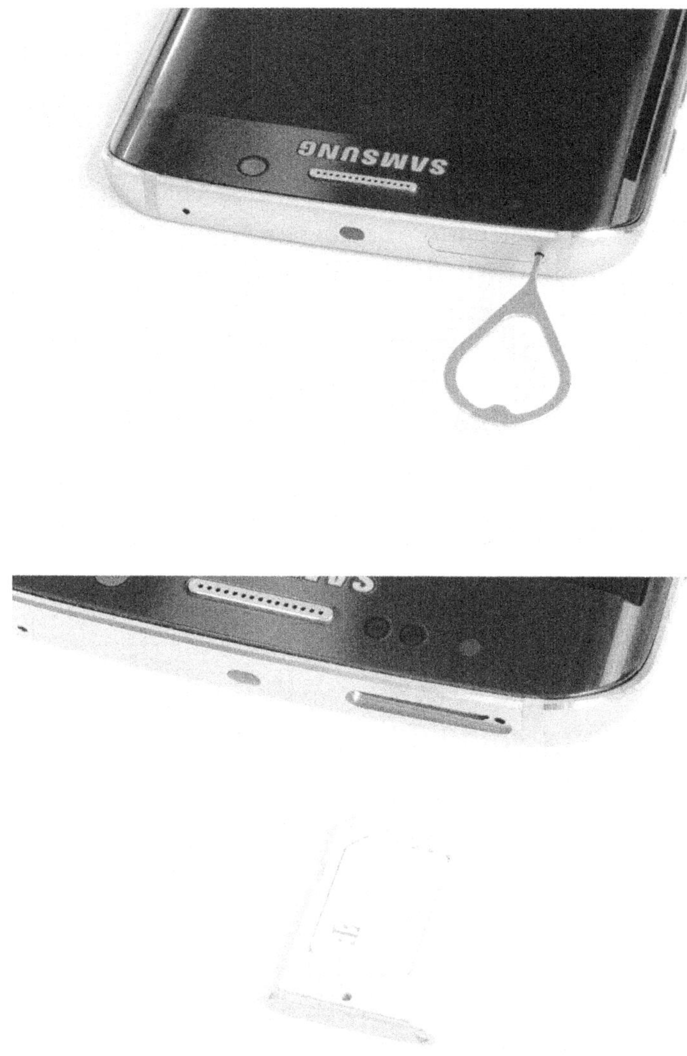

Now, you can remove the protective plastic film from your Galaxy's screen. There's also a thin and hard-to-see plastic film over the rear camera flash; make sure you remove it too.

Initial Software Setup

After you've completed the nano SIM installation process, plug in your Galaxy using the supplied power adapter and cable. An orange-red LED light on the front upper-left-hand corner of the phone will illuminate, indicating the device is charging. Turn on the Galaxy by pressing and holding the power button on the upper-right-hand edge of the device. After the device powers up for the first time, you'll see the screen pictured below.

On this screen, select your preferred language. Tap "Accessibility" if you are hard of seeing or hearing to set up some features like hearing aid support, text vocalization, and screen magnification (p. 239). Otherwise, pick your language and tap to proceed to the Wi-Fi configuration screen.

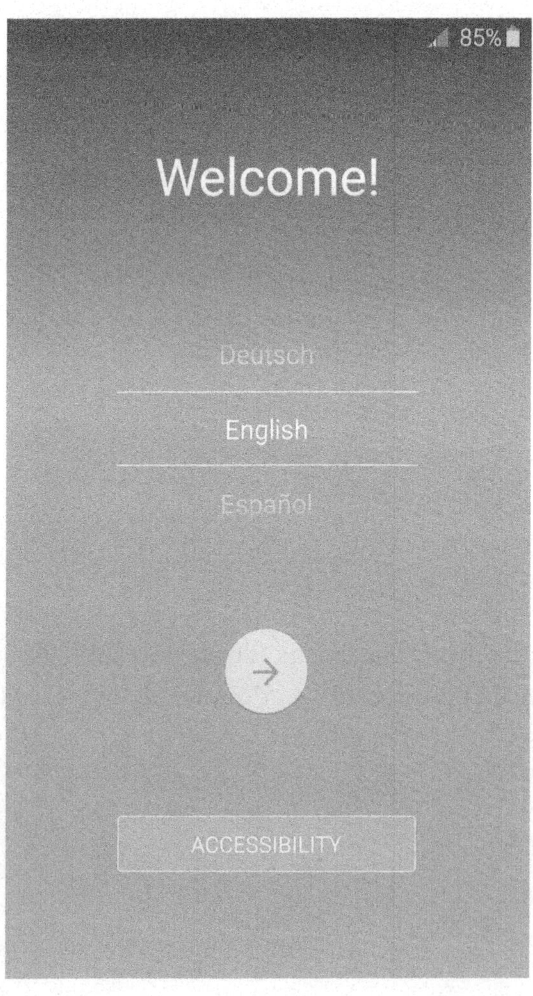

Connecting to Wi-Fi

If you have a Wi-Fi Internet connection available, first tap OFF to power on your Wi-Fi chip. Your Galaxy will search for available Wi-Fi networks and display them in a list as shown below.

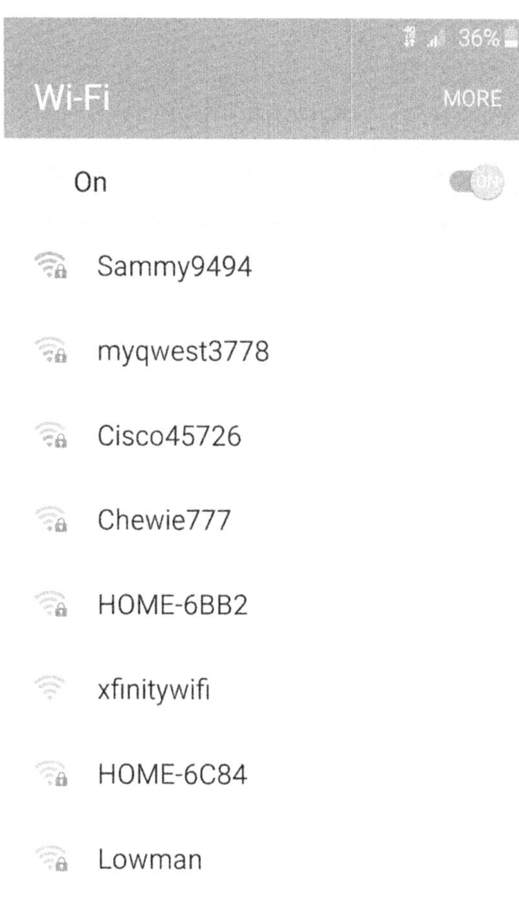

__TIP:__ If your carrier supports Wi-Fi Calling (Sprint and T-Mobile only in the United States), you may see a message about it during Wi-Fi setup. Just tap "Skip" to dismiss the message. Wi-Fi Calling lets you make and receive calls any time your Galaxy is connected to a Wi-Fi network, even when outside of cell range. If your carrier supports Wi-Fi calling, it'll be enabled by default and work automatically without any additional setup on your part. Consult your carrier if you're unsure if it offers Wi-Fi Calling.

Once you see your preferred network, tap on it. You will be prompted to enter your network's WEP/WPA password. Do so and tap "Connect." If successful, you will see a dialog box that says "Wi-Fi Connected." Tap "OK" and then NEXT >. If you enter an incorrect password, you'll be prompted to re-enter it.

If your router has a WPS button ( ), you can use it to quickly connect without entering a password. Tap MORE → "WPS push button." Then, press the button on your wireless router and your Galaxy will connect automatically.

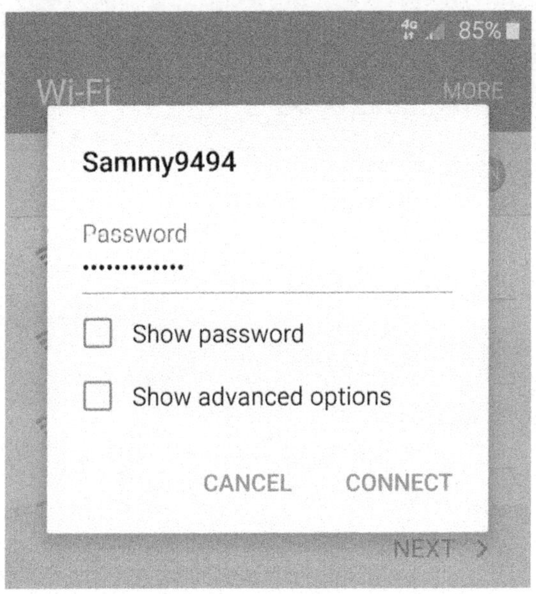

If you don't have a Wi-Fi connection available, tap NEXT > and the phone will use your carrier's wireless data connection instead. Note that this may cost you money or use up your data quota depending on your data plan. I recommend using Wi-Fi when possible.

> ***TIP:*** *If your Galaxy won't let you proceed without connecting to Wi-Fi first, it's because it doesn't yet have a cellular data connection. Give it a few minutes, or move elsewhere if you're in an area with poor cell coverage. You'll be able to proceed without a Wi-Fi connection after a cellular connection has been established.*

Accepting the Terms and Conditions

Next, you'll be prompted to accept Samsung's EULA (End User Licensing Agreement) and consent to provide diagnostic and usage data. You must accept the EULA to continue. The diagnostic and usage agreement allows Samsung to collect anonymous data to find and squash software bugs. I personally leave this feature disabled because it can slightly improve battery life. Once you've made your choice, tap NEXT > and then "Agree" to confirm.

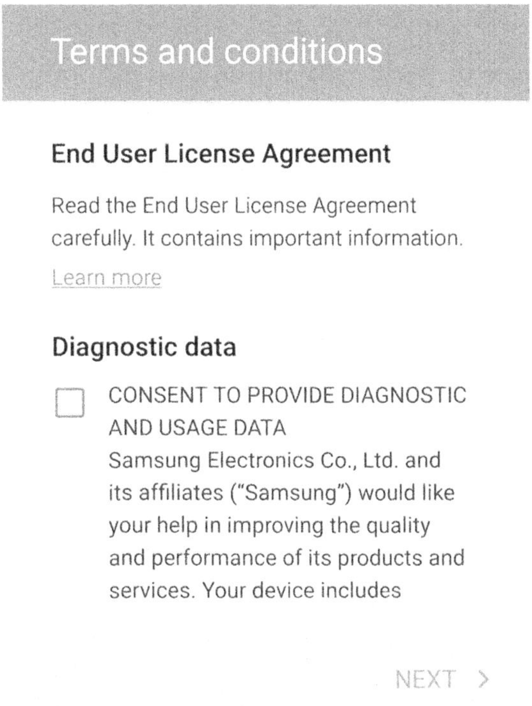

Terms and conditions

End User License Agreement

Read the End User License Agreement carefully. It contains important information.

Learn more

Diagnostic data

☐ CONSENT TO PROVIDE DIAGNOSTIC AND USAGE DATA
Samsung Electronics Co., Ltd. and its affiliates ("Samsung") would like your help in improving the quality and performance of its products and services. Your device includes

NEXT >

After tapping NEXT >, your Galaxy will verify your Internet connection and check for over-the-air (OTA) operating system updates. If one is available, tap through the dialog boxes to install it.

TIP: *At some point during the setup process, you may be prompted to enable Google's app verification service. Make sure you tap "Accept." Verify Apps is an official Google feature that runs in the background and protects your Galaxy from harmful and invasive applications. If a problem app is detected, you will be notified and prompted to remove it. Sometimes, this prompt does not appear until after the setup process, when you try to install an app from the Google Play Store.*

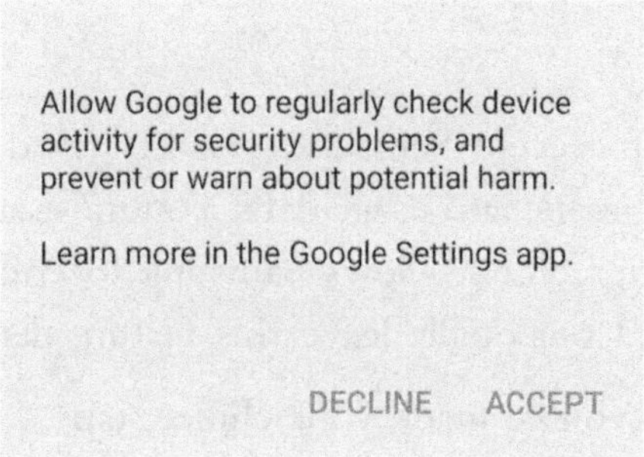

Allow Google to regularly check device activity for security problems, and prevent or warn about potential harm.

Learn more in the Google Settings app.

DECLINE ACCEPT

Transferring Data from Your Old Android Device Using Tap & Go

Next, you'll have a chance to transfer data from your old Android device using Google's "Tap & Go" data restore feature. Tap & Go is a new feature in Android 5.0 Lollipop, and I'm a fan. It works far better than the old restoration process in Android 4.0 Kit Kat, which was unreliable and unpredictable.

Tap & Go copies over your Google account, installed apps, Wi-Fi passwords, and system settings from your previous Android device with minimal hassle. Note, however, that it does *not* transfer Gallery photos or text messages, so you'll have to transfer those separately using Samsung Smart Switch (p. 82).

> ***TIP:*** *If you want to selectively transfer apps from your old phone instead of transferring them all at once, sign in the old-fashioned way (p. 36) with your username and password instead of using Tap & Go.*

Note that **Tap & Go only works if your old device supports NFC** (common on phones made in the last 3-4 years). Consult your old device's instruction manual or search Google to determine if it supports NFC.

To proceed, enable NFC in your old device's system settings and ensure the device is turned on and unlocked. Place your old device back-to-back with your new Galaxy until your hear a chime. Separate the devices and then follow prompts on both devices to initiate the data transfer.

If you don't want to use Tap & Go for any reason, then just tap "Skip."

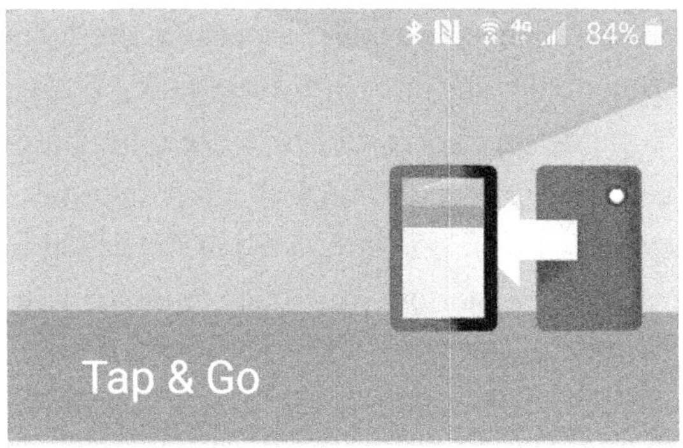

Quickly copy any Google Accounts, backed up apps and data from your existing Android device. To copy:

1. Make sure your other device is on and unlocked.

2. Briefly place the two devices back-to-back until you hear a tone, then set aside.

Learn more

< SKIP >

After the process is complete, you'll be prompted to enable a few settings like data backup and location services.

Back up your phone's apps, app data, settings, and Wi-Fi passwords using your Google Account so you can easily restore later. Learn more

Use Google's location service to

< MORE

On this screen, swipe up and down to see all available options. Personally, I leave all the boxes checked, with the exception of "Help improve your Android experience," which I disable for potential battery life benefits.

Some readers have asked me if these settings, especially the location settings, are privacy threats since they send potentially sensitive information to Google. This is a complicated discussion outside the scope of this book, but to make a long story short, my judgment is that they are not. While I do not claim that any big company like Google is entirely benevolent, I don't believe that Google is interested in meddling with your personal affairs. Rather, Google is interested in gathering your data to serve you with better information and improve its own products. Besides, let's be frank: if the NSA orders Google to monitor you, unchecking these boxes isn't going to stop them. When using a smartphone in the 21st century, you pretty much have to accept that big companies or the government can see your data if they want to. If data privacy is extremely important to you, you should rethink the idea of using a smartphone in the first place.

So, my opinion is that there's little point in crippling your Galaxy's features by disabling these services. Leave them enabled and enjoy the benefits like automatic data restoration, improved local searches, Google Now (p. 174) customization, and more. By disabling them you'll lose some pretty useful features and gain little in the way of privacy.

Signing Into Your Existing Google Account Without Using Tap & Go

If you skip Tap & Go, you'll be prompted to sign into an existing Google account the old-fashioned way with a username and password. You'll want to sign in this way if you *do* have an existing Google account, but you:

- Don't want to use Tap & Go for any reason,
- Or you can't use Tap & Go because your old Android doesn't support NFC,
- Or you want to selectively restore apps from your old Android instead of restoring them all at once,
- Or your new Galaxy is your first Android device!

If you don't have a Google account (i.e., you don't have a Gmail address), then skip to the next section: Creating a New Google Account (p. 39).

> ***TIP:*** *Not sure if you have a Google account? If you have a Gmail address, you have a Google account—your username is the part that comes before "@gmail.com."*

To sign in, enter your Gmail address or username and tap "Next."

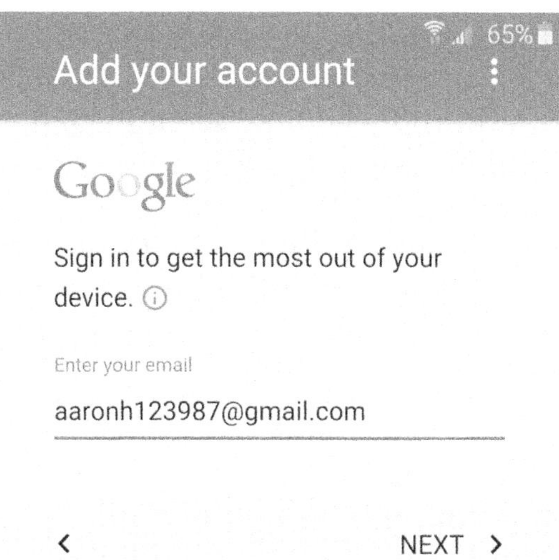

Enter your password when prompted, and then tap "Accept" to confirm and sign in. If you had any third-party apps installed on your old Android, you'll see the following screen:

Easily set up your new device by restoring from a backup of another device.

Backups include apps, app data, system settings and Wi-Fi passwords.

Restore from this backup

SM-G925T Last used today

Also include

All apps 27

NEXT

Use the "Restore from this backup" drop-down menu to select a different Android device to restore apps from, or select "Set up as new device" if you don't want to transfer any data. If you do select a device, use the "Also include" drop-down menu to selectively choose which apps from that device you want to transfer to your new Galaxy.

Note that you don't need your old device to be physically present for the restoration process—all these data are stored in your Google account on the cloud, and will be restored to your new Galaxy via the Internet.

Finally, you'll configure Google services. I recommend enabling everything except "Help improve your Android experience."

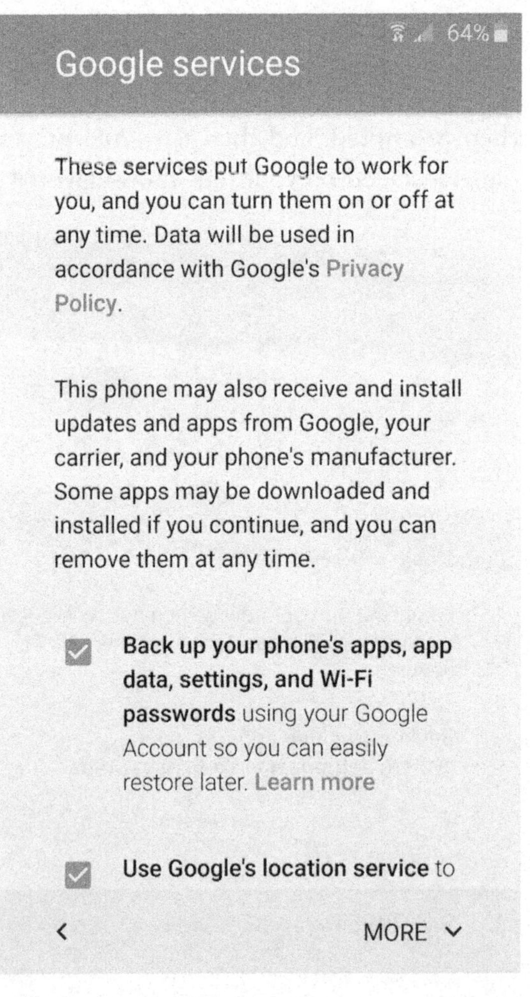

Creating a New Google Account

If you don't have a Google account (meaning, you don't have a Gmail address), then tap "Create a New Account" when you reach this screen:

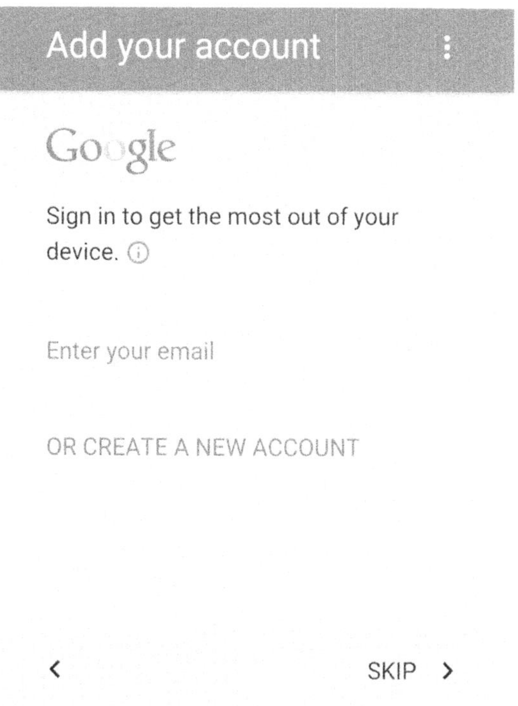

If you don't already have a Google account, create one now. I cannot stress the importance of this enough. Android is a Google product and many of the Galaxy's features require you to have a Google account. If you don't, you won't be able to download any new apps from the Google Play Store (p. 166), automatically back up your contacts, sync your bookmarks and passwords through Chrome, automatically back up your photos to Google Photos, or take advantage of many other useful features that I'll discuss throughout this book. Even if you don't use Gmail for email, you should still create a Google account to take advantage of the many other features a Google account adds to your Galaxy.

When creating a Google account, you'll have to specify a username (will be the part of your email address that comes before "@gmail.com") and password, as well as set up a phone number for emergency recovery of your account password. I recommend using your Galaxy's phone number for this. You'll also be asked to specify payment info, which lets you purchase apps and media on the Google Play Store:

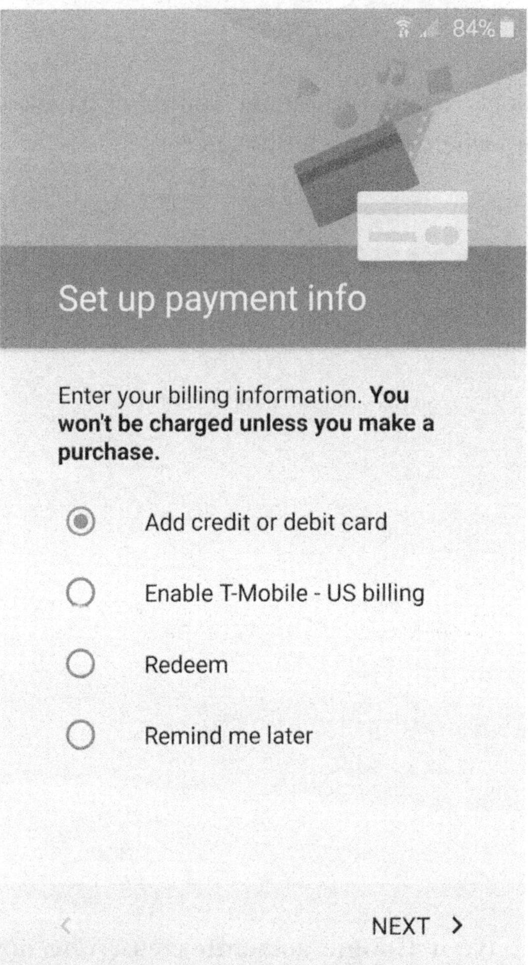

Go ahead and set up a payment method now, because you'll almost certainly buy apps or media from Google at some point. Your information will be stored securely, and you won't be charged anything until you make a purchase.

Finally, you'll configure Google services. I recommend enabling everything except "Help improve your Android experience."

Configuring Your Lock Screen

Next, you'll be prompted to set up your lock screen (p. 226), which protects your Galaxy from unauthorized access with your choice of a password, fingerprint scan, etc. When enabled, the lock screen appears every time your Galaxy is powered on, preventing anyone from using your phone without first authenticating themselves.

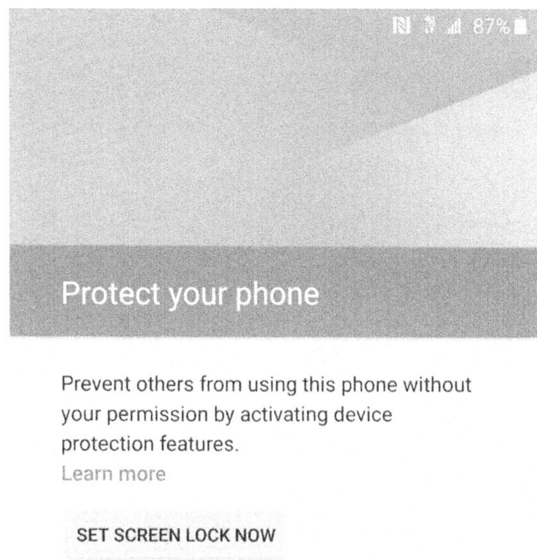

You can read a detailed comparison of lock screen methods here (p. 226), but I strongly suggest using fingerprint recognition. The Note 5 and S6 Edge+ have excellent fingerprint sensors that just require a quick tap of your thumb on the button—much quicker and easier than entering a PIN or password.

Tap "Set Screen Lock Now" → "Fingerprints" and follow the instructions to register your fingerprint and set up a backup password.

Configuring Lock Screen Notification Privacy

Next, you'll see this screen:

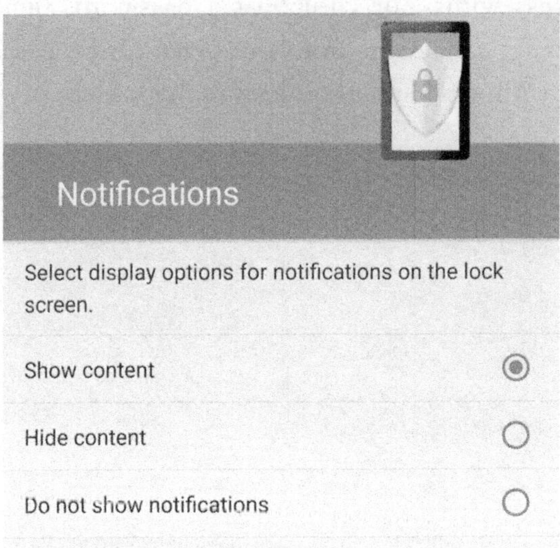

Understanding these settings requires a bit of background knowledge about the lock screen that we just configured. Normally, when your Galaxy sends you a notification (to alert you of a new text message, email, etc.) it will display a preview of that notification on the lock screen while your Galaxy is locked. This is convenient because you can just tap the power button to see what the notification is, without having to authenticate yourself and clear the lock screen first.

However, as you might imagine, some people may not want personal information to be displayed on the lock screen at all. So, these settings let you control what your Galaxy is permitted to show on the lock screen. If you don't mind your Galaxy showing some potentially sensitive info on the lock screen for the sake of convenience, select "Show content." If you want your Galaxy to only display redacted notifications on the lock screen (i.e., it will show you the type of notification, but without any personal info like sender or subject line), select "Hide Content." If you don't want your Galaxy to display any notifications whatsoever on the lock screen, select "Do not show notifications."

This is a personal decision about convenience vs. privacy—it's certainly convenient to see notifications directly on your lock screen without having to authenticate yourself—but if your phone ever fell into the wrong hands, would you be okay with a stranger seeing those notifications too?

Creating a New Samsung Account

Next, you'll have a chance to create a Samsung account, which grants you access to the Samsung Galaxy Apps store and provides some useful data backup features. In previous *100% Unofficial User Guides*, I recommended against creating a Samsung account because it worked clumsily, did little that a Google account didn't already do, and increased battery drain.. However, Samsung accounts are more efficient and functional these days and I now recommend creating one. The most useful features of a Samsung account are:

- Backing up phone logs and text messages (p. 276)
- Backing up and syncing S Health (p. 258) fitness data
- Downloading apps and updates from the Galaxy Apps Store, including themes (p. 68)

Samsung accounts also have some additional backup features that are redundant with Google account features, such as backing up contacts, backing up photos, and locating a lost Galaxy. In this book, when Google account and Samsung account features overlap, we'll be using Google. Why? Because Google accounts can be synced with *any* Android device, but Samsung accounts can only be synced with Samsung devices. If you buy a non-Samsung Android device in the future, having all your data synced to your Google account will make the data transfer process much easier.

Nevertheless, I no longer completely reject the idea of using a Samsung account as I used to. A Samsung account is important for downloading software updates from the Galaxy Apps store, and text message backup is a *great* feature that's still missing from Google accounts. Finally, if you have any interest in fitness tracking with S Health (p. 258), you'll want a Samsung account to automatically back up your data to the cloud so you don't lose it if your Galaxy is lost, damaged, or accidentally wiped.

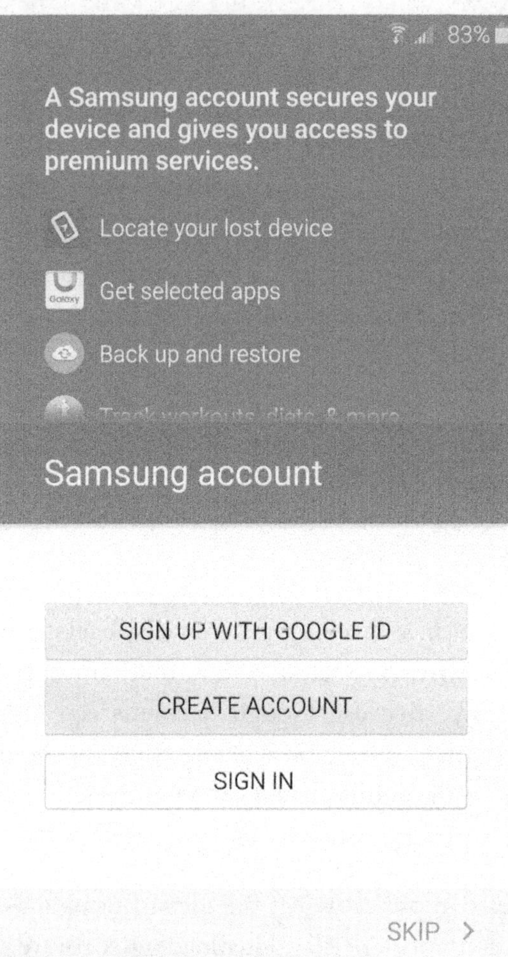

To create a Samsung account, I recommend using the "Sign up with Google ID" option. This is a new feature that lets you easily create a Samsung account with the same email address as your Google account. Follow the prompts to configure your Samsung account and sign in. Agree to all of Samsung's terms and conditions. On the following screen, tap OFF to enable "Back up and sync."

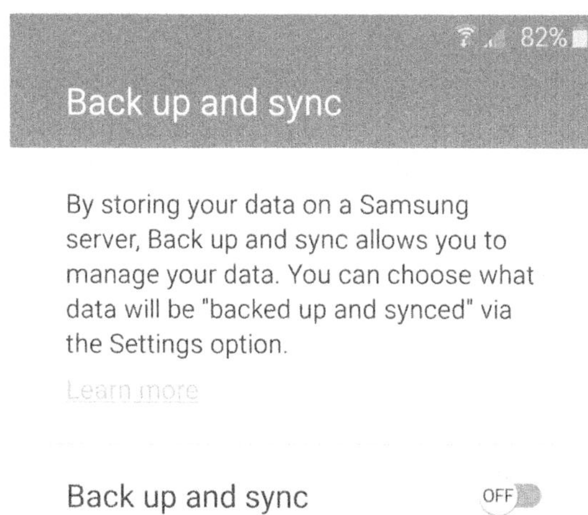

If you don't want a Samsung account, simply tap "Skip" on the initial Samsung account screen, or if you already have a Samsung account, tap "Sign In" and follow the prompts to restore data from your Samsung account.

Check here (p. 276) for a complete tutorial on backing up your Galaxy's data.

Setting a Spoken Wake-Up Command

Next, you can set up a wake-up command for your Galaxy. This process trains your phone to recognize a spoken phrase such as "Hello, Galaxy" (or anything else you want), which you can then use instead of pressing the power button. I personally prefer to stick with the old-fashioned power button and don't find a wake-up command too useful, but if you'd like to use your voice instead, tap "Set" and follow the instructions. Otherwise, tap "Later."

Set wake-up command

S Voice helps you control your device with your voice. Use your voice to easily wake up your device, open apps, make calls, and more.

LATER SET >

A wake-up command can be more useful if you plan to use it in conjunction with other voice commands, such as Car Mode (p. 242). Speaking a wake-up command to your Galaxy while you're holding it in your hand isn't too useful—it's easier to just press the power button—but a voice command *is* useful if your Galaxy is often out of reach and is configured to accept other voice commands after being unlocked via voice.

Registering Your Fingerprint

Next, you'll be prompted to register your fingerprint. Note that you won't see this screen if you already set up a lock screen (p. 41) with fingerprint authentication. Go ahead and follow the prompts to do so, as several features of the Note 5 / S6 Edge+ use fingerprint authentication.

Use your fingerprint to unlock your device and sign in to services securely without entering your password.

Easy Mode—Skip It

Finally, you'll see this screen:

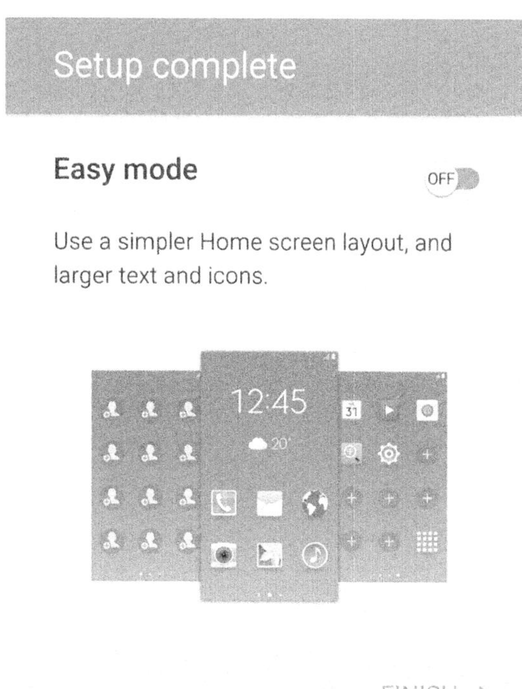

Easy Mode simplifies your Galaxy's TouchWiz (p. 50) interface by stripping out the more advanced features. Skip it—with this book, you won't need Easy Mode. And if you do enable it, you'll find that things don't match up with the images and instructions in this book.

Welcome to the Home Screen

Your Galaxy will work for a few moments and then bring you to a screen like this: the home screen.

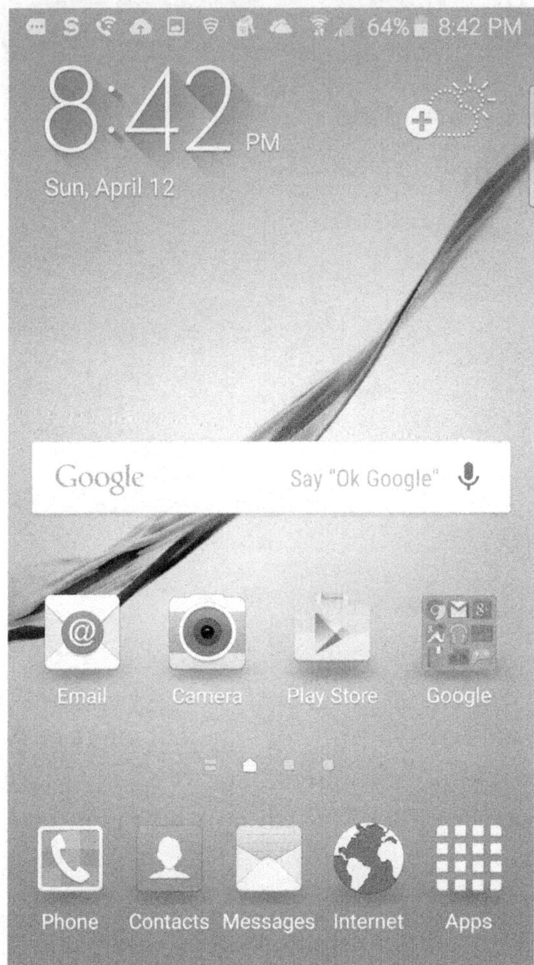

You'll be seeing a lot more of this soon, but first, a few final steps.

Final Steps

The initial setup process is finished, but there are a few more steps to take before using your Galaxy. If you're brand new to Android, feel free to come back to these steps after you've worked through the next chapter—but don't forget about them because they're important.

- First, configure your voicemail inbox. This is usually only necessary if you're a new customer to your carrier. To do so, tap the Phone app and then the "Keypad" tab.

Tap [voicemail icon] below the star ("*") key. Follow the voice prompts to set up your inbox for the first time.

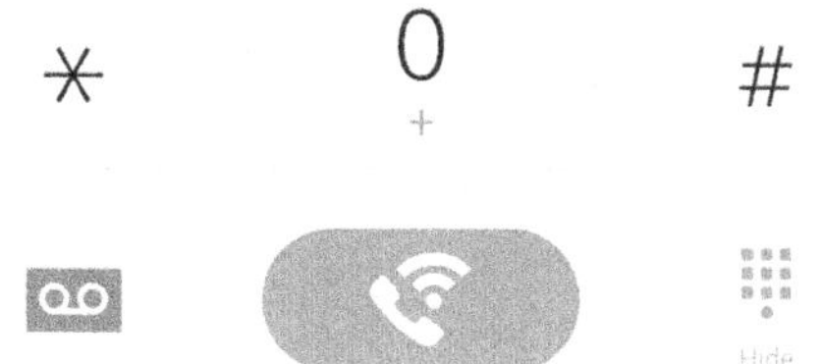

- Second, set up device tracking (p. 228) through Google. With device tracking, you'll be able to geographically locate your Galaxy if it's lost or stolen. Although this is no guarantee of recovering your Galaxy, it gives you a much greater chance of doing so than if you don't have tracking enabled.
- Third, set up SOS messages (p. 273) so you can send an emergency message with a triple press of the power button. Hopefully you'll never need to use this feature, but it's better to have it enabled and not need it than vice-versa.

With this all accomplished, you're ready to start learning more about your Galaxy.

Chapter 4: Fundamentals for New Users

Welcome to Android! More specifically, welcome to TouchWiz, Samsung's version of the Android user interface.

TouchWhat? Let me explain.

You probably know that Google makes the Android OS. Android is an operating system like Microsoft Windows or Mac OSX, but it's designed for smartphones and tablets instead of desktops and laptops. However, Google's "pure" form of Android is actually only sold with a few select devices such as Google's Nexus series. Most Android devices come from third-party companies like Samsung that put their own software "layer" on top of the Android operating system. (That's a totally different product philosophy than Apple. Apple makes 100% of the iPhones and iPads in the world, and they all run exactly the same operating system with no additional "layers".)

TouchWiz is the layer that Samsung puts on top of Google's "pure" form of the Android OS. TouchWiz isn't just an app, though—it's a collection of apps, tweaks, features, and graphics. It refers to the entirety of the changes that Samsung makes to the Android OS to make it a unique Samsung experience. Vague, I know, but let me explain further.

To be more specific, some of TouchWiz's features include:

- A custom home screen (p. 59) and app drawer (p. 78);
- A custom system settings (p. 58) menu;
- Samsung apps like S Health (p. 258);
- A better camera (p. 120) app;
- A smattering of special features like Multi Window (p. 221);
- And more.

Think of it this way: An HP computer runs the Windows OS but comes pre-loaded with HP-specific software layered on top of Windows. It's still a Windows computer but it's customized. TouchWiz refers to all the Samsung-specific stuff that's layered on top of Android. It's still the same Android operating system under the hood, but with extra features and tweaks.

To demonstrate visually, here's an example of the TouchWiz home screen (first image) compared to the pure Android home screen (second image):

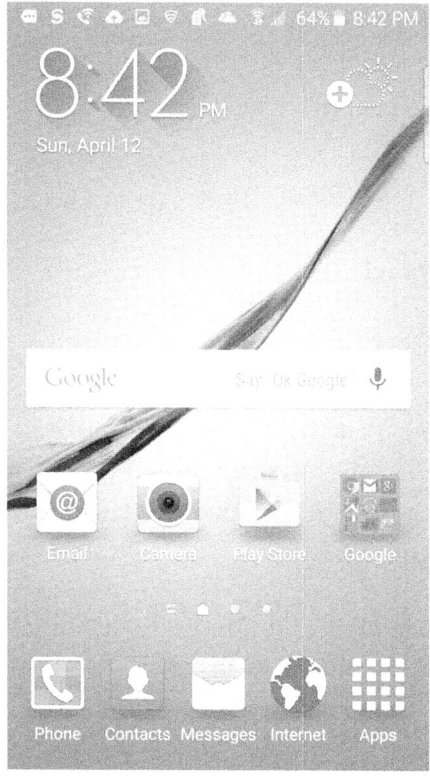

Different, but not *that* different, right? Right!

Components of the User Interface

You can think about TouchWiz in five main parts:

- **System Settings**
- **The Home Screen(s)**
- **The Notification Panel**
- **The Lock Screen**
- **The App Drawer**

Almost everything you do on your Galaxy will take place in one of these areas, or in an app. You can think of apps as your destinations and these parts of TouchWiz as the roads that get you to your destinations. In this chapter, I will teach you everything there is to know about these areas of TouchWiz.

First, though, let's briefly talk about the physical controls on your Galaxy. You need to understand these before you can efficiently use your device.

Physical Controls – For the most basic operations

The Power Button (power on/off, restart, airplane mode, & emerg. mode)

A single press of the power button wakes your Galaxy or puts it to sleep. I use the terms "wake" and "sleep" instead of "on" and "off" because your Galaxy is actually powered on even when it's asleep—it has to be, in order to receive calls and other communications.

So how do you know whether you're waking it or putting it to sleep? If the screen is on, the device is awake. A single press of the power button puts it to sleep, and the screen turns off. When the screen is off, the device is asleep. A single press of the power button wakes it again and displays your lock screen (p. 76)_(if enabled) to check that you're an authorized user.

A triple press of the power button sends an SOS message (p. 273) to a specified contact, but only if you've set up SOS messages. A long press of the power button while the device is awake brings up the following options:

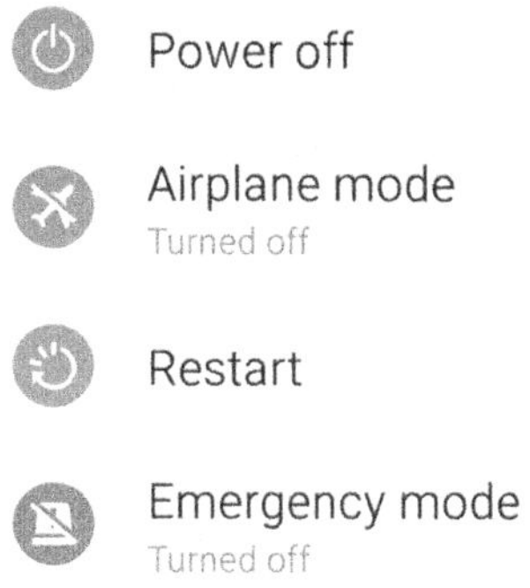

Power off

Airplane mode
Turned off

Restart

Emergency mode
Turned off

- **Power off:** Turn off the device completely. This is different than putting it to sleep with a single press of the power button. When powered off, it will no longer send or receive any communications at all. Turn the device on again with a long press of the power button.
- **Airplane mode:** Leave the device powered on, but turn off all wireless communications, including cellular, Wi-Fi, Bluetooth, NFC, and so on. Although use of electronic devices is now permitted from boarding to de-boarding on all U.S. airlines, you are still required to turn off all wireless functions during takeoff and landing. Airplane mode comes in handy for this.
- **Restart:** Reboot your Galaxy. Useful if it's exhibiting unusual or sluggish behavior. In fact, I recommend rebooting your Galaxy at least once every few days to keep it operating at its best.
- **Emergency mode:** Enable a safety and power conservation mode called Emergency Mode (p. 273). Emergency Mode places big buttons on your home screen to easily share your location or use your camera's flash as a flashlight. Emergency mode also makes your battery last as long as possible by minimizing screen brightness, displaying only black and white, and slowing down the device's CPU. Useful if you're in a bad situation, if your battery is dying, or both.

Volume Up/Down Buttons (adjust volume, vibrate & silent modes)

Your Galaxy has five separate volume settings: Ringtone, Media, Notifications, System, and In-Call volume. I know this sounds complicated, but in practice, you only have to remember one rule: **the Volume Up and Volume Down buttons generally control what you want them to control, when you want it.**

For example, if you're playing a game, they'll control the game's sound volume. If you're in a call, they'll control the speaker volume. Easy, right?

If you want the more complicated explanation, read on. You can skip the rest of this section if you're not interested in the nuances of your Galaxy's volume controls.

Still with me? Okay. Here's what each volume setting controls, in detail:

- **Ringtone Volume:** The volume of the ringtone that plays when you receive a phone call.
- **Media Volume:** The volume of audio that plays in music apps, video apps, games, etc.
- **Notification Volume:** The volume of audio alerts that play upon receiving emails, text messages, and so on.
- **System Volume:** The volume of the phone keypad tone, touch sounds, key presses, and so on.
- **In-Call Volume:** The volume of the speaker when you're in a voice call.

The Volume Up and Volume Down buttons only ever directly control Ringtone, Media, and In-Call volumes. Let me repeat that: the Volume buttons only ever directly adjust the Ringtone, Media, and In-Call volume levels, *not the notification or system volume levels.* Which setting is controlled depends on what the device is doing when you press the volume buttons. If your Galaxy is on a system screen such as a home screen or the app drawer, the buttons will adjust the Ringtone volume. If it is playing a movie or a game, the buttons will adjust the Media volume. If you are in a call, the buttons will adjust the In-Call volume.

The exception is that they *indirectly* control Notification and System volume if you turn down the Ringtone volume to zero. When the Ringtone volume is muted, Notification and System volumes are also temporarily muted. So, how do you specifically adjust the Notification and System volume levels, since the buttons don't control them? You can only do it with on-screen controls. Anytime you press Volume Up or Volume Down, tap the ⚙ icon to manually adjust these volume levels on the device, as shown below.

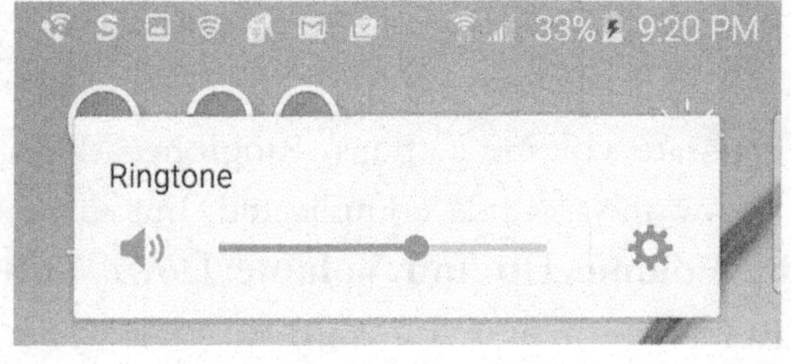

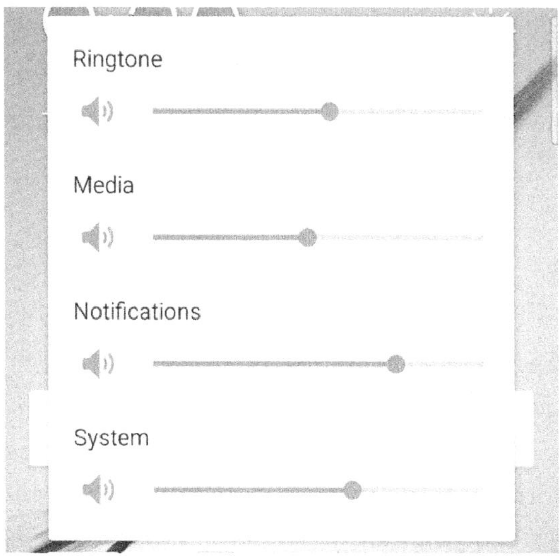

Note that In-Call volume cannot be adjusted from this menu. It can only be adjusted while a voice call is active.

Finally, you can **hold Volume Up or Volume Down** to rapidly increase or decrease the Ringtone or Media volume, but note that when holding Volume Down, the volume slider will pause at vibrate mode, which is still one notch above the mute setting. You must release the Volume Down button and press it one more time to fully mute the device. (You can also mute the device by holding the power button and tapping "Mute" on the menu that appears.)

If that all sounds complicated… well, that's because it really is. Refer to this section if you get confused about the volume settings on your device, but fortunately, you'll find what I said earlier to be true: **the Volume Up and Volume Down buttons generally control what you want them to control, when you want it.**

Home Button (go to home screen, launch Camera, open Google Now)

The physical button centered below your Galaxy's screen is the home button . Tapping it once takes you back to the home screen (p. 59) from any other screen. You can also quickly double-tap the home button to open the Camera (p. 120) (even when the device is asleep, which is extremely useful) or tap and hold it to open Google Now (p. 174), a voice command system that I will discuss in more depth later. The home button also doubles as the fingerprint scanner (p. 41).

Recent and Back Buttons (switch/quit apps, go back, Multi Window)

The recent ( ) and back ( ) buttons are soft buttons (i.e., non-click, touch buttons) to the left and right of , respectively, and are only visible when backlit.

Tapping brings up a list of all of currently running apps. From here, swipe up and down to scroll through the list. Switch to an app by tapping it, or close an app by tapping or by swiping it left or right. At the bottom of the screen is the "Close All" button, which terminates all currently running apps. Note that it's not necessary to close apps to free up memory like on a computer. Android automatically manages memory and closes unused apps as needed. Instead, the main reason you might want to swipe an app left or right is if it's acting buggy and you want to force it to quit.

As you'll notice, some apps have a button next to . This button launches the app in Multi Window (p. 221) mode.

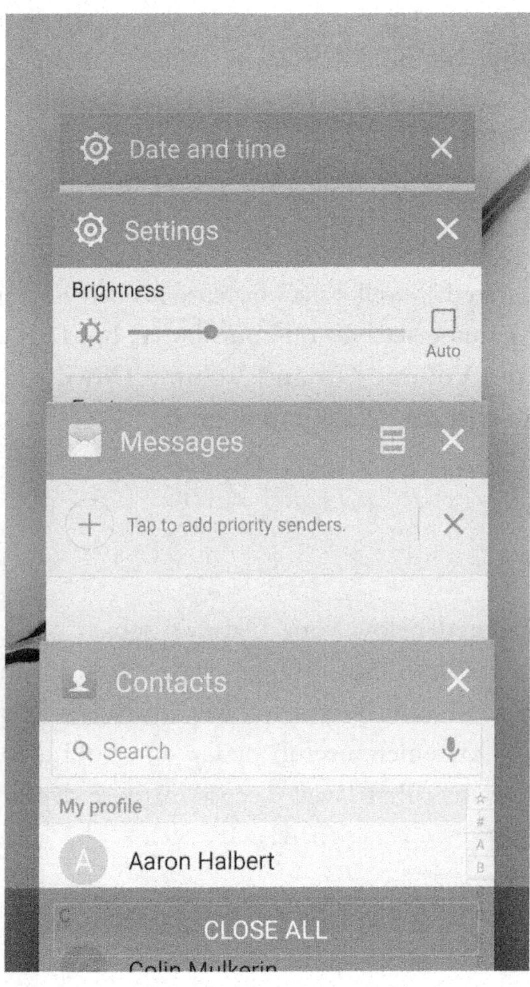

The back button ⮌, on the other hand, works sort of like a back button in a web browser, taking you to the last screen you were on. However, it sometimes does other things like hiding the on-screen keyboard or collapsing an open menu. The best way to get the hang of the back button is just to try it.

If you've owned an Android device in the past, you may be wondering where the menu button is. The answer is that it's gone, completely replaced by the recent button. Instead, look for the on-screen MORE button to see menu options. (If you're upgrading from a Kit Kat device, note that MORE has replaced Kit Kat's three-dot ⋮ on-screen menu button.)

TIP: You can also tap and hold the ⮌ button to open the menu on any screen.

Basic Touch Screen Gestures

There are six basic touch screen gestures that will be mentioned repeatedly throughout this book. Make sure you understand them:

- **Tapping:** A single tap of your finger. Commonly used to open apps, to press buttons, to type on the keyboard, and to select menu items.
- **Tapping and holding:** A tap where your finger remains on the screen for at least half a second. Commonly used to access secondary options. You can adjust the tap & hold delay in system settings → "Accessibility" → "Dexterity and interaction" → "Press and hold delay."
- **Tapping, holding, and dragging:** A tap where your finger remains on the screen for at least half a second, followed by movement without lifting your finger. Commonly used to move on-screen items.
- **Double-tapping:** A quick double-tap of your finger, where your finger completely lifts from the screen in between taps. Commonly used to zoom in and out of text in web browsers.
- **Swiping:** A fluid up, down, left, or right directional motion where your finger slides across the screen. Commonly used to scroll through menus, or page through different panels.
- **Pinching:** Using your thumb and index finger to pinch inwards or outwards. Commonly used to zoom in and out of text and photos.

System Settings – Very Important!

You need to be **very familiar** with the system settings screen on your Galaxy, because I will refer to it many times throughout this book. The system settings screen is the central control panel for your device. It includes settings for sounds, the display, wireless connections, power conservation, and much, much more.

You can access system settings in two ways. First, you can tap the "Settings" app your app drawer (p. 78): Second, you can swipe down the notification panel (p. 70) and tap ⚙.

Any time you're having trouble finding what you're looking for in the system settings, use the SEARCH feature.

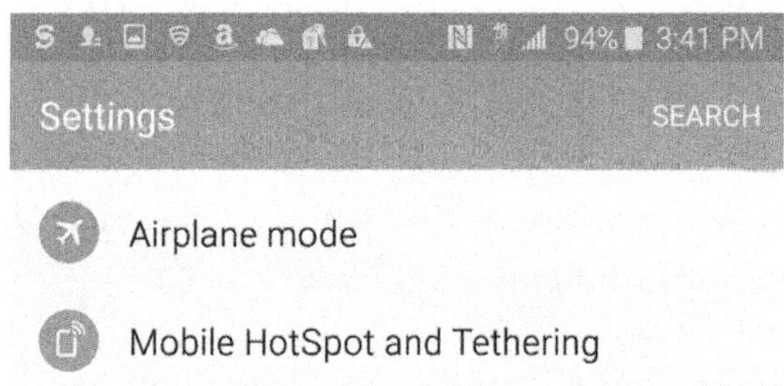

The Home Screen – Where the action starts

Now that you're familiar with the basic controls of your Galaxy, we can discuss its software. If you still have this screen pulled up, then you're on the home screen.

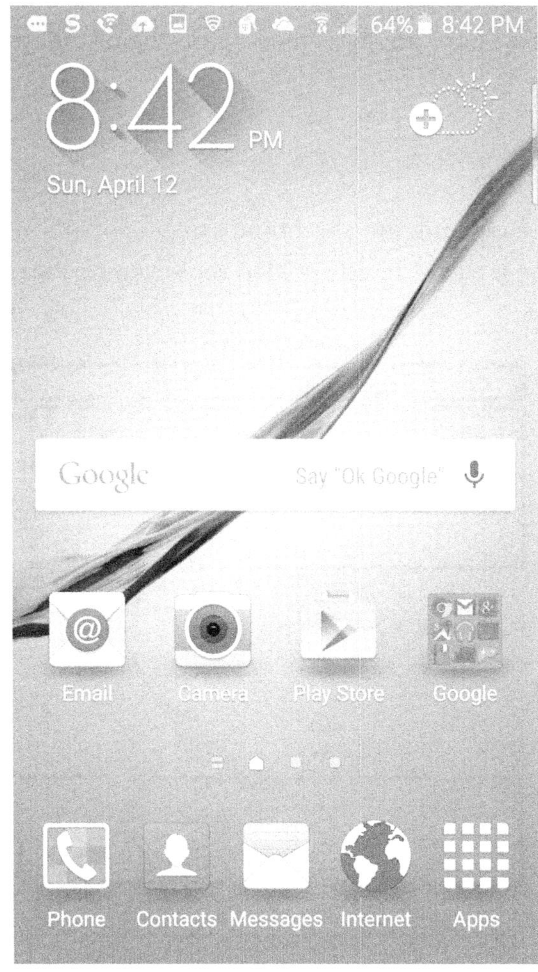

If you don't see this screen, just press and you'll get to it. Your home screen may look slightly different depending on which carrier you have and to what degree you've already customized your device.

What's the Home Screen?

The home screen is where everything starts on Android; you might compare it to the desktop of your computer. However, unlike on a computer, none of the icons you'll see on the Android home screen are files. Instead, they're all shortcuts to apps. You may be used to saving files on the desktop of your computer, but that's not possible on Android. Files can only be accessed from *within* apps.

Another difference is that Android has multiple home screens, not just a single desktop like most computers. From the home screen, try swiping left and right. This accesses secondary, adjacent home screens on which you can put additional app shortcuts and widgets. Swiping all the way left opens Briefing (p. 296), a news and social media aggregator. Briefing is technically an app, not a part of the home screen, but Briefing's developers have entered into an agreement with Samsung to feature the app very prominently.

Components of the Home Screen

There are many things happening on the home screen, so let's analyze them from top to bottom. In the following image, I have outlined the seven major parts of the default home screen.

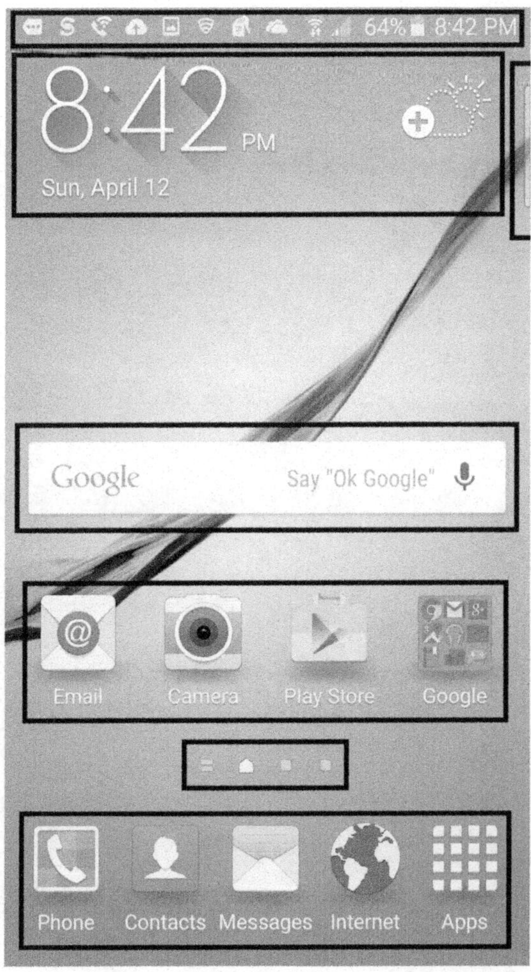

The horizontal bar at the very top of the screen is called the **status bar**. From right to left are the current time, the battery/charging indicator, the cell signal strength indicator, and the Wi-Fi signal strength indicator. The icons to the left of the Wi-Fi signal indicator all represent notifications (p. 70). Don't worry about these yet—I will explain them in more detail later in this section.

Below the status bar is a large widget (p. 63) containing the current time, date, and weather conditions. Widgets can be nearly any size and contain a variety of different content. In essence, they are mini "apps" that you can place on your home screen for easy, bite-size functionality and information. More info on widgets is coming up shortly.

The Google box below the time/weather widget is also a widget. This widget allows you to quickly perform a Google web or voice search.

Below the two widgets is a row of **app shortcuts**, including Email, Camera, Play Store, and a folder full of Google apps. These are not widgets; rather, they're shortcuts that you tap to open full apps. Samsung has placed these four shortcuts on the home screen by default, but I'll show you how to customize them shortly.

The next element is a row of symbols that includes a . In this screenshot, the is solid white, indicating that the device is currently showing the **main home screen**. Each of the icons represents a **secondary home screen**. You can switch to these secondary home screens by swiping left or right. The to the left of the house represents Briefing (p. 296).

Below is an example of a secondary home screen, accessed by swiping right from the main home screen. It's not fundamentally different than the main home screen; it just provides additional space for more app shortcuts and widgets. As you can see, this one has been preconfigured with several app shortcuts and a Galaxy Essentials/Gifts widget. Notice that one of the ■ icons is now solid white instead of ⌂, indicating that you're viewing a secondary home screen.

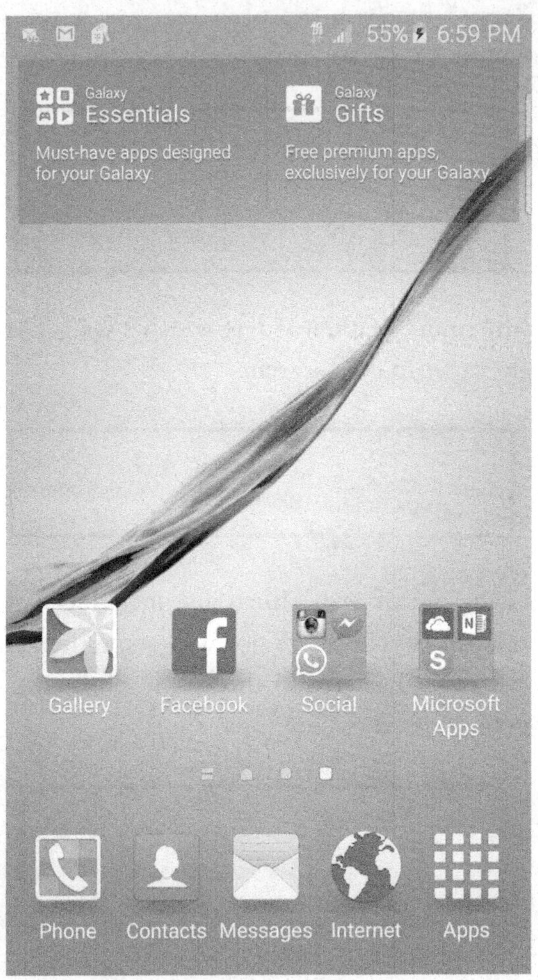

TIP: *From nearly any screen on your Galaxy, press ⬭ to return to the last home screen you were viewing. If it was a secondary home screen, press ⬭ again to return to the main home screen.*

The bottommost element of the home screen is the **app tray**. The app tray is a special place for you to place your most important app shortcuts, and unlike other app shortcuts, these stay visible on all home screens. By default, the app tray contains Phone, Contacts,

Messages, Internet, and Apps (a special shortcut to the app drawer (p. 78) that you can't remove).

TIP: As you may have noticed, the shortcuts in the app tray stay the same regardless of which home screen you're viewing, unlike the app shortcuts on the home screens themselves. This is why the app tray is a great place to put your most-used apps.

Finally, in the upper-right hand corner of the screen is the People Edge tab, if you have an S6 Edge+. Read more about People Edge in Chapter 7 (p. 213).

What Are Widgets?

You've now seen a few different widgets on the home screen—the time/date/weather widget, the Google search widget, and the Galaxy Essentials/Gifts widget. Let's define "widget" a little better.

Widgets are mini-apps that live right on your home screen. Unlike full apps, which typically have a lot of features and options and occupy the entire screen, widgets are designed to do only one or two high-priority things right from your home screen. For example, consider the time/date/weather widget that's on the main home screen by default. Without it, you'd have to open a web browser and do Google searches to get the same information—much more difficult than a simple glance on your main home screen. The time/date/weather widget is all about providing convenient access to time/date/weather information.

Simply put, widgets give you easier and faster access to information or tasks that you might need on a regular basis, so you don't have to open an app every time. There are thousands of widgets available for download from the Google Play Store (p. 166), and you can find a widget for nearly anything. For example, you can get stock tickers, news headlines, smart appliance controls, and so on. Also, many full apps come with widgets to provide convenient access to commonly used features.

Editing Existing Shortcuts and Widgets

The strength of the home screen is in its customizability, so let's talk about how to make your home screen your own by customizing your shortcuts and widgets. We'll start with the default configuration:

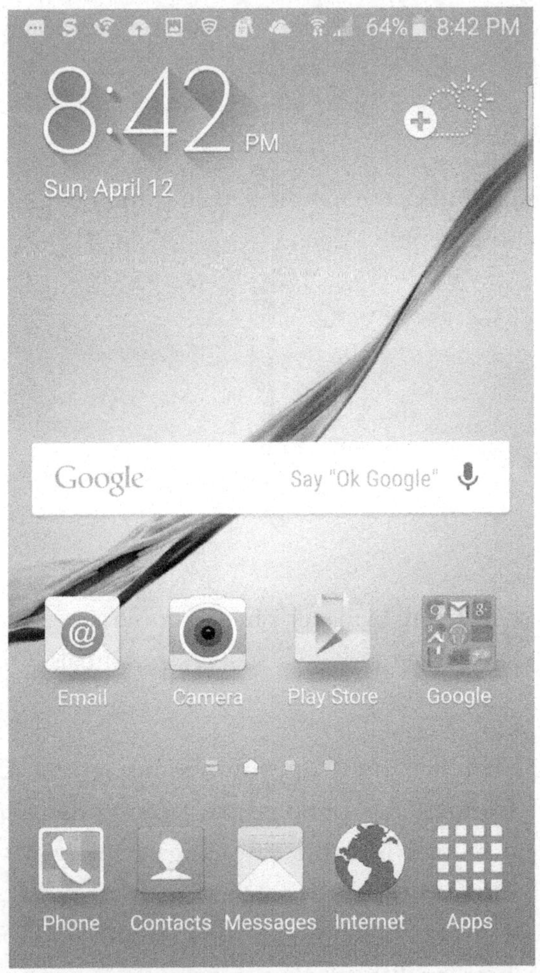

Let's say I want to rearrange the Email, Camera, Play Store, and Google folder shortcuts. Normally, this is very simple: just **tap and hold** on the shortcuts one at a time, **drag** them to their new locations, and **release**:

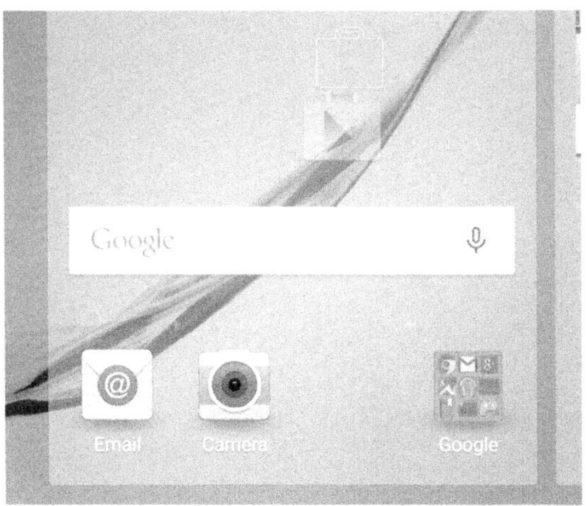

However, let's say I want to put them along the top of the screen, so there's a bit of a problem—the time/date/weather widget is in the way. It turns out that, as with app shortcuts, tapping, holding, and dragging is also the way to manipulate widgets. So, I will tap and hold the time/date/weather widget, drag it up to the "Remove" bar

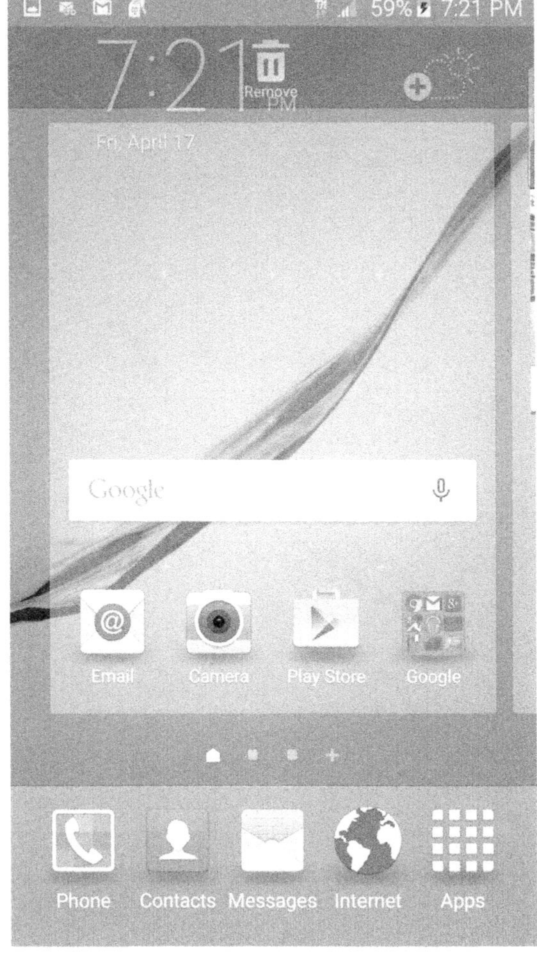

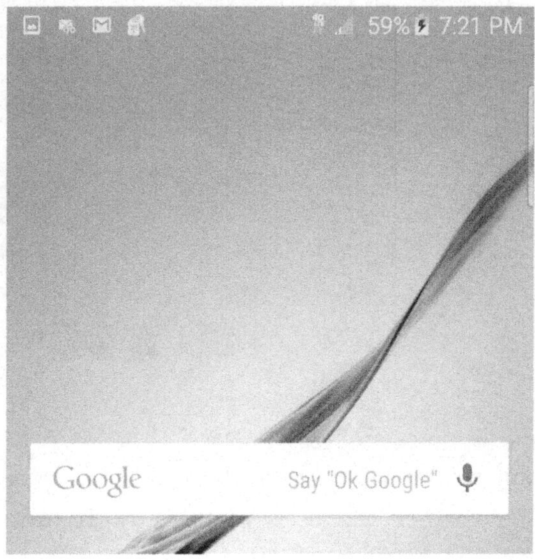

This is much better. Now, I can move my app shortcuts to the top of the screen. I will tap and hold each of these shortcuts for approximately a second, drag, and release.

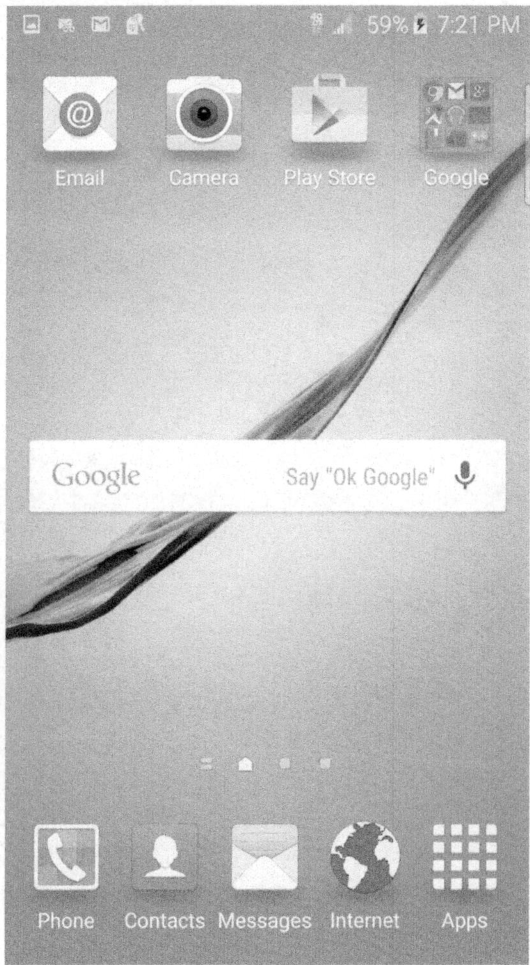

By tapping, holding, and dragging, I have rearranged the row of app shortcuts as shown above.

> ***TIP:*** *You can manipulate app shortcuts in the app tray* ***(p. 62)*** *at the bottom of the screen in the same way—just tap, hold, and drag. Note that if you drag an app shortcut over an existing app shortcut in the app tray, it will automatically create a new folder in the app tray containing both app shortcuts. To replace an app in the app tray, remove one before you add one.*

It's also possible to move app shortcuts and widgets to secondary home screens by tapping, dragging, and holding them against the left or right edge of the screen.

Adding Widgets, Changing Wallpaper & Theme, & Managing Home Screens

To add widgets (p. 63), change your background image, change your theme, or edit/add/delete secondary home screens, you need to pull up the **home screen menu**. Do so by tapping and holding any blank space on the home screen.

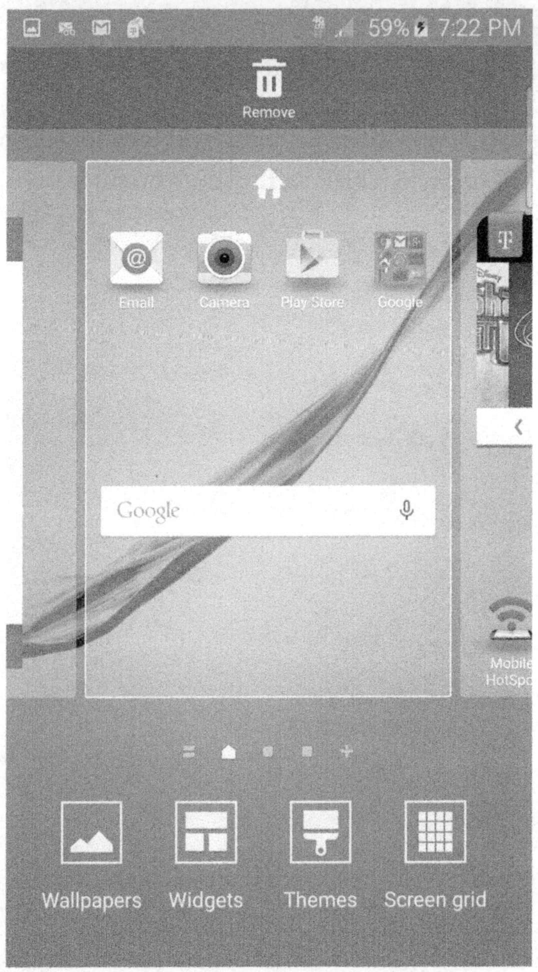

From this menu, you can:

- **Add, rearrange or remove home screens:** Swipe left and right to view and edit your currently active home screens. To remove a home screen and all of its app shortcuts and widgets, tap and hold until you feel a vibration, drag it up to the "Remove" icon, and release. To rearrange home screens, tap, hold, and drag them to the left or right sides of the screen. To add a new home screen, swipe all the way to the right and tap the plus (+) sign. You can create an unlimited number of secondary home screens, although I find that it's rarely practical to have more than five or six.

- **Change wallpaper:** Your wallpaper is the background image shown on the home screen and/or lock screen (p. 76). Tap the "Wallpapers" icon to select from a variety of other preloaded options. To use a photo taken with your device's camera instead, after you've tapped "Wallpapers," tap the "From Gallery" button in the lower-left-hand corner of the screen. When on the wallpaper selection screen, tap the down arrow next to "Home screen" to specify whether the selected wallpaper should be applied to the home screen only, the home and lock screens, or the lock screen only. Note that using darker wallpaper will increase your battery life (p. 292).
- **Add widgets:** To view all the widgets available on your device and optionally add them to your home screens, tap the "Widgets" button. From this screen, you can swipe left and right to scroll through all available widgets. Once you've found a widget you want to place on one of your home screens, tap and hold until you feel a vibration. Drag and hold your finger over the far left or right side of the screen to switch between home screens. When you've found a place for your widget, release your finger. Note that some third-party apps come with widgets, which automatically appear in this Widgets repository when the apps themselves are installed.
- **Change theme:** Theming is a new TouchWiz feature that lets you totally change the look of your Galaxy. Themes not only include wallpaper, but also replacement icons and system sounds. Tap "Themes" to download and activate themes from the Samsung store. By default, only the "Default," "Pink," and "Space" themes are shown, but tap "Theme Store" to view and download more. You'll need to be logged into your Samsung account (p. 43) to download themes.
- **Change the screen grid:** Tap "Screen grid" to change the number of app rows and columns. You can select from 4x4, 4x5, and 5x5.

TIP: *Wondering how to add new app shortcuts to the home screen? Keep reading—it's coming up in the section about the app drawer (p. 78).*

The Notification Panel – System settings & get important info

Congratulations—you've now learned almost everything there is to know about home screens on TouchWiz. Now, I'll discuss the **notification panel**, which is another very important component of your Galaxy's user interface. Place your finger on the status bar—the bar at the very top of your device's screen containing the time—and swipe down. You'll see a screen like this:

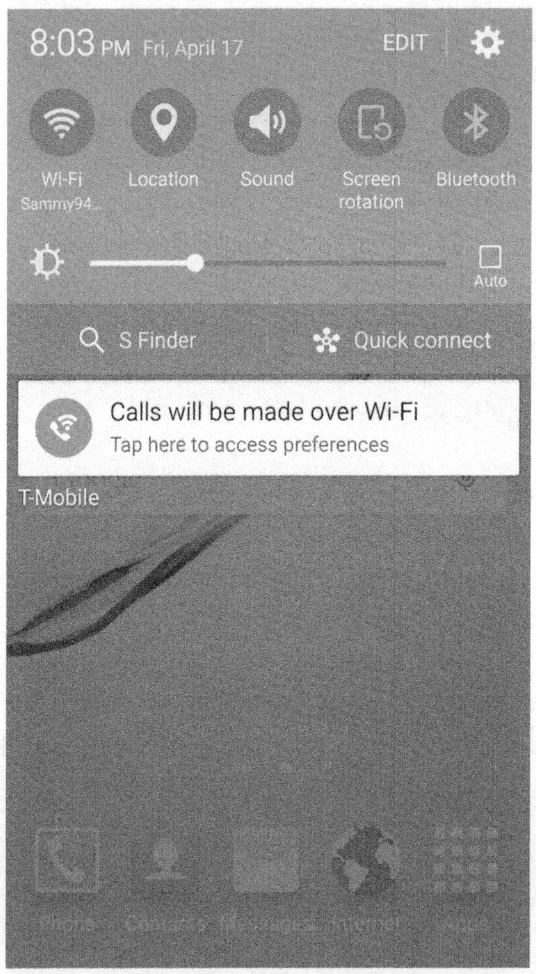

This is called the notification panel. Whereas the home screen(s) are dedicated to widgets and shortcuts for apps, the notification panel is a place where your device reports important status information and provides quick access to some commonly used settings. Let's talk about what's going on in the notification panel the same way we did for the home screen.

Components of the Notification Panel

At the top of the screen are the current time and date as well as two buttons—EDIT and ⚙.

Tapping ⚙ takes you to system settings, which is the same as accessing the "Settings" app in the app drawer (p. 78).

EDIT is used to customize the next element in the notification panel—the group of **toggle buttons** including Wi-Fi, Location, Sound, Screen Rotation, and Bluetooth. Each of these buttons is called a toggle button because it either switches a simple setting on or off, or rotates through a group of settings. For example, the Wi-Fi toggle button turns your Wi-Fi connection on or off. The Sound toggle button changes your sound settings from "Sound" (all sounds on), to "Vibrate" (sounds off; vibration on), to "Mute" (all sounds and vibration off).

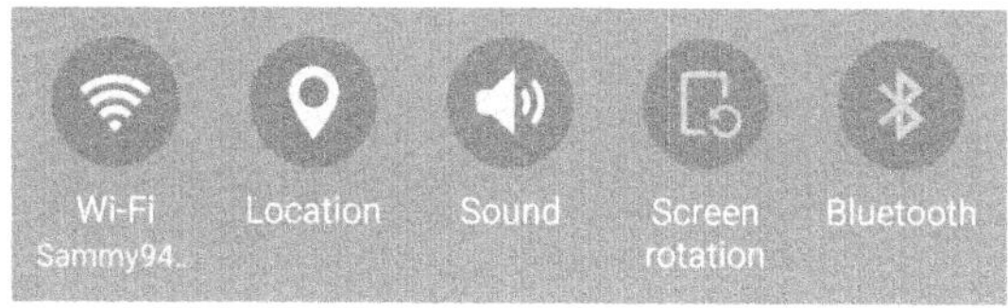

TIP: Tap and hold on any of these notification toggles to open their corresponding settings page.

Tapping EDIT opens the following screen. Tap and hold, drag, and release icons into the highlighted area to make them available in the toggle button cluster.

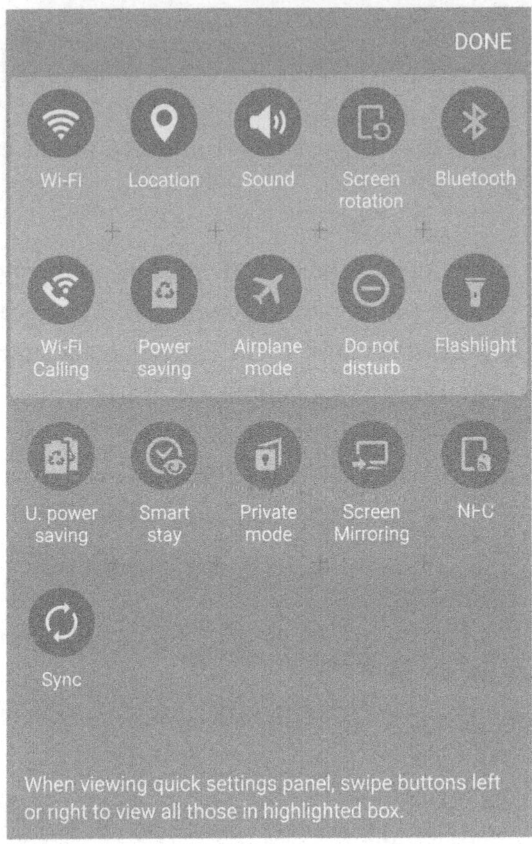

Notice how only 5 icons are shown by in the toggle button cluster by default, yet 10 total icons are shown in the highlighted area above. How do you access icons 6-10? By swiping the main group of toggle buttons left and right to gain access to the second row of toggle buttons from the expanded view. For example, here I have swiped the toggle buttons partway to the left:

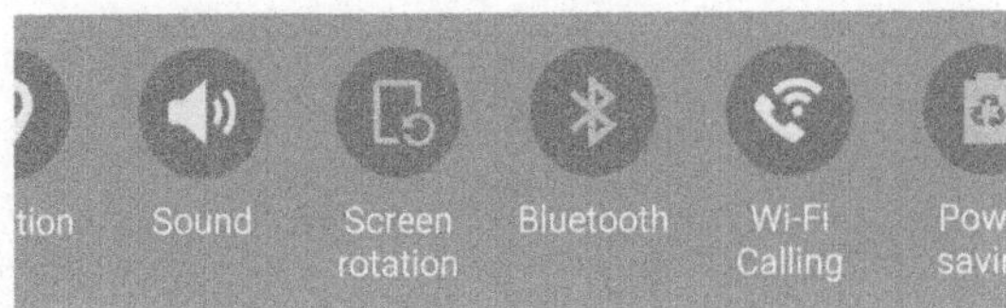

This swiping action will not access any of the additional toggle buttons in the third or fourth row of the expanded view.

Below the group of toggle buttons are the screen brightness selector and the S Finder (p. 250) and Quick Connect (p. 249) buttons. If you check the "Auto" box, your device will automatically adjust the brightness of the screen by measuring the ambient light level.

However, you can also control the brightness manually by moving the slider, and doing so will disable the "Auto" function if it is enabled.

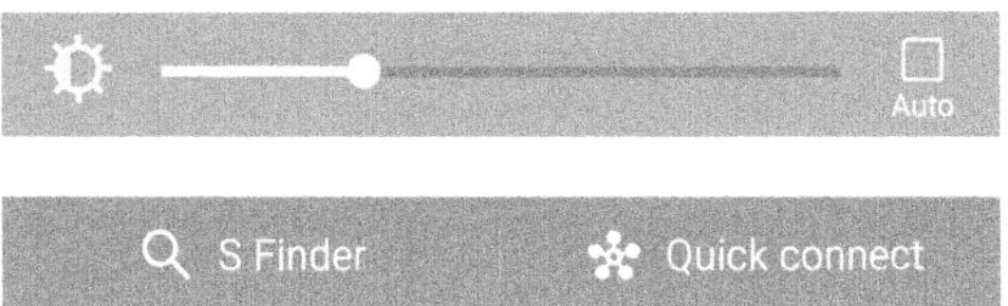

Below the screen brightness selector is the main notification area. In this area, you'll find notifications from apps or from the Android OS itself.

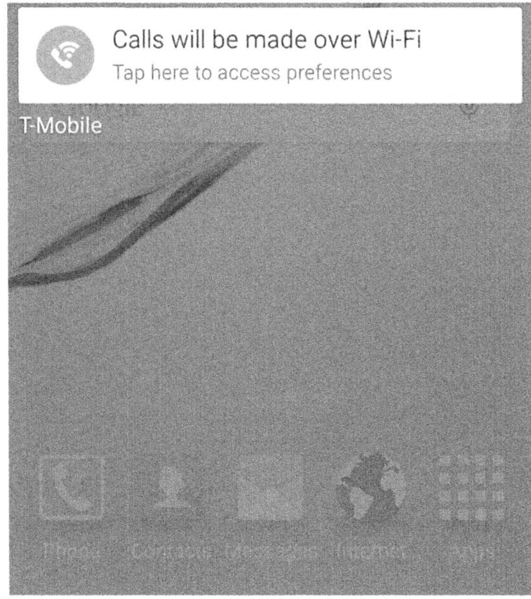

Working with Notifications

Notifications are the main way that apps communicate with you when you're not actively using them. Notifications are very important because they let your device perform valuable services in the background without your involvement. For example, by default your Galaxy's Messages app creates a notification every time you receive a text message. Other apps like stock tickers can send you alerts whenever required, such as when a stock hits a target price. In the following screenshot, I have received a notification about a text message from my friend Mike:

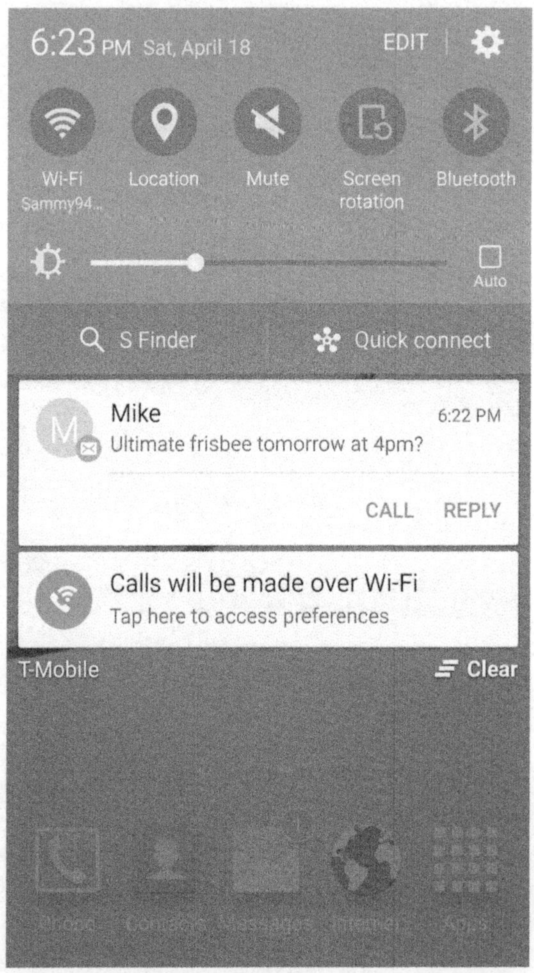

Here, I can tap "Reply" to compose a text message to Mike in the Messages app, or "Call" to place a voice call to him. Tapping the notification somewhere other than "Call" or "Reply" does the exact same thing as tapping "Reply." And indeed, most notifications do something when you tap them, even if they don't have mini action buttons like "Call" and "Reply." For example, you'll receive a notification every time you install a new app from the Google Play Store (p. 166). You won't see an explicit "Open" button, but tapping the notification will open the app. So, any time you want to follow up on a notification, but it doesn't have mini-buttons like "Call" or "Reply", just try tapping it.

Notifications generally disappear ("are dismissed") after you tap them. You can also tap the "Clear" button to dismiss all notifications without tapping them individually and triggering their actions. For example, hitting "Clear" on the screen above would dismiss the text message notification without opening the Messages app. To clear a single notification without tapping it, swipe it left or right.

> ***TIP:*** *You can expand and contract some notifications by placing two fingers on them and dragging up/down. For example, you can do this with Gmail notifications to bring up Archive and Reply buttons in the notification panel itself, or with text message notifications to show or hide the "Call" and "Reply" buttons shown above.*

Some apps create persistent notifications that cannot be cleared. For example, in the screenshot above, my carrier offers Wi-Fi calling and my device displays a persistent notification whenever it's enabled. In this case, hitting "Clear" does not remove that notification, and tapping it does nothing. It's purely informational. A USB connection notification is another example of a persistent notification.

That's everything you need to know about the notification panel. You'll find it's a very important part of your user experience. To close the notification panel, either swipe up from the bottom of the screen or tap ⮌ .

> ***TIP:*** *On some screens the status bar at the top of the screen will be hidden. Swipe down once to reveal it, and then again to open the notification panel.*

The Lock Screen – Protect your personal information

The security risk involved in owning an Android smartphone is higher than ever before because they contain so much more sensitive data than 'dumb' phones. In the past, cellphones contained only your phone book and perhaps some text messages; today, they contain your e-mail, photos, your banking information, your passwords, and so on. The lock screen is the main security mechanism to protect your data. When active, the lock screen prevents your device from being used unless you provide the appropriate authentication. Typically, the lock screen is activated every time the device goes to sleep and a password is required every time it is woken up. The screenshot below shows the lock screen with the PIN function enabled:

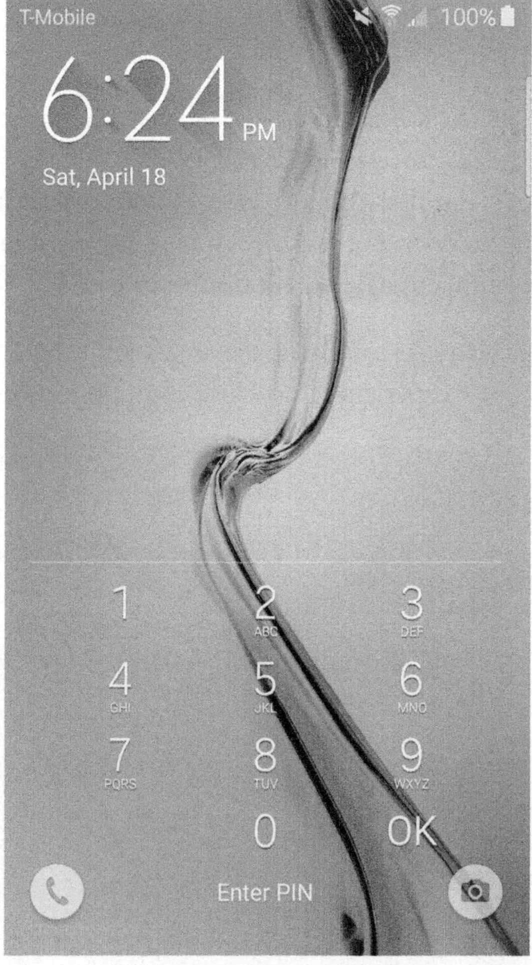

Instead of a PIN, it's also possible to use fingerprint recognition, pattern recognition, or a password. It's also possible to disable the lock screen entirely or to use a zero-security, swipe-to-unlock option, but if you value your personal information at all, I don't suggest using these options.

You'll learn how to set up your lock screen (p. 226) shortly. For now, I just want you to understand what it's for and how it works.

> ***TIP:*** *Want to customize your lock screen? Read more here* *(p. 269)*.

The App Drawer – View all apps, delete apps, & create app shortcuts

Another important part of the TouchWiz interface is the **app drawer**. It contains all the apps installed on your Galaxy, including those preloaded on your Galaxy as well as any third-party apps you have installed from the Google Play Store (p. 166) or other sources.

To open the app drawer, tap the "Apps" shortcut in the app tray:

Upon doing so, you will see a screen like this:

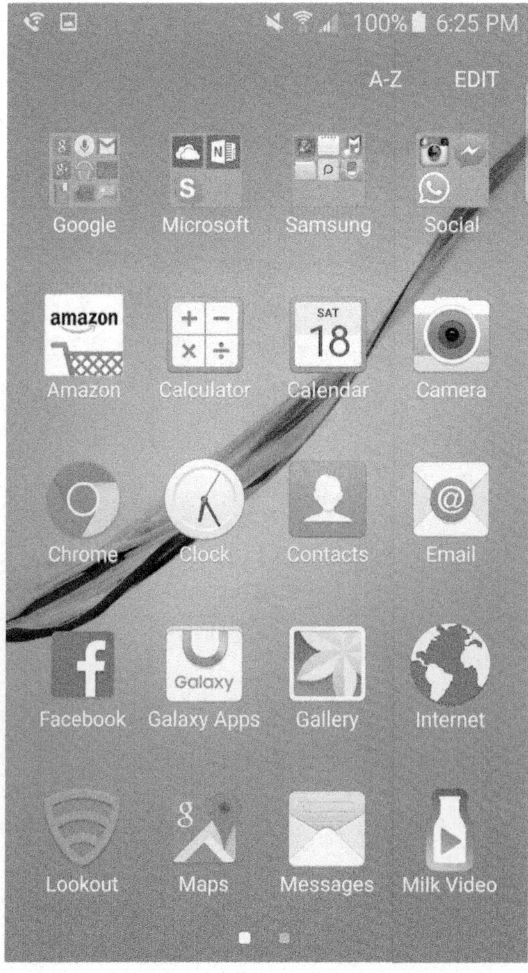

This is the **app drawer**, which contains shortcuts to *all* of the apps installed on your Galaxy, unlike the home screens, where you selectively place the shortcuts (and widgets) you want. In other words, the app drawer is a complete but less convenient way of accessing your apps.

By now, many of these elements should look familiar to you. At the top of the screen is the same status bar that's on the home screen and you can still swipe it down to reveal the notification panel (p. 70). The lion's share of the screen is covered by app shortcuts, which launch apps just as they do on the home screen. At the bottom of the screen are a couple small squares, one of which is highlighted. Similar to the home screen, this indicates you can swipe left and right to access additional screens. There is, however, no 'main' screen in the app drawer like there is with the home screens.

There are two elements in the app drawer not found on the home screen: A-Z and EDIT. Tapping A-Z alphabetizes all the apps in your app drawer. This is useful to "reset" your app drawer if you've rearranged apps using EDIT or if you've installed new apps, which by default are added at the end of your app drawer.

EDIT allows you to:

- **Organize apps in your app drawer:** To rearrange apps, tap and hold until you feel a vibration, then drag the app to its desired location and release. Note that if you want to place an app between two other apps, you have to hold it for an additional ~1 second *in between* the icons until they shift position and make room for the app you're moving. If you hold the app directly over another app instead of next to it, your device will create a new folder instead of moving the app.
- **Create a new folder to organize your apps:** To create a new folder with two or more apps, tap and hold an app until you feel a vibration, then drag the app directly over another app until you see teal highlighting. Then release. A new folder will be created containing both apps. You can move additional apps into this folder using the same tap, hold, and drag method.
- **Remove a folder:** To remove an existing folder, tap it and then tap "Delete folder." This does not delete apps inside the folder—it just returns them to the app drawer.
- **Delete or disable apps:** Tap to completely uninstall downloaded apps or disable non-essential apps (p. 267) that come preloaded on the device. Samsung does not allow you to completely uninstall preloaded apps, but disabling them freezes them and prevents them from running. I recommend disabling any built-in apps you do not use, because it frees up memory, improves system performance,

and increases battery life. In particular, feel free to disable carrier "bloatware"—any apps preloaded on your Galaxy that you know you'll never use. (I'm looking at you, "Milk.") To re-enable any disabled apps, go to system settings → "Applications" → "Application manager" and swipe right to the "Disabled" apps section.

To exit Edit mode, tap ⮌ or DONE.

Adding New App Shortcuts to Your Home Screen

When you tap and hold an app shortcut in the app drawer (p. 78), your Galaxy displays a silhouette of your home screens and gives you a chance to copy the shortcut to one of your home screens (p. 59) or the app tray (p. 62) if it has a free slot.

Below, I have tapped and held the S Health app in the app drawer, and my Galaxy is directing me to place a shortcut on my main home screen. To do so, I would simply position the S Health shortcut where I want it, and release.

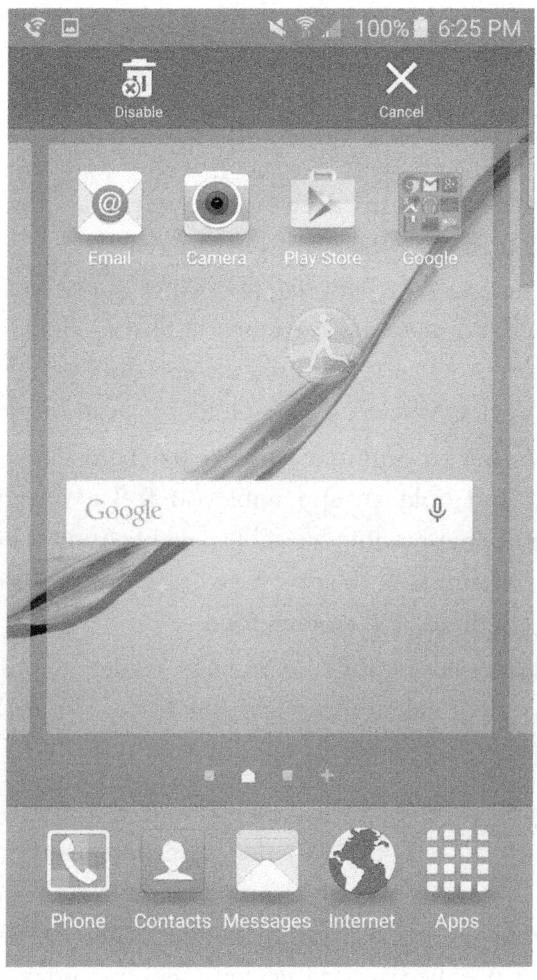

Had I wanted to place the shortcut on a secondary home screen, I would have dragged the shortcut to the far left or right edge of the screen, held it until the home screen switched over, and then released it.

As you may recall, this action is different than when you tap and hold an app shortcut that's already on a home screen—in that case, tapping and holding lets you move the shortcut around on your home screens, remove it altogether, or place it into a folder.

To summarize:

- **Tapping and holding apps in the app drawer lets you create *new* shortcuts on your home screen (p. 59) or in the app tray (p. 62).**
- **Tapping and holding app shortcuts that are already on your home screen lets you edit or move app shortcuts that have already been created.**
- **The app drawer is for comprehensive access to all your apps; home screens are for your most-used apps and widgets only.**

Transferring Your Data from Another Phone

By now, you should be getting comfortable with your Galaxy. You've seen all the major parts of the user interface and you're getting a sense of how they all work together. But there's another important topic to cover before we move on—what's the best way to transfer data from your previous phone?

From an Android That Supports NFC—Use Tap & Go

If you're switching from an Android device that supports NFC wireless communication, you can use the new Android 5.0 Lollipop "**Tap & Go**" feature to transfer your Google account, apps, app data, Wi-Fi passwords, and system settings.

A couple caveats:

- Tap & Go is only available when you first set up your device. If you want to use Tap & Go after setting up your device, you'll have to perform a factory reset (p. 274) to completely wipe your device and start from scratch as described in Chapter 3 (p. 25).
- **Tap & Go doesn't transfer your SMS/MMS messages or Gallery photos. To transfer these, use Samsung Smart Switch as described below, *after* using Tap & Go.**

Not sure if your previous Android device supports NFC? As long as it was made in the last 3-4 years, it probably does. But to be sure, consult its instruction manual or search Google.

From a non-NFC Android, iPhone, or BlackBerry—Samsung Smart Switch

If you can't or don't want to use Tap & Go, the next best option is Samsung's exclusive Smart Switch program. Samsung realized that its customers wanted an easy and fast way to transfer data to their new phones and created a good, reliable program to do just that.

It runs on both Windows and Mac OS, and allows you to transfer your data from almost any iPhone, Android, BlackBerry, or Symbian phone. In fact, if you are switching from another Android smartphone or from an iPhone and you have an iCloud account, you don't need to install any desktop software—only the Smart Switch mobile app, available from the Google Play Store (p. 166) and Apple App Store.

Smart Switch also makes it very easy to selectively transfer data, so it's a great way to selectively transfer your text messages and Gallery photos after using Tap & Go, since Tap & Go doesn't copy these things.

Whatever your situation is, the Smart Switch website has clear, step-by-step instructions. Start here:

http://www.samsung.com/us/smart-switch/

From a Dumb Phone

If your new Galaxy is your first smartphone and your last phone was a "dumb" phone, there's good and bad news. The good news is that you won't have much information to transfer—probably just phone numbers. The bad news is that data transfer programs are becoming less common as dumb phones are becoming less common. Your luck will depend on what make and model your last phone was.

Because there are hundreds, if not thousands of dumb phone models in existence, I can't offer you a one-size-fits-all solution. However, I can offer you some general advice. Here are the steps you should take to get your contacts from your dumb phone to your Galaxy:

1. First, take both phones to one of your carrier's retail stores and ask if they can help. These stores usually have special, industrial devices that can transfer your data. This is the easiest and cheapest option in most cases.

2. If the store's transfer device isn't compatible with your old phone, you can try to save your contacts to your SIM card using your dumb phone and then import them to your Galaxy. This only works if your dumb phone has a contact export feature (so consult its instruction manual), and also uses a nano-SIM card like your Galaxy (many older phones used micro- or mini-SIM cards; in that case, this method won't work). If, after consulting your old phone's instruction manual, you are able to export your contacts to your nano-SIM card, pop it back into your Galaxy and go to Contacts → MORE → "Settings" → "Import/Export contacts" → "Import" → "SIM card." Save the contacts to your Google account.
3. If you happen to have Verizon, you may be able to use its special Backup Assistant feature. Log into your Verizon account online to access it, or call customer service and ask for their help. If you have another carrier, call customer service and ask if they have a solution for your particular case.
4. If none of these methods accomplish what you need, it's time to start Googling. Search Google for **(make and model of your old phone) transferring contacts to android**. With any luck, you'll find a solution for to your particular situation. Some of them may require purchasing software or computer cables.
5. Failing that, sit down, get comfortable, and manually enter phone numbers into your Contacts (p. 135) app the old-fashioned way. Sorry!

If your old dumb phone has other data you want to transfer, like photos or MP3 files, your best bet will be to consult the phone's instruction manual to learn how to copy those files to an SD memory card. From there, you can copy those files to your computer, and then onto your Galaxy using the techniques in Chapter 9 (p. 278). Since the Note 5 and S6 Edge+ don't have a micro SD card slot, it's not possible to simply swap your old memory card into your new Galaxy.

Chapter 5: Basic Functions

So far, you've learned the basics of the TouchWiz interface, including the home screen, the notification panel, the lock screen, the app drawer, and more. Now, I'll show you how to perform basic functions such as making phone calls, sending text messages, browsing the Internet, taking pictures and video, and more.

Landscape Mode

Landscape Mode works in almost all apps—but not on the home screen, app drawer, notification panel, or lock screen. When you're in an app, just flip your Galaxy sideways and it'll automatically enter landscape mode.

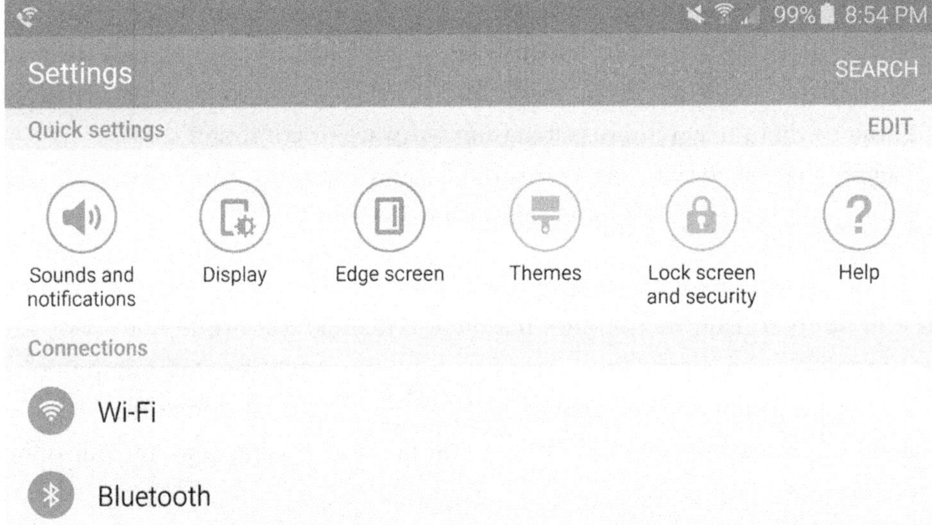

If your Galaxy doesn't enter landscape mode when you flip it sideways, swipe down the notification panel and make sure the Screen Rotation toggle button is set to "Auto rotate." You can also use this toggle button to lock the display to Portrait mode if you don't want your screen to automatically rotate.

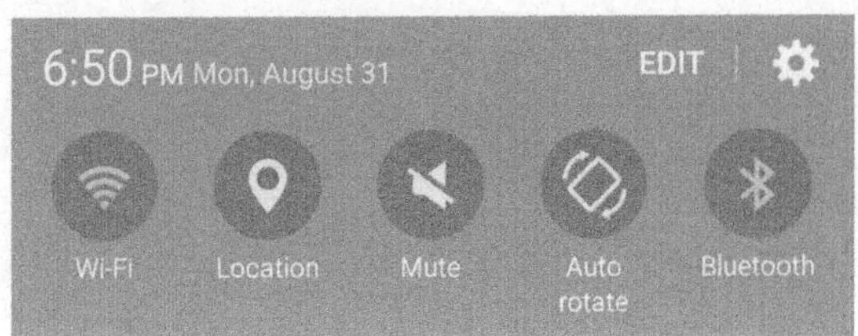

Entering Text

Inputting text is one of the most basic functions you need to know. There are several ways to do so:

- Typing with the on-screen keyboard;
- Swiping with the on-screen keyboard;
- Dictating by voice, and;
- Writing with the S Pen (Note 5 only).

Typing with the On-Screen Keyboard

The default input method is the on-screen Samsung keyboard. It looks like this:

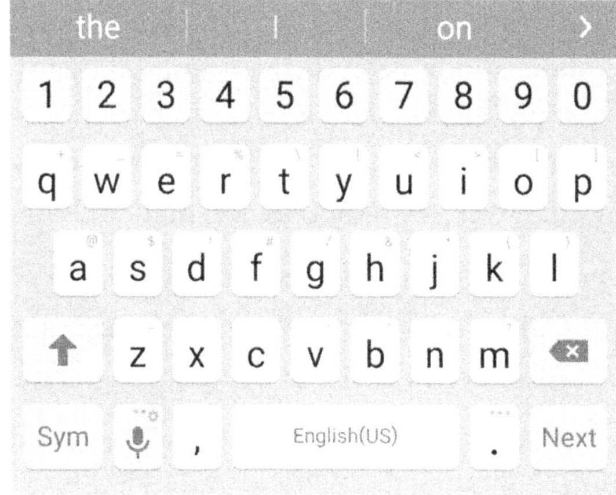

In my opinion, the Samsung keyboard is excellent. It allows both tapping and swiping (discussed below), has well-placed punctuation keys, and includes a number row that's accessible without tapping a modifier key first. I always use the Samsung keyboard.

However, the Samsung keyboard is only one of many keyboards available for Android devices. Other keyboards can be downloaded and installed from the Google Play Store, and each one looks and works a little differently. For example, the official Google keyboard has a more minimalist look and sacrifices the number row for larger letter keys:

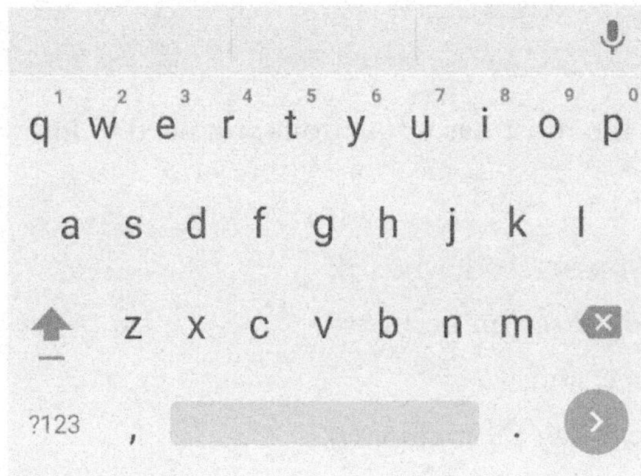

TIP: If you decide the Samsung keyboard isn't for you, try other options from the Google Play Store like the official Google Keyboard shown above, Swype, Fleksy, TouchPal, or others.

Here's what you need to know about using the Samsung keyboard:

- Tap shift ( ) to cycle through lowercase, initial uppercase, and caps lock.
- Tap and hold any character key to access accented and other secondary characters.
- Tap Sym to switch between the standard keyboard and symbols.
- As you type, your Galaxy predicts words in the gray bar above the keyboard. Tap any word to autocomplete the word you are typing. This can save a lot of time. Tap to save a new word into the dictionary, and tap to see more autocomplete options.
- Tap once to activate voice input (discussed below), or tap and hold it to access keyboard settings:

From left to right, these settings include:

- : Activate Voice Input (p. 88) (same as tapping once)
- : Activate S Pen handwriting recognition mode (Note 5 only)
- : Show Recent Clipboard Items

- ⚙: Samsung Keyboard Settings (same as going to system settings→ "Language and input" → "Samsung keyboard")

There are many settings available for the Samsung keyboard such as auto-prediction, auto-punctuation, sound and vibration, and more. You can also enable Text Shortcuts (p. 269), which let you specify abbreviations that your Galaxy will automatically expand. For example, you can configure the Samsung keyboard to expand "sth" into "something," or "bc" into "because."

Swiping for Speedy Input

In 2010, a small software developer released a keyboard called Swype. Swype was the first Android keyboard to offer typing by swiping. With this type of input, instead of tapping letters one at a time, you place your finger on the first character of the word you want and trace from letter to letter without tapping at all.

Once I tried Swype, I never looked back – as did millions of other Android users. Today, you can still download Swype from the Google Play Store, but you don't need to because Samsung includes the same functionality in the Samsung keyboard. I strongly suggest you learn to type by swiping, as it's much faster and easier than tapping. It also considerably reduces strain on your thumbs.

Below is a screenshot of me swiping the word "Hello." You can see the path of my finger over the keys.

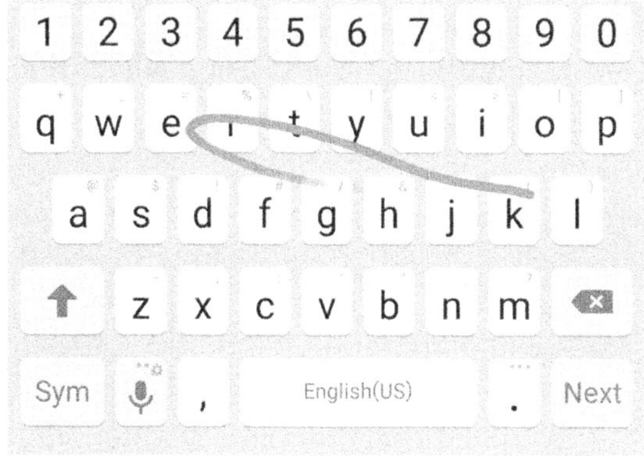

TIP: On the Note 5 and S6 Edge+, you can even type multiple words by swiping, without lifting your finger at all. Simply move your finger over the spacebar in between words.

Dictating Text Using Voice Recognition

Dictation is another way to input text. To activate voice input mode, tap on a text input field to bring up the Samsung keyboard, and then tap once. You can begin speaking as soon as the following screen appears:

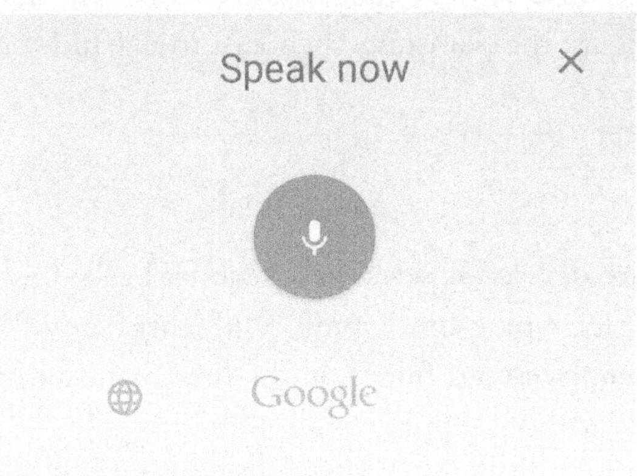

Tap to pause dictation or tap to change languages.

Voice recognition is surprisingly accurate and Google is improving it all the time. In particular, I find it very handy when I have to use my phone while driving. I suggest you give voice recognition input a shot, because it's the real deal—not a gimmick like voice recognition technology was a few years ago.

Handwriting Recognition with the S Pen (Note 5 only)

Finally, if you have a Note 5, you can input text using handwriting recognition with the S Pen. To do so, open the Samsung keyboard and tap and hold , then tap .

Read more about handwriting recognition in Chapter 6 (p. 188).

Copy and Paste

TouchWiz makes it easy to copy and paste text. First, you need to select text. Tap and hold text in apps such as Messages, Gmail, any Internet browser, and so on:

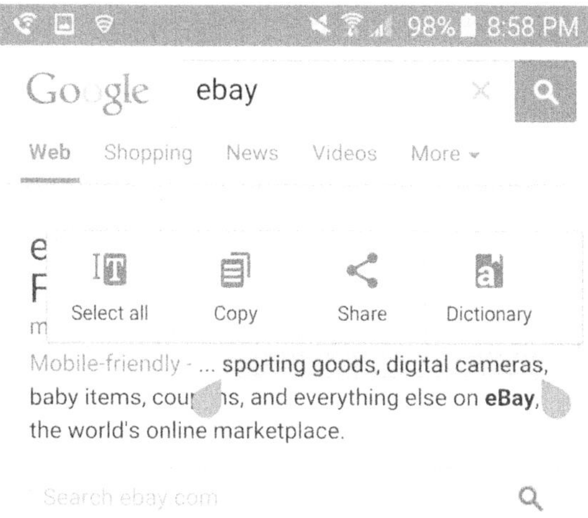

Move the blue tabs around to select the text you want to copy, and then tap "Copy." You can also swipe left and right in this toolbar to access other options.

In some apps, you may see a slightly different copy button: icon ( ), which appears along the top of the screen. The other two icons on this toolbar are "Cut" ( ) and "Select All" ( ), respectively. closes the toolbar.

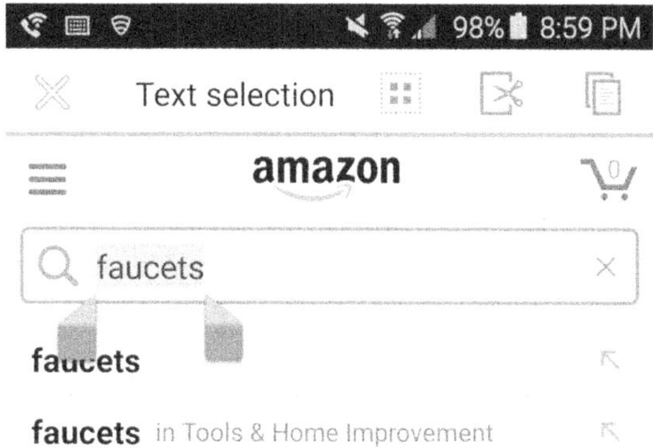

After you've copied your text, tap and hold in the text field you want to paste into, and then tap "Paste." Alternatively, to access data that you previously copied, tap "Clipboard" and then the content you want to paste.

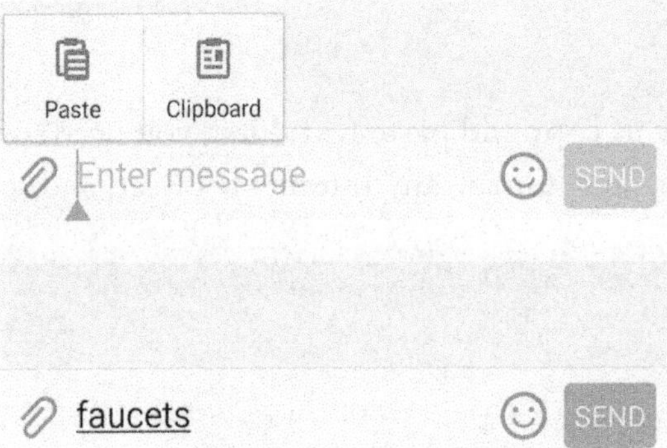

In some apps, you may see the following paste button instead:

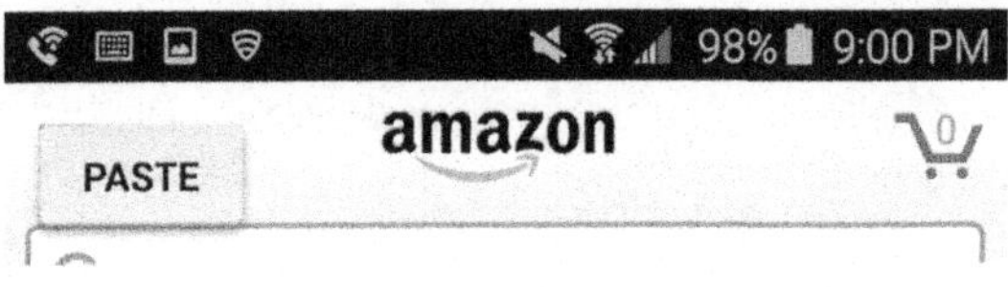

The Share Via Tool

You'll see the Share Via tool in nearly every app, so you need to understand how it works. The Share Via icon looks like this:

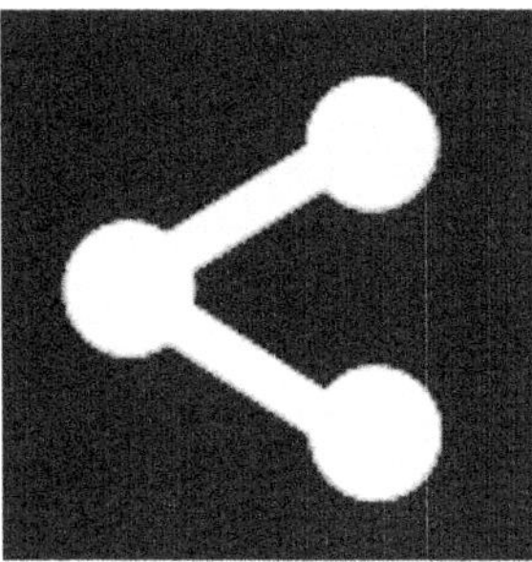

Tapping this icon lets you **send content from one app to another, in order to do something with it**. For example, in the following screenshot I have tapped while viewing a photo in the Gallery app:

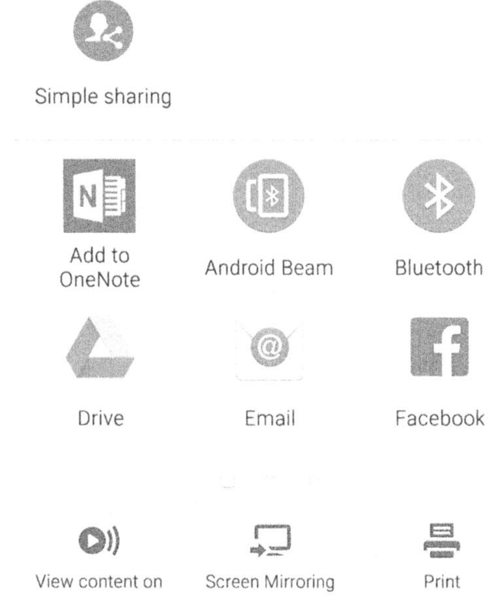

Using the Share Via tool, I can:

- Send the file to Google Drive to upload it to cloud storage;
- Send the file to the Facebook app to post it on social media;
- Send it to another Android with Android Beam (p. 232)
- Print it;
- and so on.

Swipe left and right to see more options, like sending it to the Messages app to include in a text message, or sending it to the Gmail app to send as an email attachment.

> ***TIP:*** *"Simple sharing" uploads your content to a Samsung server and then sends a link to the person you shared it with. In my opinion, "Simple sharing" is an unnecessary middle step. Skip "Simple sharing" and share files as email attachments instead by swiping right and selecting "Gmail" (or "Email" if you've set up a non-Gmail POP3 or IMAP account).*

As I mentioned, you'll see this tool all over your Galaxy. Sometimes it may be listed as "Share" in a MORE menu instead of being labeled with . But its purpose is always the same: to send content from one app to another. It's kind of like a replacement for files and folders on a desktop computer. For example, if you want to email an attachment on a desktop computer, you'd click "Attach" and then browse your hard drive to find the desired file. On Android, files and folders are all hidden behind the scenes. Instead, you'd just open the desired file in its respective app (e.g., Gallery for photos) and then use the Share Via tool to send it to the Gmail app for use as an attachment.

The bottom line is, **if you need to get a file from one app to another, look for the Share Via tool.**

Connecting to a Wi-Fi Network

Need to connect to a wireless network at home, in an airport, in a coffee shop, etc.? Make sure the Wi-Fi toggle button is enabled in the notification panel and go to system settings → "Wi-Fi." You will see a list of available networks:

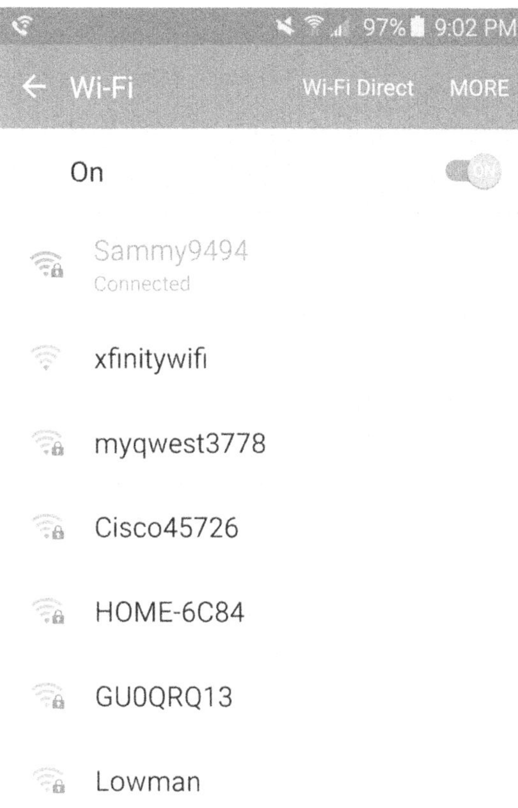

Tap on any network and follow the prompts to connect. If the network is secured, you'll be asked to enter a WEP/WPA password first.

Alternatively, to connect to a router using WPS technology, press the WPS button ( ) on your router. Then, on your Galaxy tap MORE → "WPS push button." If your router supports WPS, this method lets you connect to the network without typing in a password. Most modern routers support WPS and I personally like to use it when possible.

If your network does not appear in the list, try toggling Wi-Fi off and on again and/or power-cycling your router.

***TIP:** For some commercial Wi-Fi hotspots, such as the ones at Starbucks, you'll be able to connect to the network without a password, but after you're connected you'll need to open your browser and accept terms & conditions before you actually get Internet access. You will usually receive a notification in your notification panel that you need to log in, but not always. So, if you connect to a public Wi-Fi hotspot but data isn't working, open your browser and try to load a web page. You should be redirected to a login page, and after logging in, you will have Internet access.*

Browsing the Internet

The Note 5 and S6 Edge+ come pre-loaded with two Internet browsers. The first is aptly titled "Internet," and the second is the mobile version of Google Chrome. Although the stock Internet browser is not a bad browser, my suggestion is to skip it and go straight to Chrome—*especially* if you use Chrome on your desktop computer. Chrome is updated more often, is faster, and integrates with your Google account to automatically sync your desktop bookmarks, saved passwords, history, browser tabs, and more.

You'll find Chrome in your app drawer. If, for some reason, your Galaxy did not come with Chrome, download it free from the Google Play Store (p. 166).

***TIP:** Internet has a couple notable features that Chrome lacks: saving webpages for offline viewing and using fingerprint authentication to store website logins. If either of these features is very important to you, consider using Internet instead of Chrome.*

Upon opening Chrome for the first time, you'll need to accept Google's Terms of Service to continue. Do so, and then proceed to sign in with your Google account. When you're done, you'll see the Google homepage:

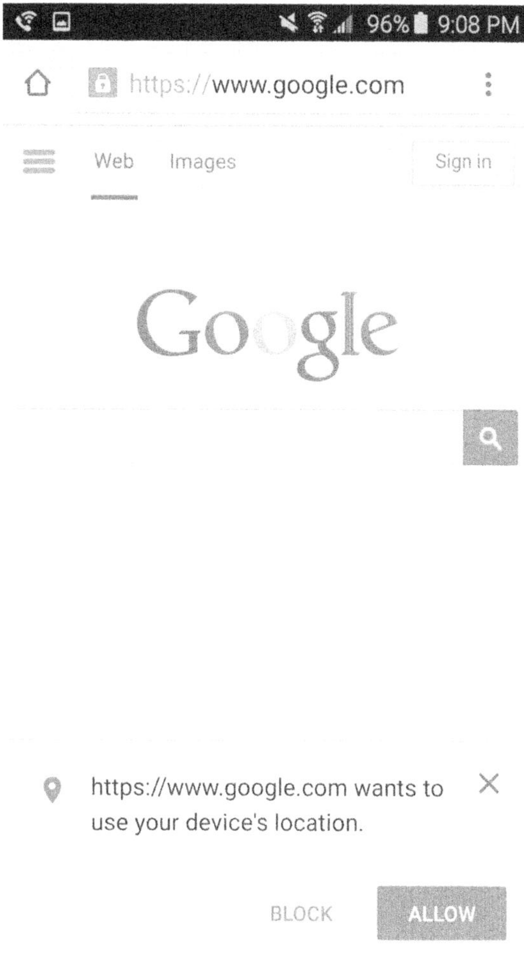

To browse the web, enter web addresses (.com's, etc.) in the search box at the top of the screen, or simply enter keywords to search Google. While browsing, you can double-tap paragraphs to auto-fit-to-screen, pinch in and out with two fingers to zoom manually, copy and paste text (p. 89), and tap and hold links to bring up additional options. To view open tabs, tap ▭ and you'll see them listed alongside your currently running apps. Tap ⋮ to see the menu, where you can access other options including:

- Open a new tab;
- Open a new incognito tab (p. 98);
- Access bookmarks;
- View browsing history;
- Share the current tab with the Share Via (p. 91) tool;
- Print (p. 262) the current tab;
- Find text in the current tab;
- Request the desktop version of a mobile site;

- Access Chrome's settings;
- and more.

> ***TIP:*** *Auto-fit and pinch-to-zoom usually only work when you're viewing desktop sites in mobile Chrome. If you're viewing a mobile-optimized site, often you'll find that these features don't work. If this is a problem, you can force all websites to allow zooming. Tap ⋮ → "Settings" → "Accessibility" and check "Force enable zoom." From this screen you can also change the default text size to make websites easier to read on the device's screen.*

Tabbed Browsing

Chrome lets you have multiple tabs open at the same time, much like on a desktop browser. This is a convenient way to quickly jump back and forth between multiple web pages. On Android 5.0 Lollipop, Chrome tabs are shown alongside your currently running apps, so to see them and switch between them, tap the recent key (▭) to the left of ⬭.

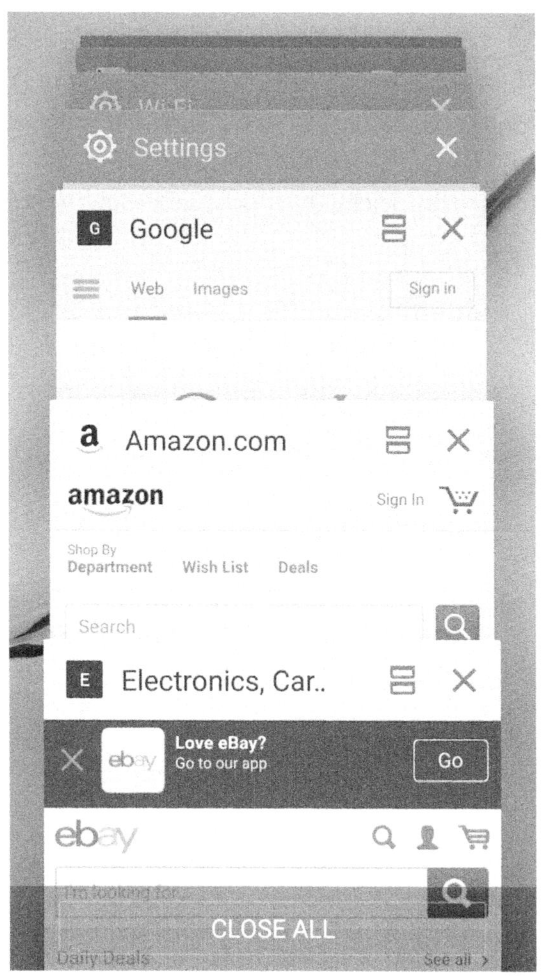

Tap a tab to make it full screen.

TIP: If you want to separate your tabs from your currently running apps, go to ⋮ → "Settings" → "Merge tabs and apps" and turn the slider off. Now, your tabs will be accessible through the window switcher icon (3) next to ⋮.

Adding and Viewing Bookmarks

To bookmark an open web page, tap ⋮ → ☆. Tap "Save." To manage your bookmarks, tap ⋮ → "Bookmarks." Tap on folders to open them, and tap ↩ to go to the previous folder. Tap and hold individual bookmarks to rename them ("Edit bookmark") or to delete them ("Delete bookmark"). Unfortunately, there is no way to move bookmarks between folders on your Galaxy. You either have to use the Bookmark Manager on the desktop version of Chrome, or delete the bookmarks and recreate them in the correct folder one at a time.

> ★ ***TIP:*** *If you add, remove, or edit bookmarks in the desktop version of Chrome, the changes will be automatically synced to mobile Chrome, usually within 5-10 minutes. You don't need to take a manual action to synchronize the two browsers. The same principle holds true for other data that Chrome syncs, such as saved passwords, history, open tabs, and more.*

Private Browsing with Incognito Mode

Sometimes, you might want to browse without leaving a trace in your history. No judgment. To do so, tap ⋮ → "New incognito tab." This new tab, which has a black background, lets you browse without recording your history, cookies, or any other record of the web pages you visit.

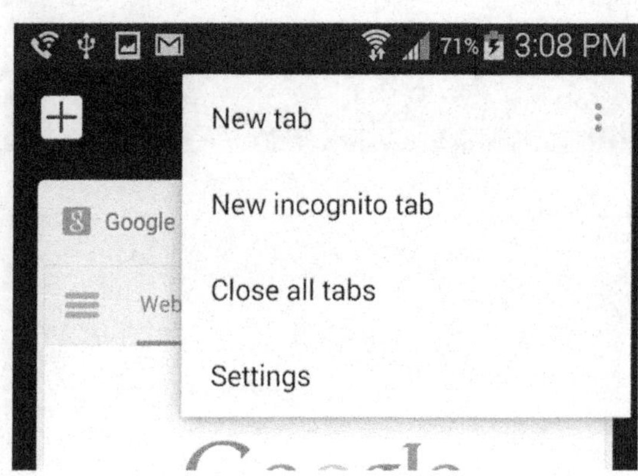

Viewing Open Tabs on Your Desktop Computer

As long as your desktop Google Chrome is set to sync open tabs (in desktop Chrome settings → "Advanced Sync Settings"), you can access your currently open desktop tabs using your Galaxy. To do so, tap ⋮ → "Recent tabs." You'll see a list of devices synced with your Google account—look for your desktop computer and tap the tab you want to open on your Galaxy. This is a very convenient way to pick up where you left off on your desktop computer while on the go.

Overriding Mobile Web Themes

While some websites have great mobile versions, others are just detestable, broken wastelands or are missing critical features. Not all businesses are up to date with the importance of mobile websites. If this happens, you can attempt to override the website's mobile theme by tapping ⋮ → "Request desktop site." This doesn't always work, but it usually does.

Extensions: Nope

One very popular feature of the desktop Chrome browser is its vast library of extensions, such as ad blockers and password managers. Although there is often speculation about if and when Google will implement extensions for the Android version of Chrome, at this time there is no way to run Chrome extensions on your Galaxy.

Clearing History and Cookies

To clear your private browsing data, tap ⋮ → "Settings" → "Privacy." Tap "Clear browsing data" at the bottom of the screen, select the types of data you want to delete, and then tap "Clear."

Tweaking Other Chrome Settings

Chrome has additional settings and features we haven't discussed in detail. Some of these include:

- Changing the **default search engine** to something other than Google;
- Enabling/disabling **save passwords** and **autofill** (of order forms, etc.) of your personal information;
- Setting a **home page**;

- Enabling web page **pre-fetching** on Wi-Fi (anticipates links you might click and caches their content to speed up browsing);
- Using Google's Data Saver feature to **compress your browsing data** and save bandwidth on your cell plan;
- Blocking **pop-up windows**;
- Disabling **JavaScript**;
- Configuring foreign language **translation settings**;
- and more.

You can investigate and customize these options yourself by tapping ⋮ → "Settings" and exploring the settings sub-menus.

Making Calls

Calls are made through the Phone app. It's in your app tray and app drawer by default.

Making and Ending Calls

To place a call, open the Phone app and tap the keypad icon ( ). Dial the outgoing number as you would on a normal phone, and then tap to place the call. If you make an error while entering the number, tap to delete the last digit entered.

There are several other ways to make calls as well:

- Tap the "Log" tab to view recent calls, tap a name or number, and then .
- Tap the "Favorites" tab to view your most frequently called contacts, tap a contact's name, and then .

- Tap the "Contacts" tab to view your entire phone book, tap a contact's name, and then .
- To speed dial a contact, see the Speed Dial (p. 105) section below.
- Voice dial a contact using Google Now (p. 174) or S Voice (p. 181).
- Tap a 10-digit phone number on a webpage in Internet or Chrome, and then  .

__TIP:__ Swipe left on any contact in your call log or Contacts to quickly text message them, or swipe right to call them. If you don't like this feature, disable it in Phone → MORE → "Settings" → "Swipe to call or send messages."

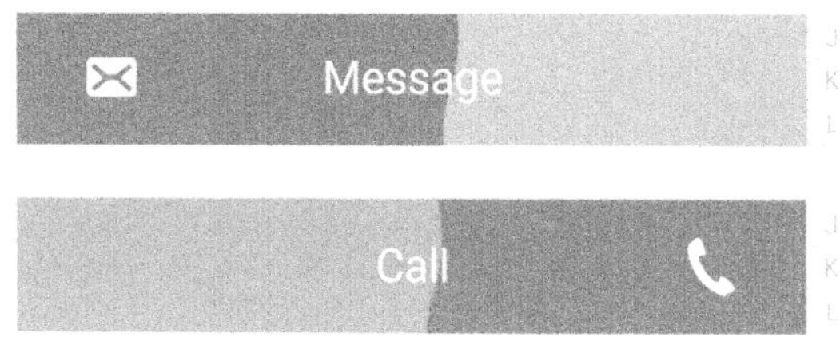

Answering and Rejecting Calls

To answer an incoming call, tap and hold and drag it right. To reject an incoming call, tap and hold and drag it left.

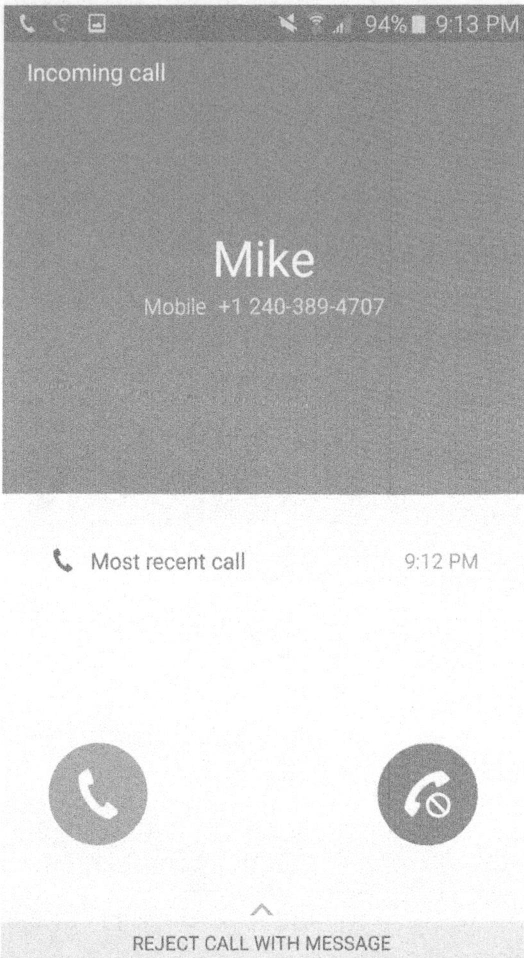

Alternatively, swipe the "Reject call with message" tab upward, and then tap the message you wish to send. Your Galaxy will reject the call and dispatch a text message to the caller.

To customize rejection messages, go to Phone → MORE → "Settings" → "Call blocking" → "Call-reject messages."

TIP: *If you receive a call while an app is open on your screen, you'll only see a small pop-up instead of a full-screen notification that kicks you out of your app: In this case, just tap "Answer" or "Reject." No swiping necessary.*

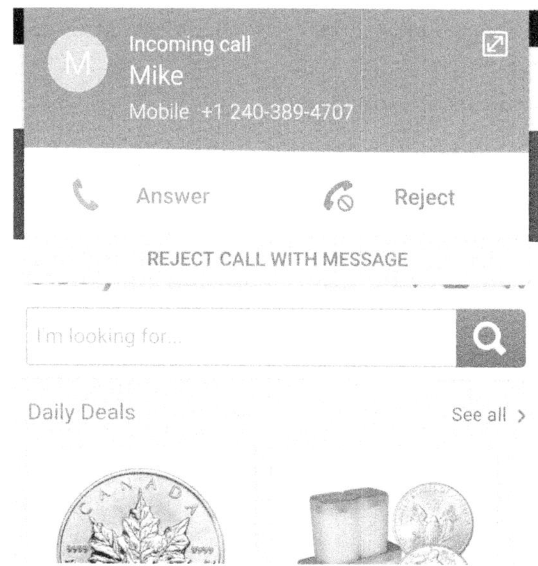

In-Call Controls

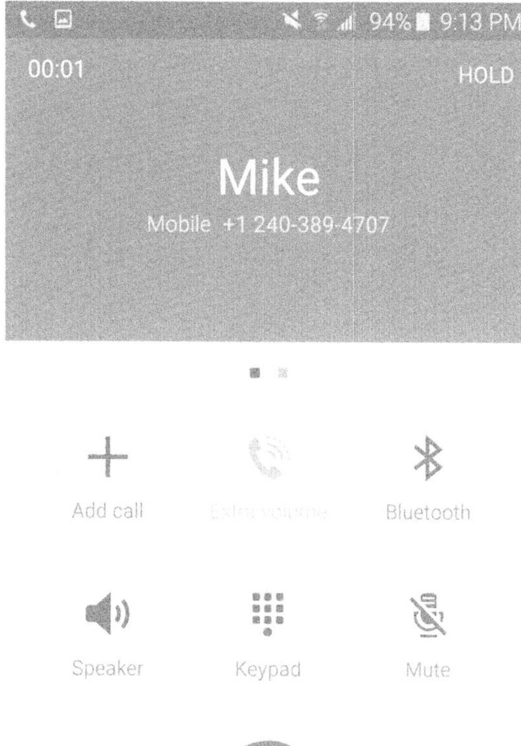

Once you're in an active call, you have the options shown above:

- "Add call" lets you dial in a third party.
- "Bluetooth" switches the call to a Bluetooth headset or car stereo, if one has been paired (p. 234).
- "Speaker" switches to speakerphone.
- "Keypad" brings up a number pad so you can enter numbers on automated phone lines.
- "Mute" turns off your microphone, so the other party cannot hear you.

> ★ ***TIP:*** *You'll also notice a* HOLD *option in the upper-right-hand corner of the screen. In my experience, Hold doesn't work well on Android. It often causes the call to disconnect. Just use Mute instead—it accomplishes the same thing.*

You can also adjust the call volume using the Volume Up and Down buttons, or tap ▭ to see your home screen and open other apps while keeping your call connected. Or, swipe right to access some common apps while on a call (works best when you're using the speakerphone).

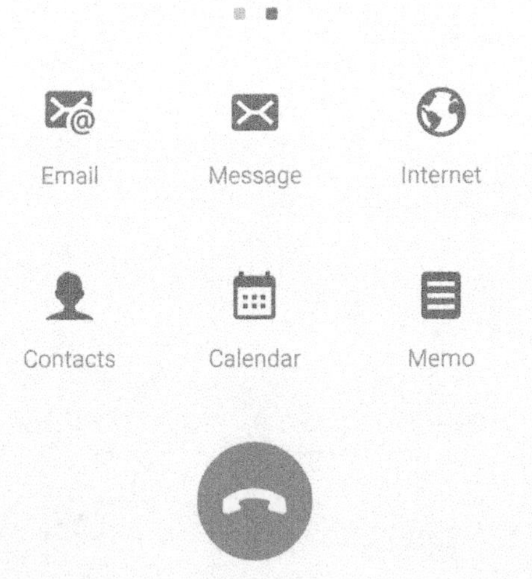

Screening Calls Discreetly

Sometimes, you might want to discretely reject a call—let it go to voicemail, but let it ring normally first. Obviously all you have to do is not answer—but there's a good trick to know. While your Galaxy is ringing, just tap the Volume Down key to silence the ringtone, but let the call continue to voicemail normally. This way, the caller won't think you're rejecting their call after one or two rings, and you won't have to listen to the phone ring all the way to voicemail.

Checking and Returning Missed Calls

If you miss a call, you'll receive a notification in your notification panel. Swipe down the notification panel and tap the notification to view the caller's details and return their call if you wish. If you don't see the "Call back" and "Message" shortcuts, place two fingers on the notification and drag down.

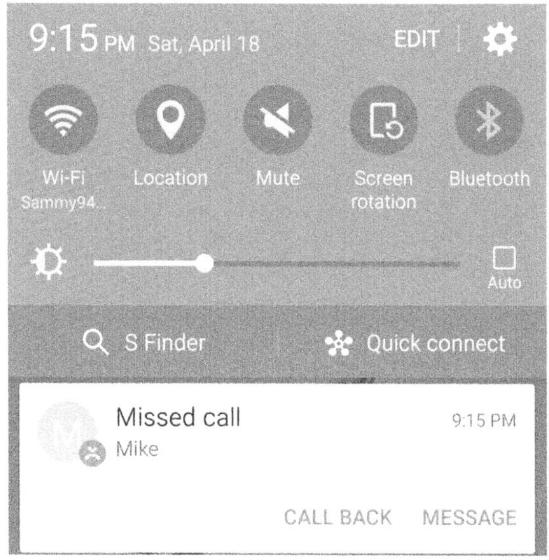

Speed Dial

To create a new speed dial contact, go to Phone → ⠿ → MORE → "Speed dial." From this page, tap the number to which you wish to assign a contact and select the appropriate contact/phone number from your contacts.

To dial a speed dial contact after it has been assigned, go to Phone → ⠿ and dial the speed dial number, holding the last digit until the contact is dialed. For example, to dial the contact associated with speed dial "2," simply tap and hold 2. To dial the contact associated with speed dial "25," tap 2, then tap and hold 5.

To remove a speed dial contact, go to Phone → ⠿ → MORE → "Speed dial." From this page, tap ▬ next to the speed dial contact you wish to remove.

Video Calls

At the time of writing, some carriers are rolling out a new video calling feature on the Note 5 and S6 Edge+. This feature is built directly into the Phone app and uses your Galaxy's front camera. To place a video call, open the Phone app, dial the intended number, and then tap . Although this is a very cool feature, currently you can only video call other Note 5 and S6 Edge+ owners who are on the same carrier as you, so in practice its usefulness may be limited.

> ***TIP:*** *If you want to video call someone who's not a Note 5 / S6 Edge+ user on your carrier, try Google's pre-installed Hangouts app instead. Video calling someone using the Hangouts app only requires that they have an Android device with Hangouts installed.*

Checking Voicemail

To check your voicemail, open the Phone app and tap the "Keypad" tab. Tap and follow the prompts. The first time you call your voicemail, you may need to set a PIN and record a greeting depending on your carrier's procedures.

Visual Voicemail

Depending on your carrier, you may have a visual voicemail app in your app drawer. Visual voicemail apps list your voicemails on-screen like emails and let you selectively listen to or delete them. If your carrier includes such an app, try it out—it's a big step up from traditional voicemail.

Sending Text Messages (SMS) and Picture Messages (MMS)

Text messages are sent through the Messages app, which is in your app tray by default.

Tap an existing conversation thread to open it, or tap to compose a new text message.

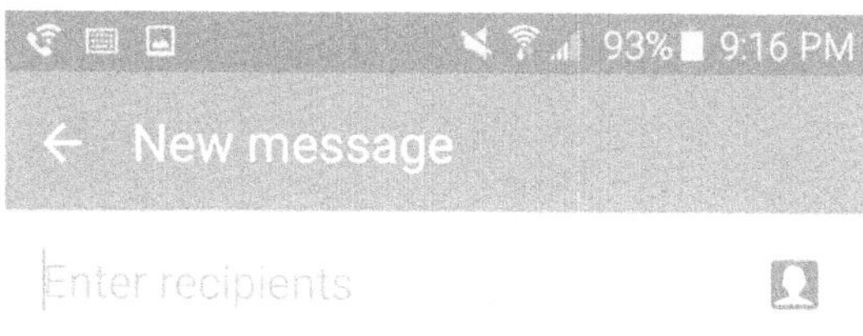

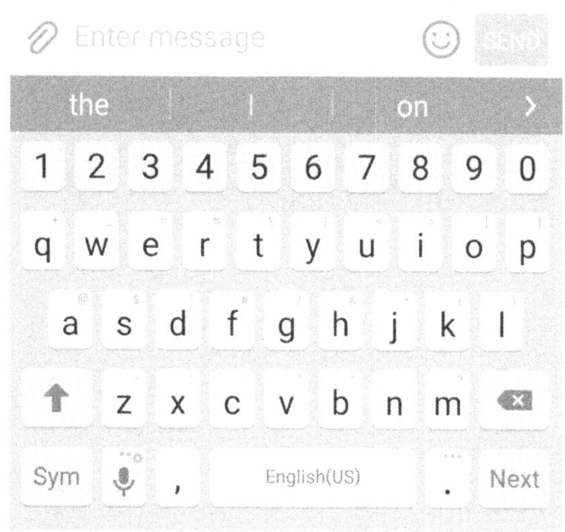

TIP: To easily change the font size in the Messages app using the volume keys, go to MORE → "Font size." You can also pinch-to-zoom, but only after you've opened a conversation thread—this won't work in the main Messages screen.

To specify a recipient, tap in the "Enter recipients" field and type a phone number or name in your contacts. Alternatively, tap and select a contact from your phone book. You can enter multiple recipients. Some carriers support group messaging, meaning that if you include multiple recipients, any replies sent to you will also be sent to *all* your original recipients. Be careful with this feature—it's very useful but potentially very awkward if you don't understand it. (To disable this feature, go to MORE → "Settings" → "More settings" → "Multimedia messages" and turn off "Group conversation.")

To enter a message, tap in the "Enter message" field and type your message. You can attach a photo by tapping → "Image" → "Gallery" and then selecting a picture and tapping "Done." This is how to send a picture message, otherwise known as an MMS.

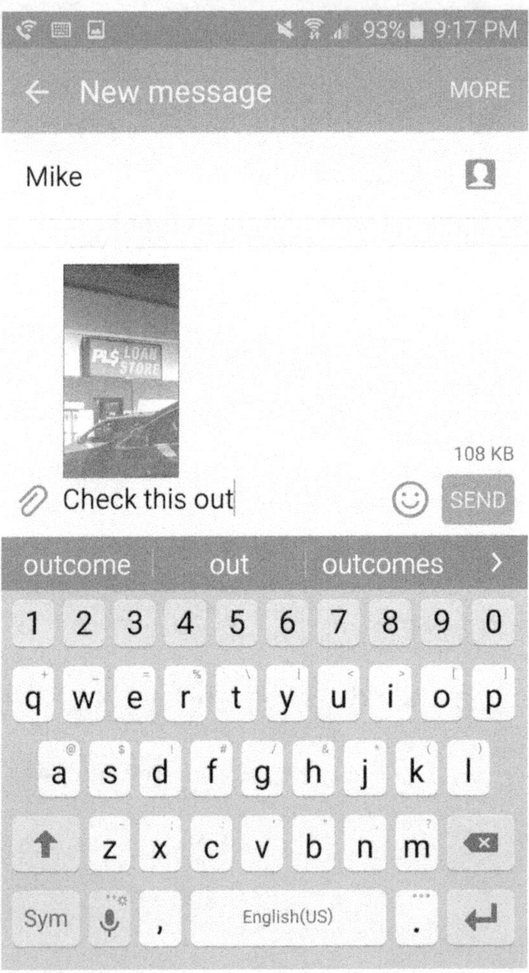

After you've selected a recipient and composed a message, tap SEND to dispatch your message.

When you receive a response to a text message, you'll receive a notification in your notification panel.

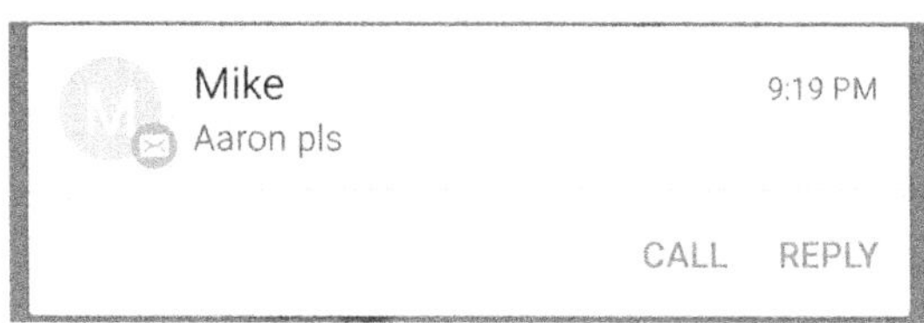

Tap the notification to open the text message thread, or use the "Call" and "Reply" shortcuts to quickly respond to the text. If you don't see the "Call" and "Reply" buttons, place two fingers on the notification and drag down.

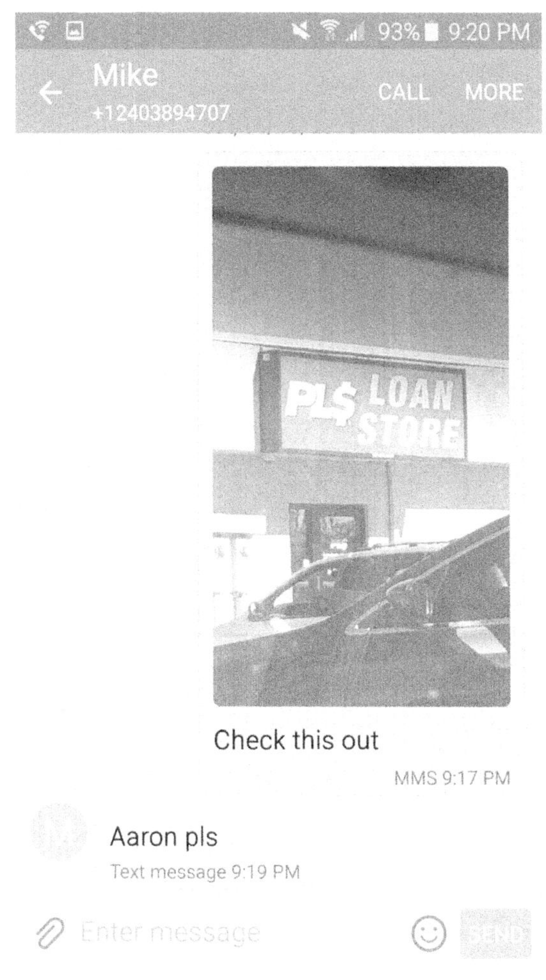

Compose further replies in the same manner described above.

Setting Up Priority Senders to Text Quickly

Priority Senders lets you compose new texts to your favorite people with a single tap. To set it up, tap + in the Messages app.

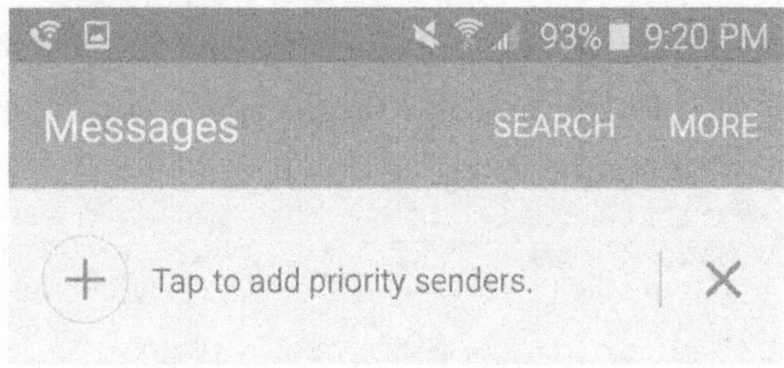

Locate the contact(s) that you wish to place in your Priority Senders area, select them, and then tap DONE in the upper-right-hand corner of the screen. Your contact(s) will appear in the Priority Senders area. Tap one to quickly compose a new text message, or tap + to add additional Priority Senders.

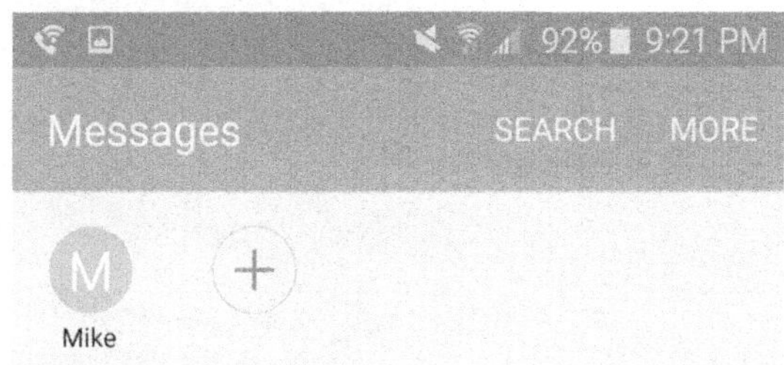

Customizing the Appearance of the Messages App

To customize the appearance of conversation threads in the Messages app, tap MORE → "Settings" → "Backgrounds and bubbles." Make your desired changes, and then tap ↩ to save your changes.

To change the font size inside conversation threads, pinch in and out to zoom. To change the font size on the main Messages screen, tap MORE → "Font size."

Blocking Numbers

To block a number from sending you texts, open the conversation thread and tap MORE → "Block number." To manage your blocked numbers, return to the main Messages screen and tap MORE → "Settings" → "Block messages" → "Block list."

Deleting Messages

To delete a conversation thread, tap and hold it on the main Messages screen so you see a ☑ next to it. Then tap DELETE. To delete a single message inside a conversation thread, tap and hold it and then tap "Delete."

Locking Messages to Prevent Accidental Deletion

You can lock individual messages inside conversation threads so they cannot accidentally be deleted, even if you attempt to delete the entire thread. (However, entire threads cannot be locked.) To do so, tap and hold a single message inside a conversation thread, and then tap "Lock."

Using the Gmail App

On the Note 5 and S6 Edge+, there are two preloaded apps from which you can send and receive emails: Gmail and Email. Gmail is designed for people who have and regularly use a @gmail.com email address, whereas Email is designed for people who have non-Gmail email addresses. However, the Gmail app now supports all email address as well—not just Gmail—and in my opinion it's a better app than Email anyway. So, my advice is to use the Gmail app and completely disregard the Email app regardless of whether you have a @gmail.com email address. The only exception is if you have an Outlook work account you want to set up on your Galaxy. In that case, I suggest using a third-party Outlook client called TouchDown (p. 320).

Setting Up the Gmail Inbox

When you first launch the Gmail app, you'll see the following screen.

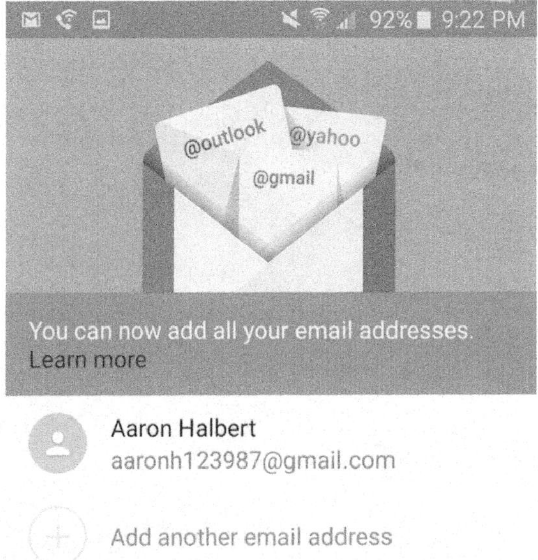

If you set up your Google account in Chapter 3 (p. 25), your Gmail address will already be listed like mine is above. If you want to set up additional email addresses for use with the Gmail app, tap "Add another email address." When you're done, tap "take me to Gmail."

TIP: *Unlike the Phone and Messages apps, the Gmail app is not in the app tray by default—you'll find it in the app drawer, inside the "Google" folder. I suggest creating a shortcut in the app tray or on your home screen so you don't have to open your app drawer every time you want to open your inbox.*

Welcome to the Gmail inbox. Let's discuss the controls available.

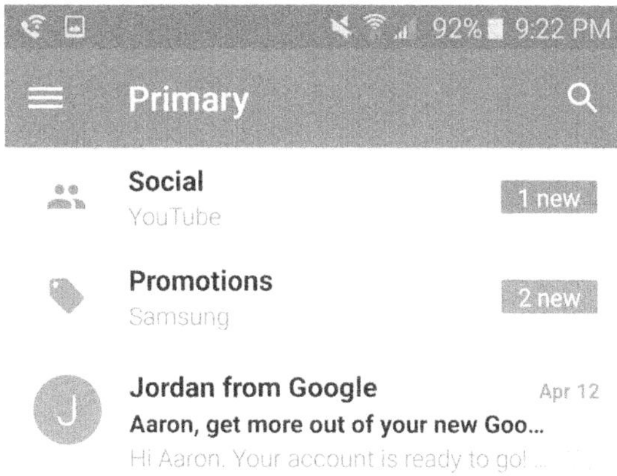

- Tap on any email to open it. Once you open an email, you can reply to it or forward it (p. 116).
- Swipe an email left or right to archive it. If you accidentally archive an email, just tap "Undo." Want to disable this feature? Read here (p. 118).
- To select one or more emails, tap the sender image(s) on the left-hand side of the screen. (If no image is specified, you'll just see the first letter of the sender's name, like the "J" above.) Then, use the controls along the top of the screen to take action on the selected emails.
    - : Deselect all emails.
    - : Archive selected emails.
    - : Delete selected emails.
    - / : Mark email(s) as read or unread, respectively.

- ⋮: Access additional options, including move, change label, add star, mark important, mute, and report spam.

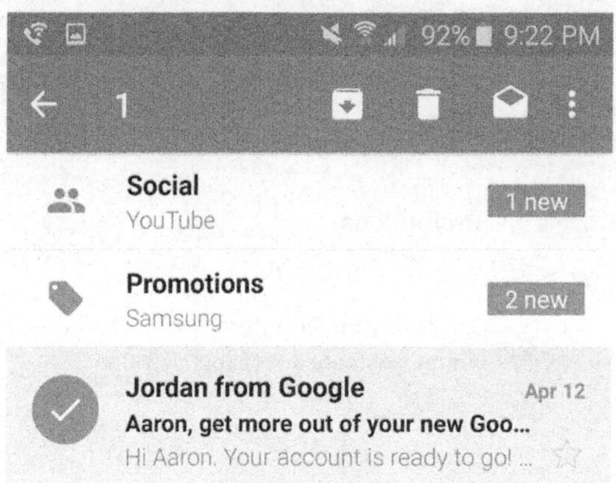

- Swipe from the far left edge of the screen right, or tap ☰ to pull up the main menu. Swipe up and down to scroll through your folders and labels, and tap one to open it. Note that Gmail's settings page is tucked away at the bottom of this menu.
- Tap ✎ in the lower-right-hand corner of the screen to compose a new email.
- Tap 🔍 to search your emails.

Reading Emails

When reading an email, the controls at the top of the screen include, from left to right:

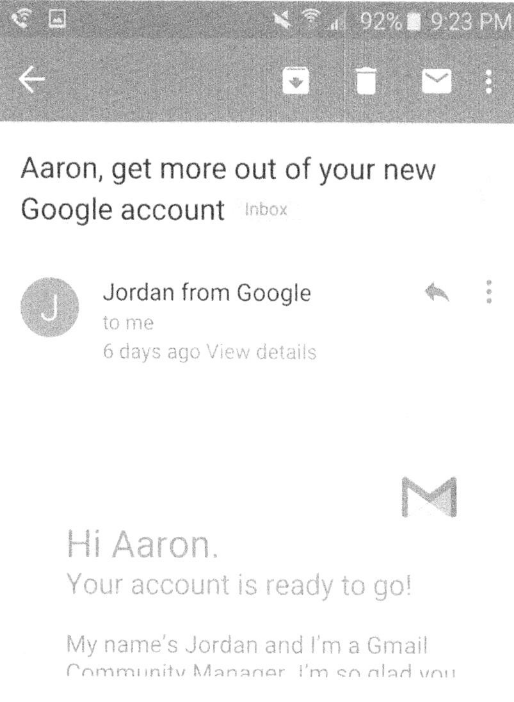

- : Back to inbox.
- : Archive email.
- : Delete email.
- : Mark as unread.
- : Additional options.

Compose a reply by tapping , or reply-all or forward the email by tapping . Tap the sender image to create a new contact or add the sender's email address to an existing contact. Tap to star the email. You can also pinch with two fingers to zoom in and out on the email body itself.

Composing and Sending an Email

When composing a new email, you'll see a screen like this:

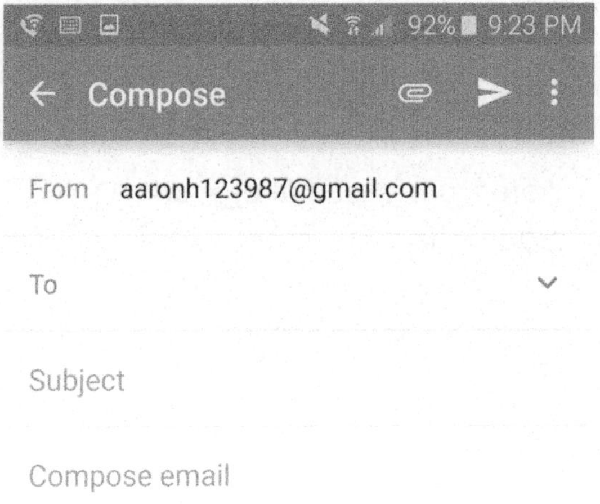

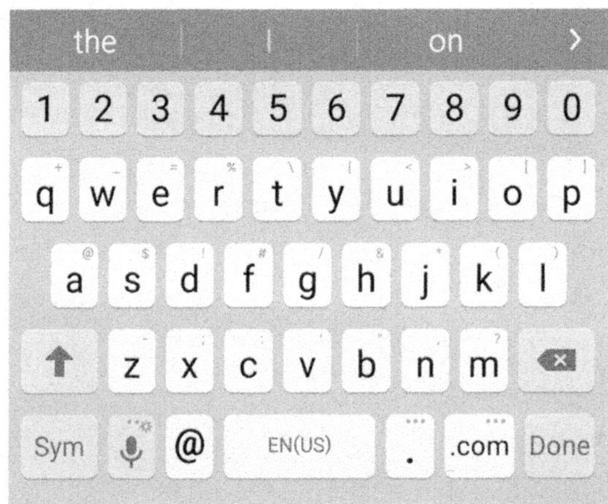

The "To," "Subject," and "Compose" email fields are self-explanatory. After you have composed and addressed your email, attach files to it by tapping , tap for additional options, or send the email with .

Composing a reply is almost exactly the same process, with one notable difference. Instead of seeing "Compose" in the upper-left-hand corner, you will see "Reply." Tap "Reply" to change the mode of the email to reply-all or forward.

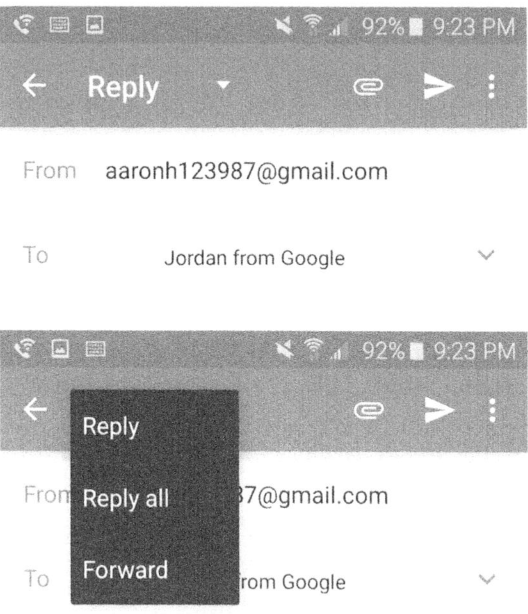

Attaching Files

On older Android phones, it was only possible to attach image or video files to Gmail messages. Fortunately, this has been corrected and it's now possible to attach nearly any type of file saved on your Galaxy or in your Google Drive. To attach a file to a Gmail message, tap while composing an email. Choose the appropriate source ("Attach file" lets you select a file saved on your Galaxy's internal memory) and follow the prompts to select the desired file. Can't find the file you want to attach? Read here (p. **Error! Bookmark not defined.**).

Refreshing Your Inbox

The Gmail app periodically gets clogged up and stops receiving new emails. If this happens, bring it back into sync by refreshing your inbox. In the main inbox view, place your finger in the middle of the screen and drag down. You will see a swirling arrow appear, and when it disappears again, your inbox will be in sync. If this does not fix the problem, restart your Galaxy (p. 53).

A similar problem sometimes occurs when sending a message with a large attachment; it gets stuck in the outbox folder and never sends. If this happens, restart your Galaxy and it will finish sending the email. The Gmail app has been notorious for this behavior for years, and Google has never quite managed to squash the software bug. Fortunately, a restart almost always does the trick.

Storing More Emails Offline

By default, your Galaxy stores your last 30 days of emails in its internal memory. To access anything older than that, it has to connect to Google's servers. This isn't normally a problem unless you spend a lot of time in dead cell zones. If you do, consider increasing this setting. Tap ☰ → "Settings" → (Your email address) → "Days of mail to sync."

Getting a Notification for Every New Email

By default, if you receive multiple emails in a short period of time, your Galaxy sounds a notification only the first time. This can be bad if there's an urgent chain of emails, because you might not realize you've received more than one. To make your Galaxy sound a notification for every new email, tap ☰ → (Your email address) → "Inbox sound & vibrate" and check "Notify for every message."

Disabling Swipe-to-Archive to Prevent Accidents

As I showed you earlier, by default you can swipe an email in your inbox right or left to archive it. While this is convenient, unfortunately it is far too easy to accidentally swipe a message away and miss the window to tap "Undo." Unlike accidentally deleting an email, there is no way to know which email you archived this way! There have been many times where I accidentally archived an email that I knew was important, but couldn't figure out what it was. To prevent this, tap ☰ → "Settings" → "General settings" and disable "Swipe actions."

Confirming Before Sending

In a professional setting, few things are worse than sending an email you didn't mean to send. To avoid this, tap ☰ → "Settings" → "General settings" and enable "Confirm before sending." You'll receive a confirmation dialog every time you attempt to send a message, preventing a potential classic career-ending faux pas. Just make sure not to accidentally reply-all—another classic email mistake.

Customizing Your Inbox Categories

Google recently introduced a Gmail feature that splits your inbox into various categories such as "Social" and "Promotional." If you detest this feature as much as I do, it's easy to switch off. Tap ☰ → "Settings" → (Your email address) → "Inbox categories" and uncheck the categories you don't want.

Setting a Signature

To set a signature for all emails sent from your Galaxy, tap → "Settings" → (Your email address) → "Signature."

Muting Conversations

The Gmail app includes a "mute" feature, which automatically archives all future emails in a given conversation, skipping your inbox entirely. This is a great feature if you've been CC'd on an ongoing email thread you don't care about. To mute a conversation, open it, and tap → "Mute."

> ***TIP:*** *If you use Microsoft Outlook at work, I strongly recommend you purchase and use the app TouchDown. It is a fantastic, full-featured Outlook client for Android, and keeps all of your work information nicely contained in one app. Read more about it* *here (p. 320)*.

Managing and Adding Email Accounts

Want to add a new email address to the Gmail app? Tap → , then "Add account" or "Manage accounts." Remember, the Gmail app now supports all email addresses, not just @gmail.com email addresses.

Tweaking Other Gmail Settings

Gmail has dozens of settings available that let you customize the interface to work exactly as you please. I've already discussed many of the most important settings, but I suggest you explore all Gmail settings to perfectly configure the app for your needs. To do so, go to → "Settings." Some settings are under "General settings" and others are under (your email address), so explore both menus.

Taking Photos with the Camera App

Photos and video are taken using the Camera app, found on your home screen by default. The Note 5 and S6 Edge+ have a 16-megapixel rear camera with an f/1.9 aperture, 1/2.6" sensor, 4K video, and optical image stabilization (OIS). Their 5-megapixel front camera has a wide-angle lens (120 degree) also with an f/1.9 aperture. Translation: the cameras on the Note 5 and S6 Edge+ are among the best smartphone cameras to date.

> ★ ***TIP:*** *A full discussion of digital photography concepts is outside the scope of this section. If you want to learn more about basic photography concepts like metering and ISO, I suggest starting with Google.*

By default, the Camera app opens into stills (as opposed to video) mode. Let's discuss the features available on this screen.

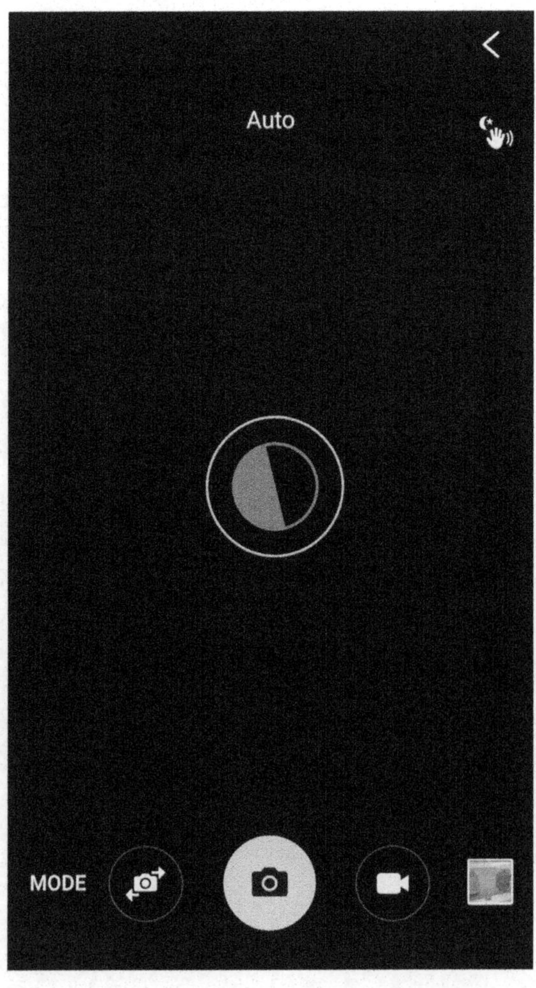

- : Expand the quick actions bar. Quick actions include:
    a. : Open advanced camera settings.
    b. : Set the photo resolution (# of megapixels).
    c. : Adjust the beautification filter, which softens facial features. Only available in front camera mode.
    d. : Toggle the flash mode between "always off," "automatic," and "always on."
    e. : Set the shutter self-timer.
    f. : Enable/disable HDR mode. HDR stands for "High Dynamic Range," and uses software techniques to improve the exposure and color in your photos. Basically, digital cameras capture only a portion of the lighting situations that the human eye can see, and HDR tries to correct this. If your photo includes both very bright and very dark objects, you will normally get either some over-exposed, blown out areas, or some under-exposed, dark areas, or both. HDR helps fix this problem. Experiment with this setting to see what looks best.
    g. : Apply filters like grayscale, faded color, cartoon, etc.
- : Indicates the camera is in low-light mode (the device sets this automatically based on the surrounding lighting conditions). Tapping this does nothing.
- MODE: Choose from a variety of camera modes, including panorama, selective focus, slow-motion, fast-motion, Video Collage (p. 129), Live Broadcast (p. 128), and more. Tap "Download" to get more mode plug-ins from Samsung. There is also a new "Pro" mode that provides on-screen exposure, ISO, and white balance settings. Pro Mode is discussed further below (p. 123).
- : Switch between the front and rear cameras.
- : Shutter button. Tap to take a picture, or tap and hold to take burst shots in quick succession.
- : Video button. Switches into video mode and starts recording.
- : Open the Gallery app to view previously taken photos.
- The circle in the center of the screen is the **autofocus and metering area**. Tap anywhere on the screen to autofocus and meter on it. Tap and hold to autofocus, meter, and lock settings. If you want to lock autofocus only and adjust metering separately, you can do so with Pro Mode (p. 123).

- To **zoom in or out**, punch with two fingers. Note that zooming is accomplished digitally, not optically, so quality degrades quickly as you zoom in.

Opening the Camera in 0.7 Seconds for Quick Shots

The Note 5 and S6 Edge+ have a fantastic new way to capture fleeting moments. Just double-press  any time, even when the device is off. It'll launch the camera in about 0.7 seconds so you don't miss your snapshot. I'm a huge fan of this feature. It goes a long way toward solving one of the worst flaws of smartphone cameras—how slow they usually are to launch.

Enabling Advanced Controls with Pro Mode

Pro Mode is a new feature that provides easy-to-access advanced camera settings. If you like to manually set ISO, exposure, metering, and so on, you'll enjoy how Pro Mode moves all these settings directly onto the viewfinder screen so they're no longer hidden away in menus.

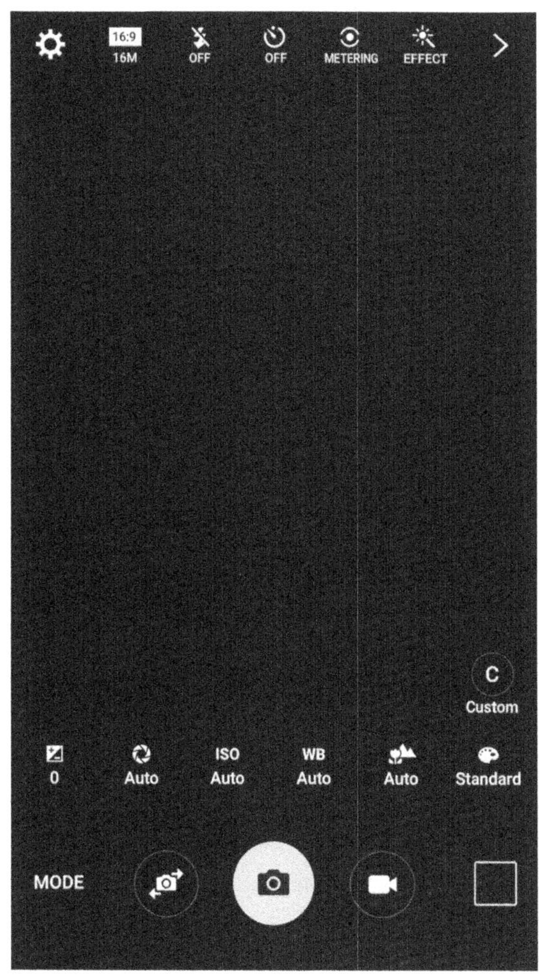

To enable Pro Mode, tap **MODE** → [icon].

TIP: Another helpful feature of Pro Mode is autofocus and auto exposure separation. While in Pro Mode, tap and hold to lock the AF and AE. Then release your finger, and tap and hold again to move AE independently of AF.

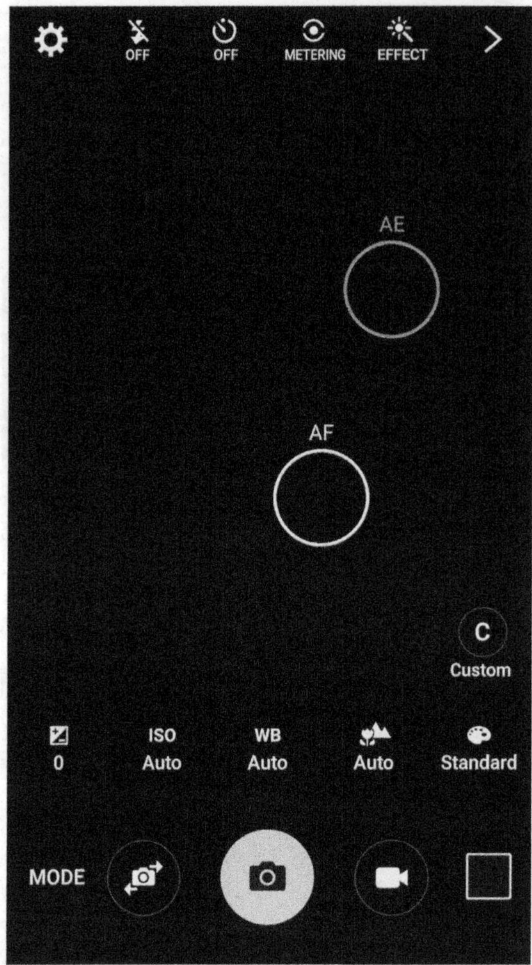

Capturing Fast Action Using Burst Shot

The Note 5 and S6 Edge+ are capable of taking multiple shots in rapid succession, which is useful for fast action scenes. To use burst shot, tap and hold [camera icon]. You'll see a counter appear on the screen, showing how many shots have been taken up to a maximum of 30.

Tagging Your Photos with Location Data

Ever forget where you took a photo? Try location tagging. It embeds GPS coordinates in your image files. To enable it, tap [back icon] → [settings icon] and turn "Location tags" on. You can view these coordinates using an advanced image viewer like Adobe Lightroom on a computer, or by viewing the photo in the Gallery (p. 130) app and tapping MORE → "Details."

If you enable this feature, remember that GPS information will be embedded in the file metadata of any photos you post online! Be careful not to expose personal information by posting photos with your home's GPS coordinates embedded in them. Also, keep in mind that this feature works best when your Location toggle button is switched on in your notification panel and your location method is set to "GPS, Wi-Fi, and mobile networks" in system settings → "Privacy and safety" → "Location" → "Locating method."

Using the Self-Timer for Group Shots

The self-timer mode is great for taking group shots. To use it, tap → . Choose your preferred duration. The only tricky part is figuring out how to prop up your Galaxy without a tripod…

Flipping Front Camera Images Automatically

By default, your Galaxy's front camera takes reverse-mirror-image pictures, meaning that you'll see selfies the way other people see you—not how you see yourself in a mirror. If you want to flip your selfies to mirror-image orientation, tap to enter front camera mode, then → → "Save pictures as previewed."

Muting the Shutter Sound

Sometimes you might want to take pictures discreetly. Pretty creepy… but I'm not here to judge. To disable the shutter sound, tap → and then turn off "Shutter sound."

Taking Panoramic Shots

To take a panoramic shot (super-wide-angle), for example of a landscape, tap MODE → "Panorama." Aim your Galaxy at the far left or right edge of the scene you want to capture. Tap once, and then slowly move your Galaxy across the scene. Tap when you're finished. Note that you'll need to tap MODE again to put your camera back into the default "Auto" mode.

Taking HDR Shots

As I noted earlier, the Note 5 and S6 Edge+ have an HDR mode that simulates the high-saturation, high-dynamic range shots that have recently become popular among digital photographers. To use it, tap → HDR AUTO. HDR mode can improve exposure in highlights and shadows, as well as give you punchier, more saturated colors. Keep in mind, though, this HDR mode is all software based, and is therefore more limited than true HDR techniques that involve multiple exposures. It can improve some shots on your but don't expect the same look of HDR photographs taken with DSLRs and processed with dedicated HDR computer software.

Getting Great Bokeh and Editing Bokeh Using Selective Focus

Selective Focus mode lets you do two different but related things. First, it lets you take a photo of an object or person with a blurred background (called "bokeh"), a popular technique in portrait photography. Second, it allows you to change the point of focus *after* the photo has been taken, i.e., to blur the foreground and bring the background into focus. To take a shot using Selective Focus mode, tap MODE → "Selective focus."

For selective focus mode to work best, the object in the foreground must be within 1.5 feet of the camera, and the background must be at least 4.5 feet beyond the object.

To change the focal point of a picture after it has been taken, open the photo in the Gallery app and tap in the center of the screen. You can only do this if you took the picture with Selective Focus mode on.

Applying Color Filters, Including Faded Color, Vintage, and Grayscale

The camera app has several built-in color filters. To use these, tap → EFFECT and choose the effect you want. You can only use effects while in "Auto" mode.

Setting the Flash Mode

By default, the flash is always off. To change it to always on (ON) or automatic (AUTO), tap → OFF.

Enabling Picture Review

Want to review each picture after you take it? Tap → and turn on "Review pictures." After taking a photo, your Galaxy will show a pop-up window for about 2 seconds. Tap to dismiss the pop-up window, or to delete the image.

Taking Photos Using Voice Control

Another cool Camera trick is Voice Control. Turn it on by tapping → and turning on "Voice control." Once enabled, you can take photos by saying "Smile," "Cheese,"

"Capture," or "Shoot," or record a video by saying "Record video." This is a handy alternative to the self-timer for group shots. It can also help steady your shots, since it eliminates the need to tap the on-screen shutter button.

Taking Photos Using the Volume Buttons

If you prefer pressing a physical button to take pictures, you're in luck—your Galaxy lets you use either of the volume buttons as your shutter button. To enable this feature, tap → → "Volume keys function." You can also set the volume buttons to zoom or record video.

Taking Selfies with the Heart Rate Sensor

When you're using the front camera, you can take pictures by quickly tapping your finger on the heart rate sensor, next to the rear camera. It's usually easier to just tap , but try the heart rate sensor method if you find the regular shutter button clumsy.

Tracking a Moving Object with Tracking AF

If you're taking photos of a moving object, you can automatically track it with Tracking AF. The camera will automatically adjust its focus as the object moves. To use Tracking AF, tap → and turn on "Tracking AF." Then, tap an object to lock onto it. You'll see yellow brackets to indicate that tracking is active.

Downloading New Camera Modes

To download additional camera modes like surround shot (virtual tour), food shot, dual camera, and more, tap MODE → "Download." You'll need to be logged into your Samsung account to download these modes. Once installed, these modes will be accessible from the MODE screen.

Saving Photos in RAW Format

If you're a digital photography enthusiast, you've no doubt worked with RAW files and post processing software like Adobe Lightroom. Happily, the Note 5 / S6 Edge+ support saving RAW files so you can post process your Galaxy's photos just like your DSLR's photos. To use this feature, tap MODE → "Pro" to enter Pro mode. Then tap → and enable "Save as RAW file."

Capturing Video with the Camera App

Tap to enter video recording mode.

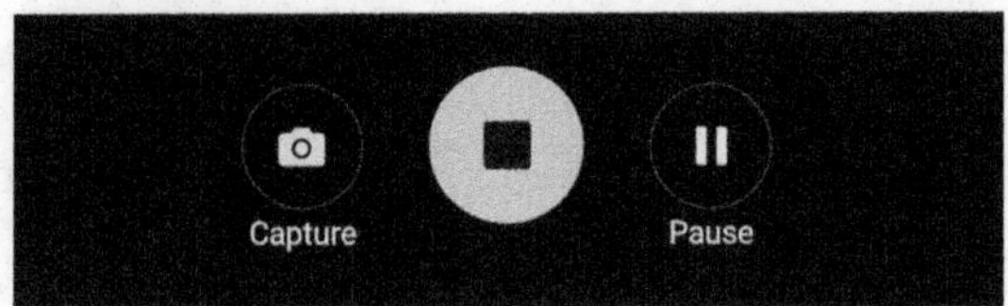

Recording will begin as soon as you enter video mode. Tap to pause/resume recording, or to stop recording and save the video. Tap to take a still shot without interrupting recording. Tap to exit video mode.

> ***TIP:*** *Counter-intuitively, all video-related settings are adjusted while the Camera app is in stills mode. All video settings are in → .*

Taking 4K (UHD) Video

One of the selling points of the Note 5 / S6 Edge+ is their ability to capture 4K video for playback on the latest high-resolution TVs. But, there's no obvious 4K setting. What you need to do is tap → .→ "Video size" and change the resolution to UHD 3840x2160 pixels. That's 4K!

Taking Slow-Mo and Fast-Mo Video

To take slow-motion or fast-motion video, tap MODE while in stills mode and then "Slow motion" or "Fast motion." The Camera app will automatically enter video mode with the chosen effect.

Enabling Video Stabilization

Video stabilization reduces shake and improves video quality in low-light settings. To enable it, tap → and turn on "Video stabilization."

Live Broadcasting to YouTube

Want to live broadcast camera footage to YouTube to share with friends, family, or followers? The Camera app now has this functionality directly built in. To use it, open the

Camera app and tap MODE → "Live broadcast." The first time you select this option, you'll have to agree to Samsung's terms of service and grant the Camera app access to your YouTube account. Once this is done, though, you can live broadcast any time just by selecting this setting.

By default, the stream will be private—you'll have to manually invite users by tapping "Invite" or make your stream public by tapping ⚙. Once you're ready, just tap "LIVE."

Creating a Video Collage

Video Collages are another new feature on the Note 5 / S6 Edge+. A video collage lets you take four six-second videos and combine them into a single six-second video, displayed as a 2x2 grid. However, you cannot use previously recorded video, nor can you choose any length of time other than six seconds. To create a video collage, tap MODE → "Video collage" and tap the record button to begin the process. After each six-second clip, tap the record button again to start the next clip. When you've recorded all four clips, optionally select background music and tap SAVE to complete your video collage.

Viewing Your Photos & Videos with the Gallery App

So, you've taken some photos or videos using the Camera app and now you want to view them. Do so using the Gallery app. You can access it from your app drawer or from the Camera app itself by tapping the thumbnail image in the lower-right-hand corner of the screen.

Navigating the Gallery

Below is a screenshot of the main Gallery screen.

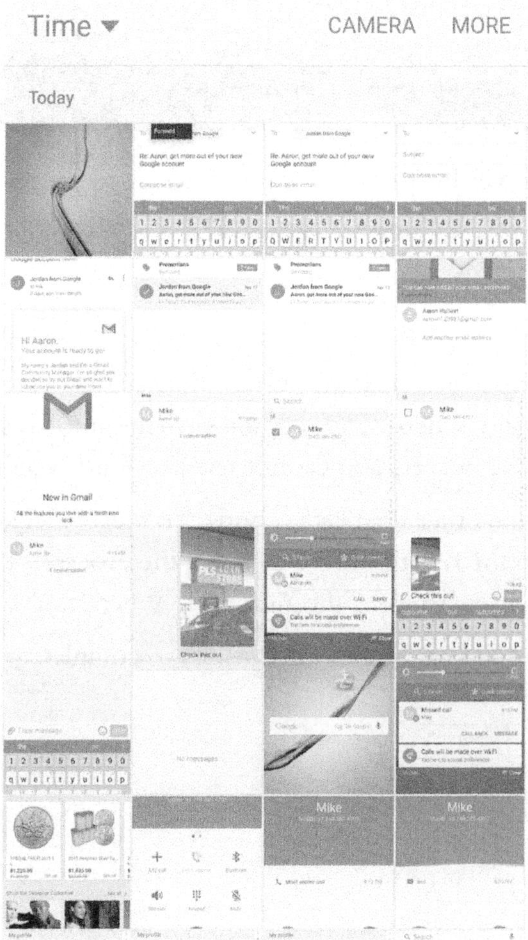

- Swipe up and down to view your photos and videos. By default they are sorted by newest to oldest.
- Tap any photo or video thumbnail to open it in full-screen view. Tap ↩ to return to the main screen.
- Time ▾: Sort your photos by time, album, event (location (p. 124)), or category (camera mode), or favorites (only visible when you've marked 1+ photos as favorite).
- CAMERA: Quickly launch the Camera app.
- MORE: Access additional options, including Edit (enters Selection Mode (p. 131)), Share (p. 91), Search, and Help.
- Tap and hold any photo/video thumbnail to enter Selection Mode (p. 131) (same as tapping MORE → "Edit").
- Pinch with two fingers to zoom in or out, increasing or decreasing the size of the photo/video thumbnails.

Selection Mode

Selection Mode lets you organize and manipulate your photos/videos in batches instead of one at a time. To enter Selection Mode, tap and hold a photo/video thumbnail, or tap MORE → "Edit."

After entering selection mode, select additional photos/videos by tapping their thumbnails. Selected photos are indicated by a green checkmark: ☑. Once one or more photos/videos are selected, tap DELETE to delete them, SHARE to share them, or MORE to copy or move them to a different album.

In the screenshot below, I have selected three thumbnails, indicated by the three checkmarks.

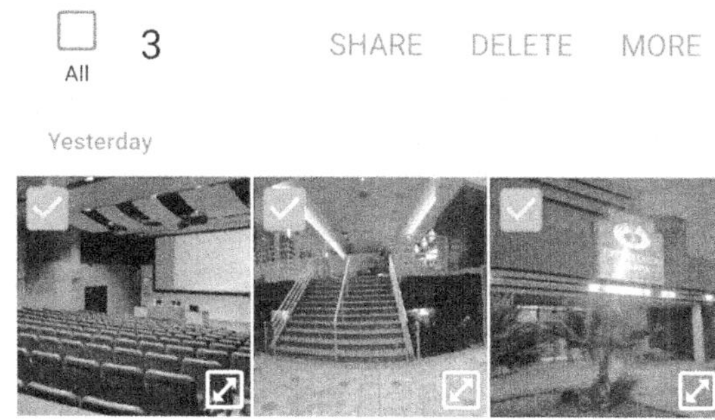

TIP: To quickly select multiple photos, tap the first thumbnail, hold, and drag your finger up/down/left/right over other thumbnails.

Viewing and Editing Photos & Videos

To view a single photo/video and perform basic edits such as rotation and cropping, exit Selection Mode and tap a photo/video once without holding. It'll open in full-screen mode:

- Tap anywhere on the photo/video to show/hide the top and bottom menu bars.
- ←: Back to main Gallery screen.
- CAMERA: Quickly open the Camera app.
- MORE: View photo/video file details, including location data, or start a slideshow.

- : Mark photo/video as favorite. (Filter favorites by tapping Time ▾ in Gallery.)
- : Share photo/video with Share Via (p. 91) tool.
- : Edit photo/video in the Photo/Video Editor (read more below).
- : Delete photo/video.

Advanced Photo/Video Editing with the Photo Editor and Video Editor

The Photo and Video Editors are adapted from the "Studio" feature on the Galaxy S5 and Note 4. They're much more powerful than the editing tools included with earlier Galaxy devices. For example, they allow you to:

- Rotate, straighten, crop, and resize photos;
- Adjust contrast, saturation, color temperature, hue, and brightness;
- Add tone filters like "vintage" and "grayscale";
- Remove red eye;
- Airbrush faces;
- Add frames;
- Trim video clips;
- Apply filters to video clips;
- Edit audio in video clips;
- … and more.

The Photo Editor and Video Editor are easy to miss if you don't know they exist. To access the Photo Editor, open any photo in the Gallery and tap "Edit" → "Photo Editor." To access the Video Editor, open any video in the Gallery app and tap "Editor" → "Video Editor." The first time you attempt to open the Video Editor, you'll be prompted to download supporting files from the Galaxy Apps store. Proceed with the download and installation to access the Video Editor.

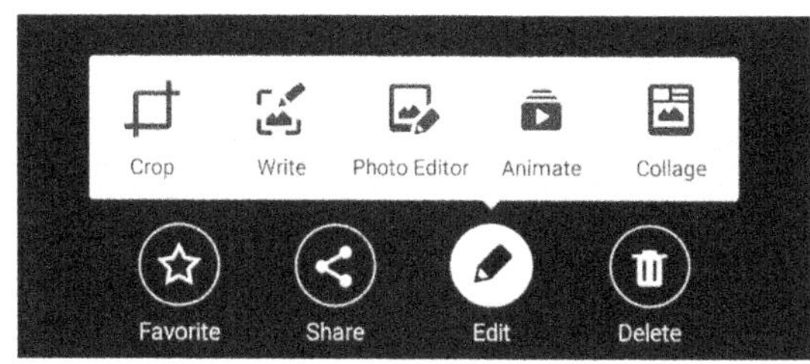

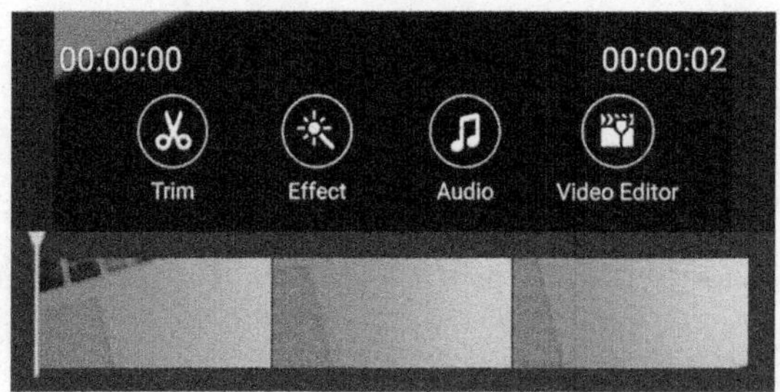

Creating .GIF Animations

The Gallery on the Note 5 / S6 Edge+ has a new feature that lets you create .GIF animations using photos on your device. Note that its capabilities are quite limited—you can only add/reorder images and change the speed of the animation. There are no text effects or other special effects.

To create an animation, open the first photo in the Gallery you'd like to feature in your animation, and then tap "Edit" → "Animate." From this screen, tap + to add more photos to the animation. Tap, hold, and drag photos to reorder them in the animation. When you're finished, tap DONE to preview and finalize the animation.

Creating Photo Collages

In addition to creating .GIF animations, you can also create static photo collages, which let you combine up to 5 photos from the Gallery into a single image with a decorative custom layout, border, and background artwork.

To create a photo collage, open the first photo in the Gallery you'd like to feature in your collage, and then tap "Edit" → "Collage." From this screen, tap + or ADD to add more photos to the collage. Customize the collage with the "Aspect ratio," "Layout," "Border," and "Background" buttons along the bottom of the screen, or tap SHUFFLE to randomize the collage's design. When you're finished, tap SAVE.

Managing Contacts

The Contacts app is your phone book. Use it to store names, numbers, email addresses, and other information for your friends, family, and business contacts.

You can access the Contacts app in a couple ways. You'll find it in your app tray by default, and you can also access it by opening the Phone app and then tapping the Contacts tab.

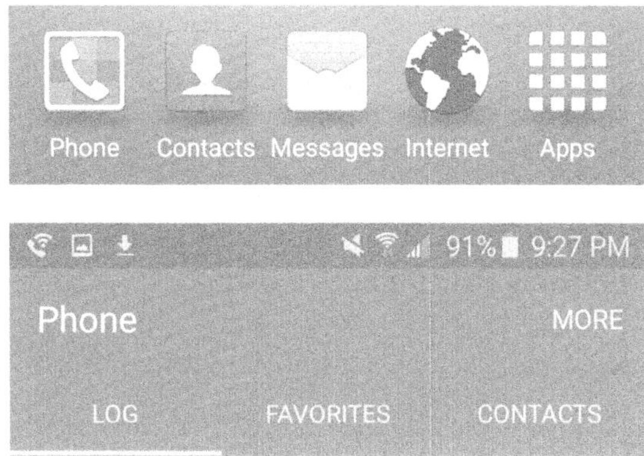

While on the main Contacts screen, swipe up and down to scroll through your contacts, or tap a letter along the right edge of the screen to skip to that section. Tap a contact to view his or her details.

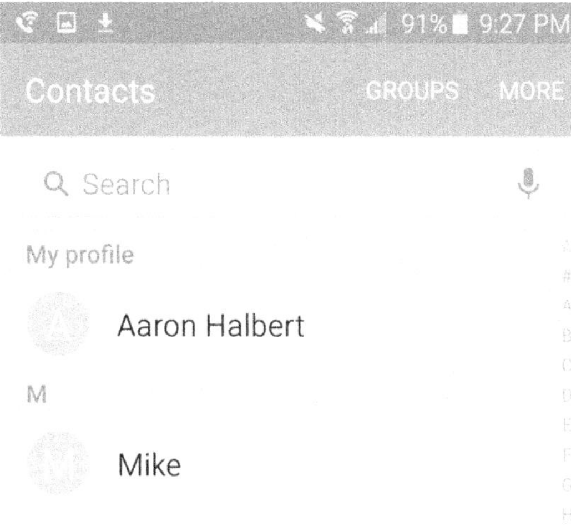

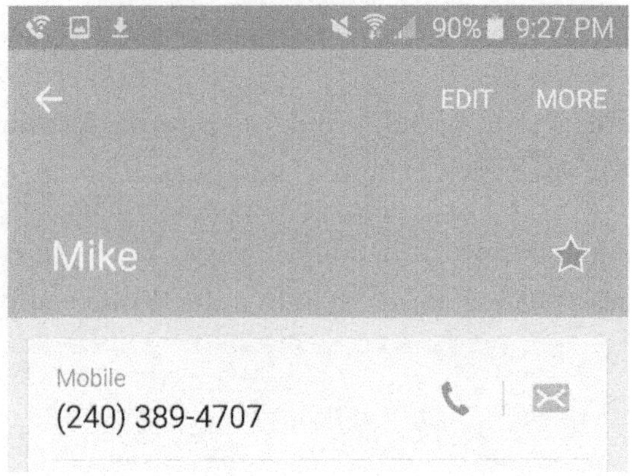

Selection Mode

Selection Mode lets you organize and manipulate your contacts in batches instead of one at a time. To enter Selection Mode, tap and hold a contact.

After entering Selection Mode, select additional contacts by tapping them. Selected contacts are indicated by a green checkmark: . Once one or more contacts are selected, tap DELETE to delete them, or SHARE to share them.

Adding New Contacts

To add a new contact, tap . You will be prompted to choose where to save the contact. **I strongly suggest you keep all contacts saved to your Google account** so they will be consolidated in one place and can be automatically restored if you ever lose your data or if you upgrade to a new phone. I recommend against saving contacts directly to the device or to the SIM card, because if you lose your device, you'll also lose your data. As I've noted previously, I also don't recommend saving contacts to your Samsung account, because they won't be easy to restore if you ever buy a non-Samsung Android device.

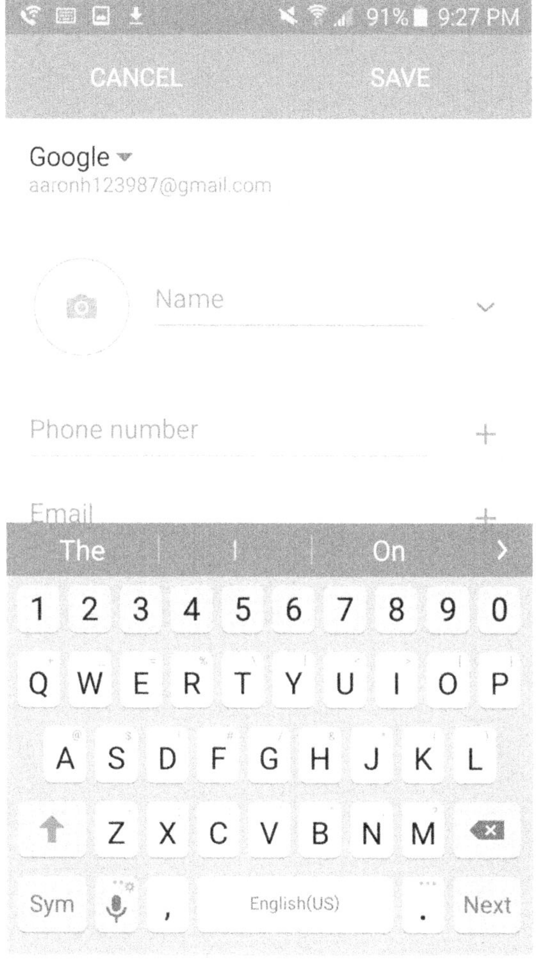

After selecting a save destination, enter the contact's information. Tap + to add additional phone numbers or email addresses to the record, and tap to assign a photo from your Gallery to the contact. To add another field like "IM account" or "Organization," scroll to the bottom of the screen and tap "Add another field." When you're done, tap SAVE.

Editing Existing Contacts

To edit a contact's details, tap the contact's name and then EDIT. Then, follow the instructions in the previous section, "Adding New Contacts."

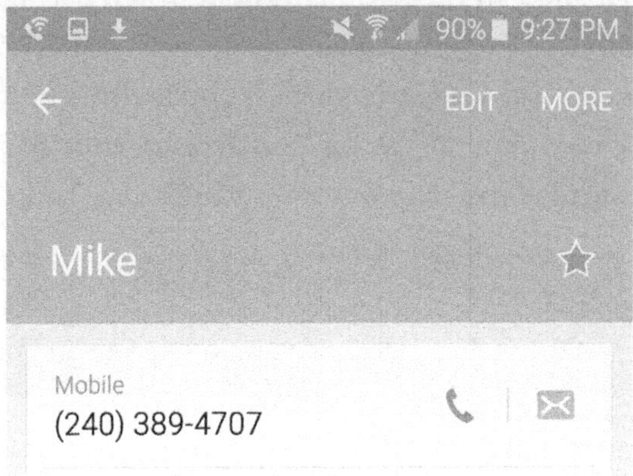

Deleting Contacts

To delete a contact, tap and hold the contact's name on the main Contacts screen to enter Selection Mode, check any other contacts you wish to delete, and then tap DELETE.

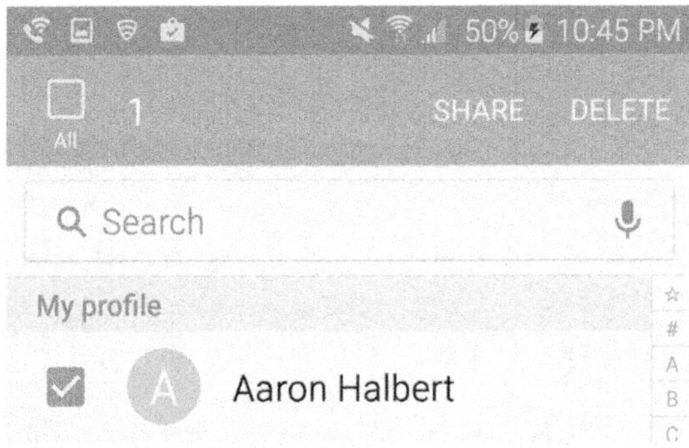

Merging Duplicate Contacts

When duplicates occur in your contact list, the easiest way to remove them is by going to https://contacts.google.com on your desktop computer and using the Find Duplicates feature. (Of course, this only works if all your contacts are saved to your Google account like I've repeatedly recommended.)

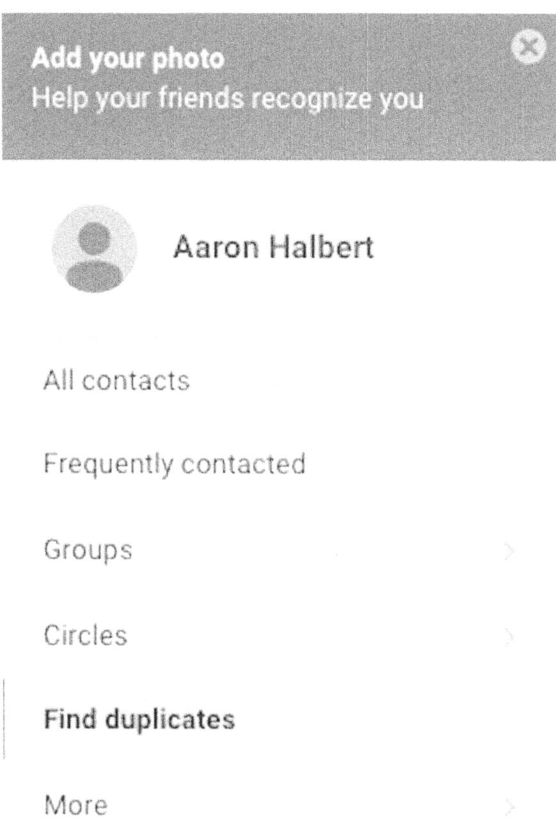

However, apps like Facebook and LinkedIn can sometimes create duplicate entries in your Galaxy's internal memory. Since these are not saved to Google's servers, Google's contact tools won't detect them. Instead, you can use the built-in "Merge contacts" feature, which allows you to manage multiple contacts as a single contact. (However, it does not save the results to your Google account, which is why Google's Find Duplicates feature is a more preferable and permanent solution.)

To use this feature, tap MORE → "Merge contacts." Select the contacts you want to link and tap "Merge." If you don't see any contacts in the list, it's because no duplicate entries were detected.

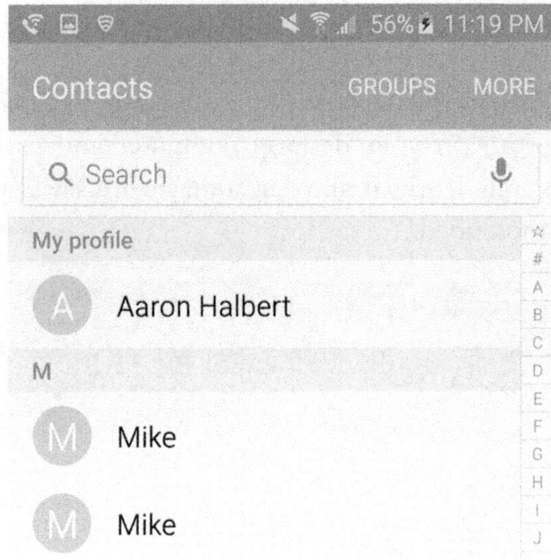
56% 11:19 PM
Contacts
GROUPS
MORE
Search
My profile
Aaron Halbert
M
Mike
Mike

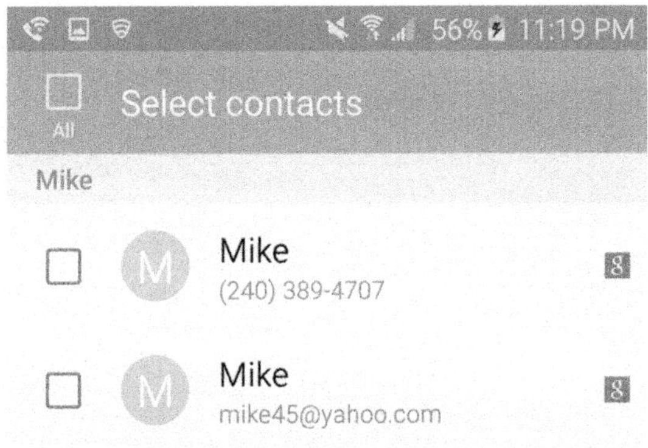
56% 11:19 PM
All
Select contacts
Mike
Mike
(240) 389-4707
Mike
mike45@yahoo.com

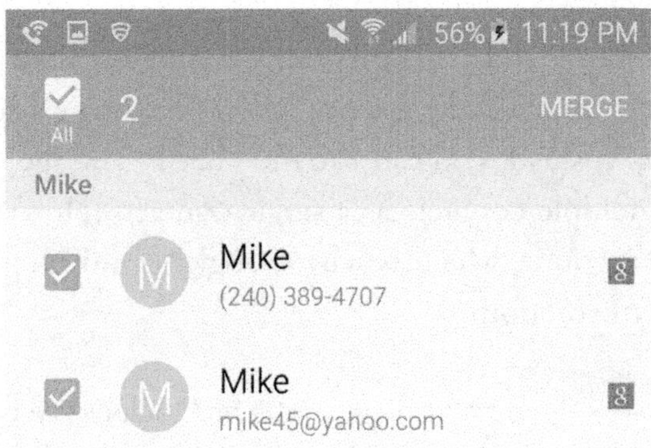
56% 11:19 PM
All
2
MERGE
Mike
Mike
(240) 389-4707
Mike
mike45@yahoo.com

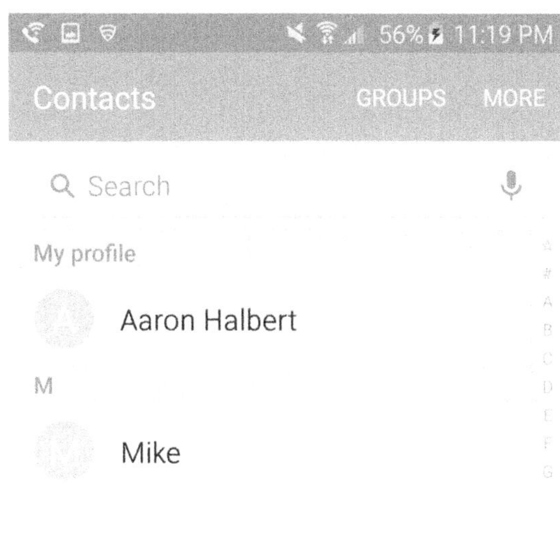

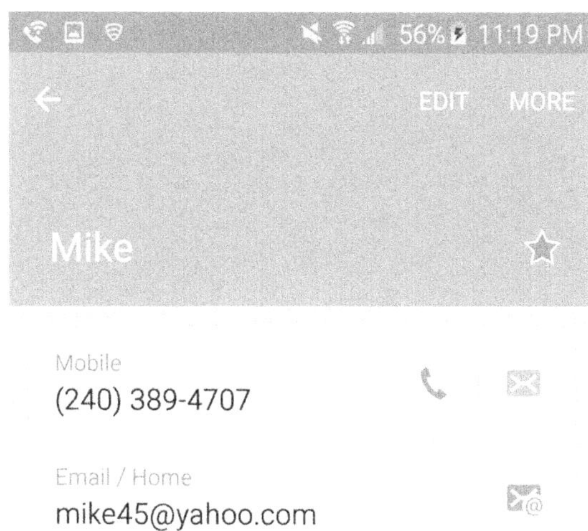

To unlink contacts, open a linked contact and tap . Tap next to each contact you want to unlink, and then tap to exit this screen.

Sharing Contacts

To share a contact in the standard vCard format, tap a contact in your contact list. Then, tap MORE → "Share contact."

Setting Custom Ringtones for Contacts

To assign a custom ringtone for a contact, first download an MP3 of the desired ringtone or song using a web browser on your Galaxy or transfer an MP3 by USB (p. 278). If you have an MP3 file on your desktop computer, you can also email it to yourself as an attachment and then save it using the Gmail app. It does not matter what folder you save the file to.

Once you have an MP3 file on your device, download the app "Ringtone Maker," by Big Banc Inc. from the Google Play Store. This app lets you customize the portion of the song that plays when you get a call (e.g., the chorus).

Once you open Ringtone Maker, tap next to the song you want to use as a ringtone. Tap "Edit." You will see the following screen. Move the sliders around to choose the portion of the song to use for your ringtone. (Press to preview the clip, or and to zoom in and out.)

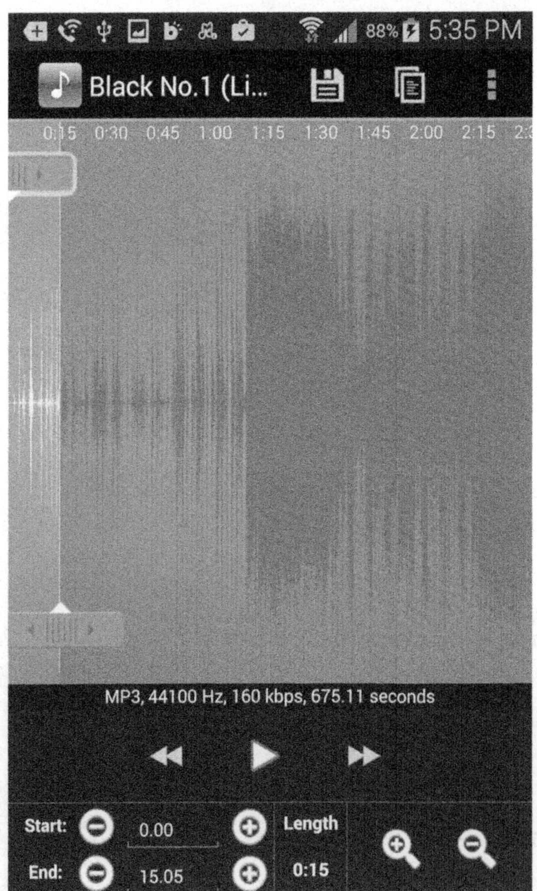

Once you are happy with your selection, tap to finish.

Rename your ringtone if you wish and tap "Save." Finally, choose whether you want to make it your default ringtone for all contacts, or assign it only to a single contact.

Managing Alarms and Timers

The Clock app is great for setting wake-up alarms or countdown timers. I frequently use the timer feature when I'm cooking; my only complaint is that you can't set more than one timer at once. (But you can with Kitchen Timer (p. 312), which I discuss in Chapter 11 (p. 306).)

Alarms

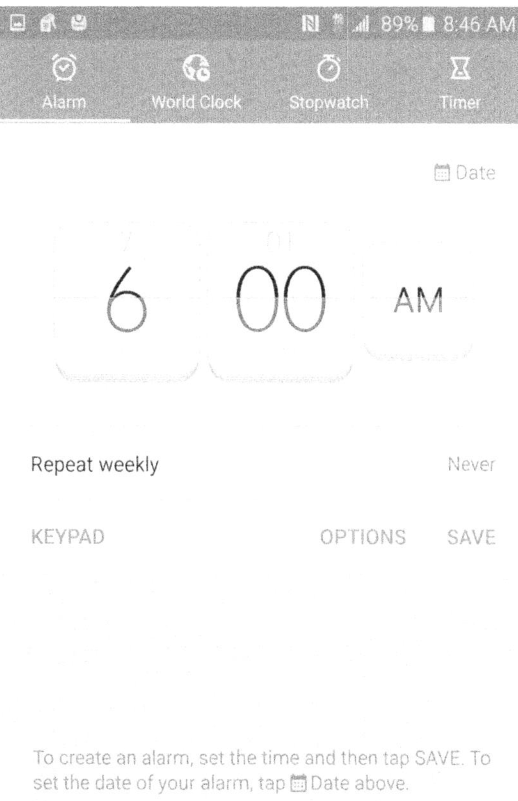

To set an alarm for a specific time, first select the "Alarm" tab. Tap the upper and lower halves of the hour, minute, and AM/PM boxes to set the hour and minute for your alarm (or use the KEYPAD). Tap Date to specify a day for the alarm, or tap "Repeat" to make the alarm recur on certain day(s) of the week. Tap OPTIONS to set the volume, tone, snooze interval, and more. If you want to clear everything and start over, tap ⮌ → CANCEL. To save and activate the alarm, tap SAVE.

Here, I've set an alarm for 7:15am every weekday. I would delete it by tapping X, or disable/enable it by tapping ON.

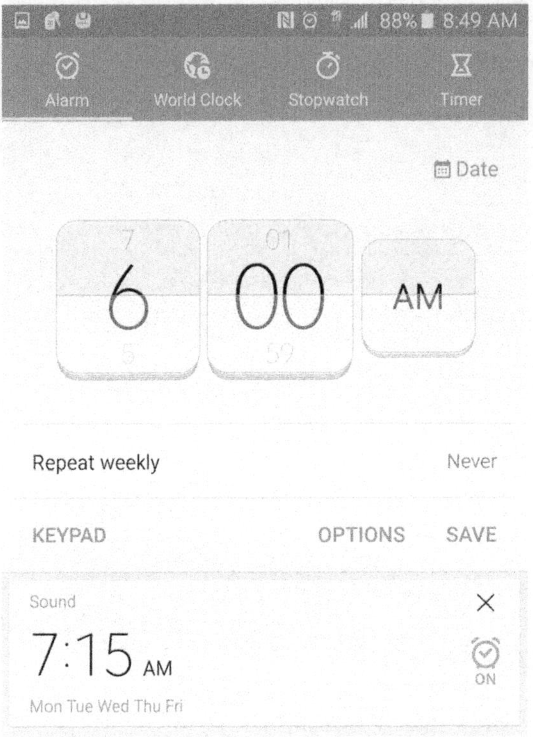

Timers

To set a timer, tap the "Timer" tab. Tap the upper and lower halves of the hour, minute, and seconds boxes to specify hours, minutes, and seconds, or tap KEYPAD to manually enter numbers. Tap "Start" to start the timer.

Stopwatch

To use the stopwatch, tap the "Stopwatch" tab. Tap "Start" to begin, "Lap" to record the current time, "Stop" to pause, and "Reset" to zero out the stopwatch.

Playing Music

There are many ways to play music on your Galaxy. You can stream music from apps like Pandora or Spotify, purchase it from Google Play, import your existing MP3 collection to Google Play Music, or just copy your existing MP3 files to your Galaxy and play them with the Music app. Let's talk about each option.

Pandora

Pandora is a popular music streaming service that allows you to stream an unlimited amount of music every month for free. However, you don't get to choose every song or artist you listen to. Rather, you create different "stations" based on artists, songs, and genres that you like, and Pandora automatically plays related music it thinks you will like. You can only skip 6 songs per station, per hour, up to a total of 24 skips per day.

On one hand, this can be disappointing if you want to be able to freely pick and choose songs and artists, but on the other hand, it can be an amazing way to discover new music. Either way, because it's completely free, you don't have much to lose. The premium version, Pandora One, costs $4.99 per month but eliminates all advertisements, heightens quality, and allows more total skips per day.

Download Pandora from the Google Play Store. You'll need an active Internet connection (cellular or Wi-Fi) to use it, so if you have a limited data plan, be careful not to plow through your data allowance.

Spotify

Spotify is another popular music streaming service that gives you more control than Pandora. The free version provides unlimited streaming, and on the mobile app you can listen to any artist's catalog for free on shuffle mode. (That means if you want to only hear one artist, you can, but you can't control the exact songs you hear.) Like Pandora, you get 6 skips per hour and there are advertisements between songs. To remove advertisements and be able to play any song you want, at any time with no skip limit, you must upgrade to Spotify Premium for $9.99 per month. Spotify Premium also has an offline mode, so you can download music to play on the go without using your cellular data.

Personally, I think Spotify offers the best value of all options mentioned in this section.

Download Spotify from the Google Play Store.

Google Play Music All Access

All Access is a new service from Google intended to compete with Spotify. Like Spotify, All Access costs $9.99 per month, and has nearly as good a selection of streaming music. Its main advantage over Spotify is that you can also upload your own MP3s, which is very convenient if you have music in your collection that's not available for streaming. (Note that you can still upload your MP3s to Google Music for streaming in the Play Music app even if you're not subscribed to All Access—see the "Importing Your Existing Collection" section below for more information).

For now, I still prefer Spotify since I've found its catalog to be slightly more complete, but All Access could overtake Spotify in the future.

You can sign up for All Access through the Play Music app—no additional download required.

Purchasing Music from the Google Play Store

If you prefer purchasing music instead of streaming it, your best option is the Google Play Store (p. 166). Tracks from the Google Play Store are $1.29 and albums are usually $9.49. For offline listening, you can download purchased tracks to your Galaxy using the Play Music app.

However, although songs bought from Google Play belong to you and have no listening limitations, the cost of a single album is nearly the cost of a full month of Spotify Premium, which in my opinion is a much better deal. Keep this in mind before you buy from Google Play.

Importing Your Existing Collection to Google Music

If you already have a large library of MP3 or other audio files on your computer, you can upload up to 20,000 songs to Google Music for free. Those songs can then be streamed or downloaded using the Play Music app on your Galaxy.

To get started with Google Music, go to the link below on your desktop computer and follow the directions to install Google Play Music for Chrome and upload your music collection to the cloud. When you're done, access it using the Google Play Music app on your Galaxy.

https://support.google.com/googleplay/answer/4627259?hl=en

(Short link: http://goo.gl/mgqV4o)

Playing MP3 Files with the Music App

Finally, if you just want to copy a couple songs or albums from your desktop computer to your Galaxy, you can simply copy the files over USB (p. 278) and play them using the preloaded "Music" app.

To do so, establish a USB connection with your computer using the directions in Chapter 9 (p. 278). Create a new folder entitled "Music" and copy your MP3 files directly to it. On many popular desktop music players like iTunes, you can copy your music files simply by dragging them from the program's interface into the appropriate folder on your device. Note that these files may not play on your Galaxy if they were purchased from a music store that uses digital rights management (DRM).

After your files are copied, simply open your Music app and your music will be ready to play. The Music app looks like this:

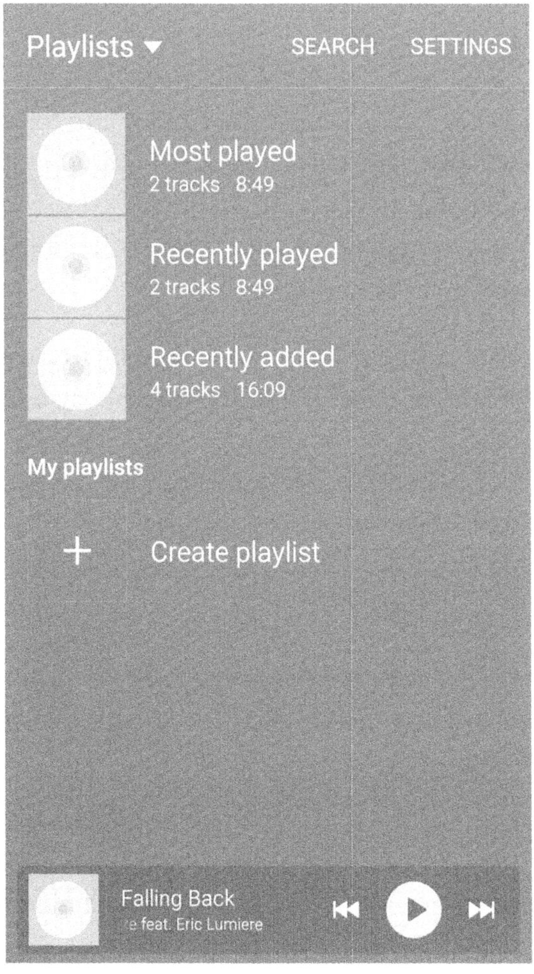

- Tap to sort your music by playlist, track, album, artist, genre, etc.

- Tap a playlist name, artist name, song name, etc., to browse through and play your tracks.
- Pause, rewind, and fast forward tracks using the control panel at the bottom of the screen.
- Create a new playlist by tapping + while in "Playlists" view. Check all songs you want to add, and then tap DONE.
- Tap SEARCH to search by song, artist, or album name.
- Tap MORE → "Settings" to access the equalizer and other settings.

TIP: *The music player supports most common file formats, not just MP3s. However, it's a very basic music player. If you're looking for a more full-featured music player, I recommend Play Music or Poweramp from the Google Play Store.*

Customizing Sound Output for Your Ears

The Note 5 and S6 Edge+ have a very interesting and useful feature that performs a mini-hearing test to customize audio output to your ears and headphones. To set it up, plug in the pair of headphones you plan to use with the device, go to a quiet room, and start the process by going to system settings → "Sounds and notifications" → "Sound quality and effects" →"Adapt Sound."

Note that this process tests your ability to hear different frequencies—not volumes—so listen very carefully and tap "Yes" even if you can only barely hear the beeping. Once you have completed the hearing test, you can specify whether to use the customized settings for calls, music playback, or both, as well as configure your most frequently used ear if you often use only one ear bud. Make sure to try the "Preview Adapt Sound" feature to test the results—it makes a big difference for me, and many other users have reported similarly good results.

Unfortunately, for music playback this feature only works with Samsung's stock Music app, so if you use third-party programs like Poweramp, you will not be able to take advantage of Adapt Sound.

Preventing Accidental Battery Drain with Music Auto-Off

It's very easy to accidentally leave music playing—I do it all the time after workouts. With the headphones plugged in, your battery can waste away for hours. To prevent this, enable "Music auto off" in the Music app's settings. Again, this setting only applies if you are using the Music app to listen to your music.

Exiting the Music App

While the Music app is playing songs, tapping [home button icon] will allow you to multitask while your music continues to play. To exit the app and stop all music playback, pull down the notification panel and tap the "X" next to the persistent Music notification.

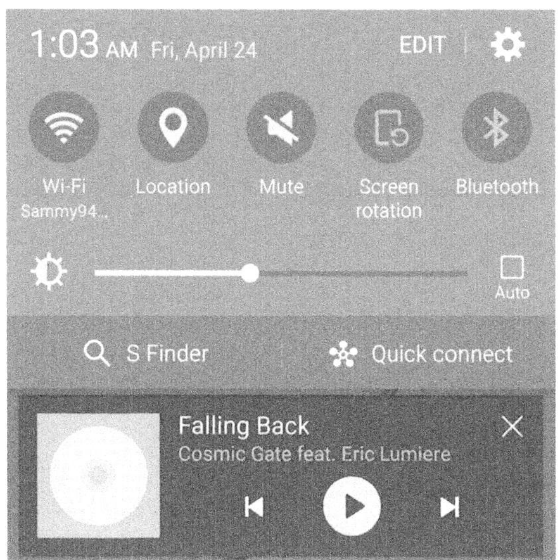

Playing Music Using Bluetooth Speakers

To pair your Galaxy with Bluetooth speakers (e.g., Bluetooth headphones or a car stereo), go to system settings → "Bluetooth." If Bluetooth is off, turn it on. Put the Bluetooth speakers in pairing/discoverable mode (consult the instruction manual if needed), and wait until the name of the device appears on your Galaxy. Tap it and follow the prompts to pair the devices. Your media will play through your Bluetooth speaker as long as Bluetooth is enabled in the notification panel. To revert to the internal speaker, just turn Bluetooth off. If your media doesn't play through your Bluetooth speaker when Bluetooth is on, go to system settings → "Bluetooth" and tap on the name of the device. Make sure it is enabled.

Navigating Using Maps and the GPS

The Maps app is an excellent co-pilot. It provides directions for driving, walking, bicycling, and public transit, and even offers real-time voice-guided navigation. To use it, open the Maps app in your app drawer.

Basic Controls

Below is a screenshot of the main Maps screen, zoomed out to show the United States.

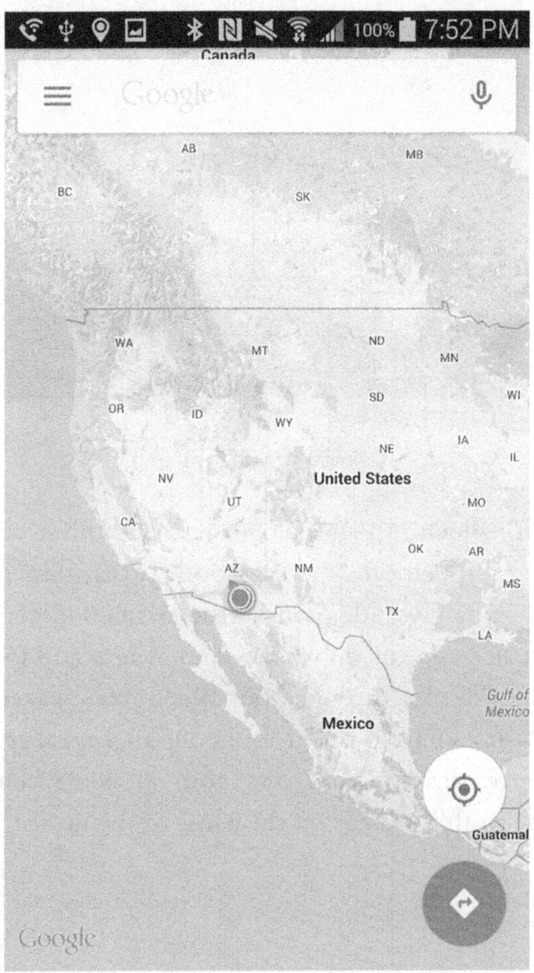

Controls include:

- Pinch to zoom in and out.
- Move your finger around the screen to pan.
- Tap ☰ to open the main menu.
- Tap ⊙ to locate your current position on the map.

- Tap to get directions.
- To find locations, addresses, or establishment names, tap the search bar at the top of the screen and type in the name of your destination, or tap and speak your search term. You don't have to enter a specific destination. You can type in a general search term like "Italian restaurants," "gas stations," or "ATMs" and Maps will show you all the results in your area.

The Main Menu

Access the main Maps menu by tapping :

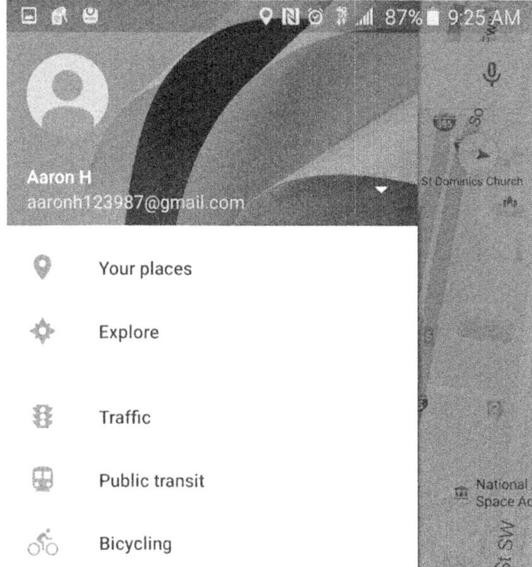

- The options "Traffic" through "Terrain" are all layers. Tap one to enable or disable it. When enabled, information will be overlaid on the main map.
- "Your places" allows you to specify your home and work addresses and save maps for offline use (p. 159).
- "Explore" shows you nearby restaurants and attractions.
- "Settings" opens the app's settings page. The most useful settings are discussed later in this section.

Finding Nearby Destinations

Let's say you're in Tucson, AZ and you want to go to The UPS Store. Tap the search bar and enter your search term:

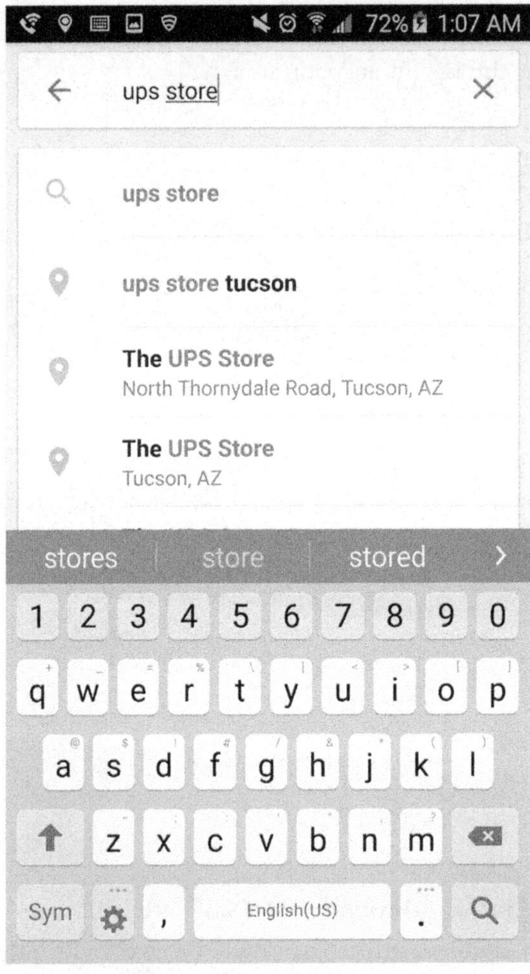

As you type, you'll see results appear below the search bar. In this case, Google has done its job well and the closest UPS Store, on Thornydale Road, is displayed in the list. Tap it to view it on a map.

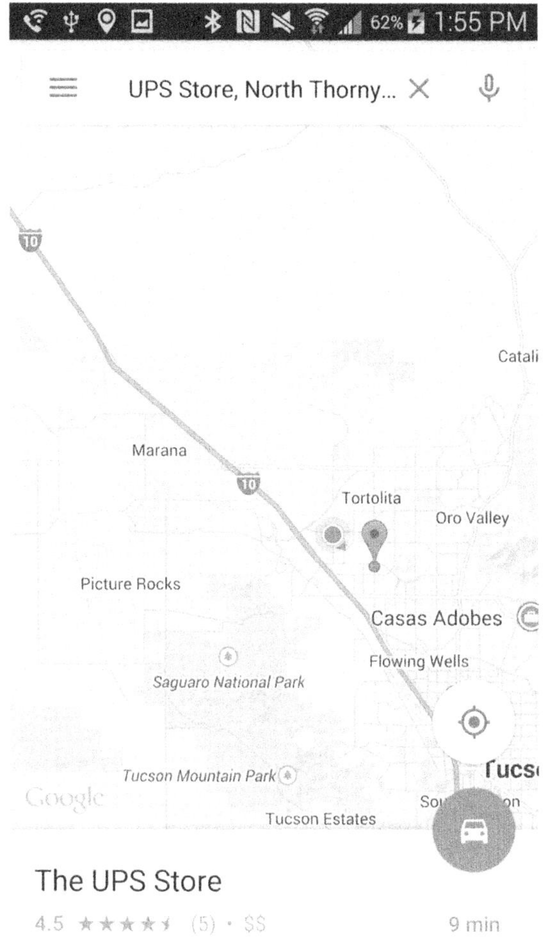

- From this screen, tap [directions icon] to get directions to your destination. If you have previously set a mode of transportation, this icon may be different. Above, it's displayed as a car because I have previously requested driving directions.
- Swipe up the white bottom bar to see detailed location information such as phone number, address, and more. Tap [back icon] to close it and return to the map.
- You can also search for generic keywords instead of specific destination names. For example, here I have searched for nearby pizza joints:

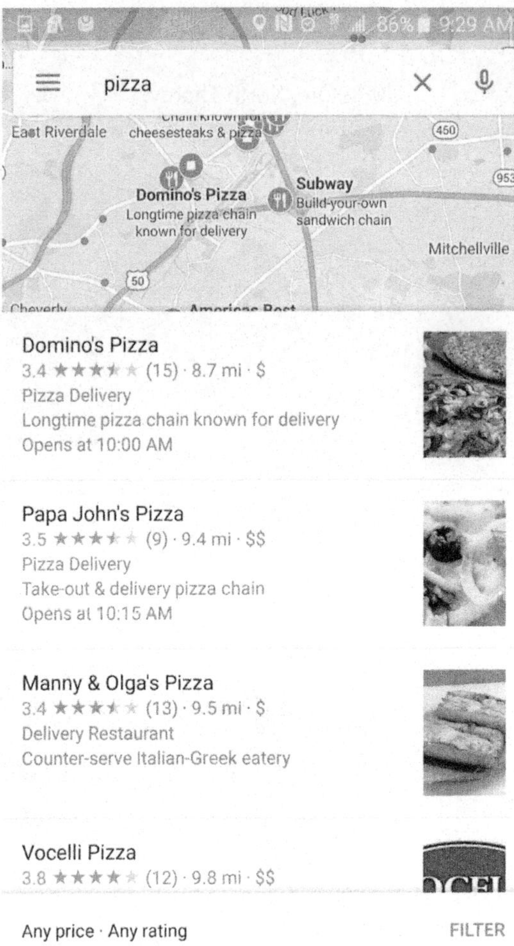

Tap "Filter" to narrow down your search by hours, price, etc., or tap a location to see detailed location information. Tap ✕ to clear the search.

> ★ ***TIP:*** *If Maps returns search results that aren't near your location, go to the main Maps screen, tap ◎ to refresh your current location, and try your search again.*

Detailed Location Information

As I just mentioned, detailed location information is accessed tapping a location in "List Results." The detailed location information screen looks like this:

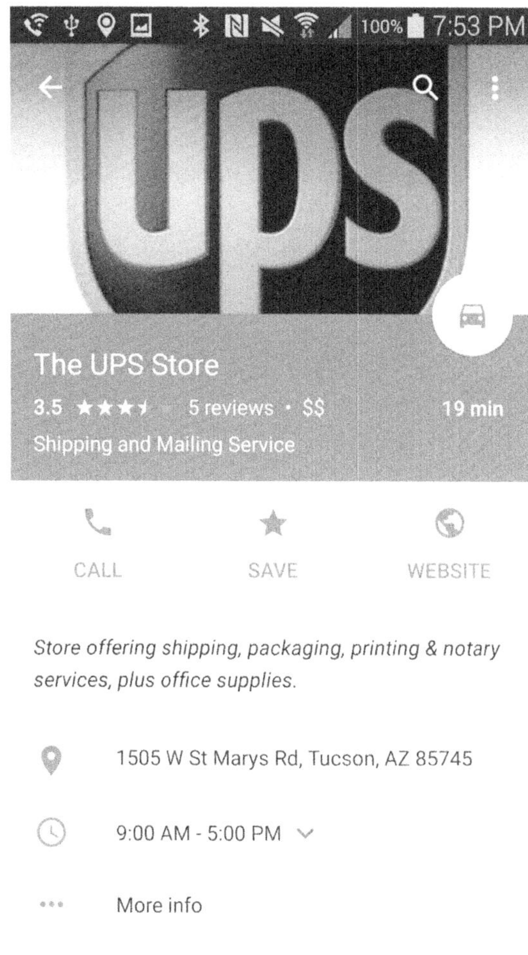

Scroll up and down to see hours, address, the Call button, and so on. To get directions to the destination, tap [icon]. Again, this icon may be displayed as a car, bike, etc. depending on how you've previously gotten directions. (In the screenshot above, it's displayed as a car.)

Getting Directions and Using Voice-Guided Turn-by-Turn Navigation

To get directions to a destination, tap (sometimes displayed as a car, bike, etc.) on a detailed location information screen (p. 155) or on the main Maps screen. You'll see this screen:

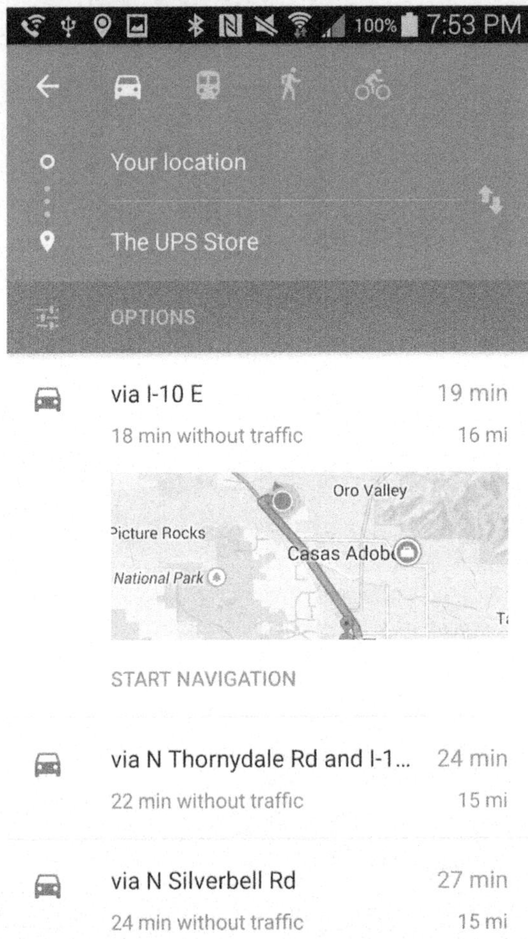

Tap the icons at the top of the screen to change the mode of transportation, or just below that, edit the starting and ending locations. The bottom portion of the screen shows different routes you can specify. "Start Navigation" is automatically displayed under the recommended route. Tapping it once immediately starts voice-guided navigation:

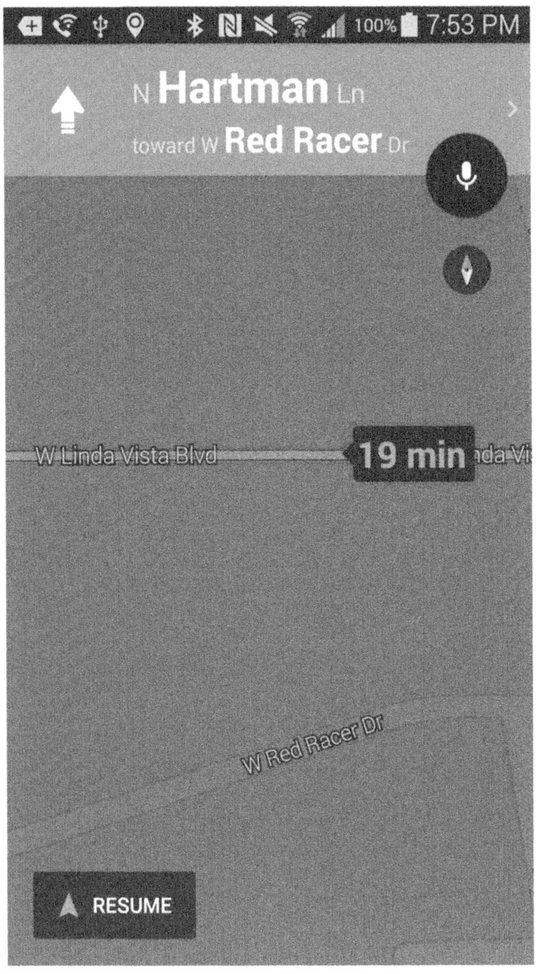

Alternatively, tap the text for one of the destinations (for example, "via I-10 E") to preview the route without starting voice-guided navigation:

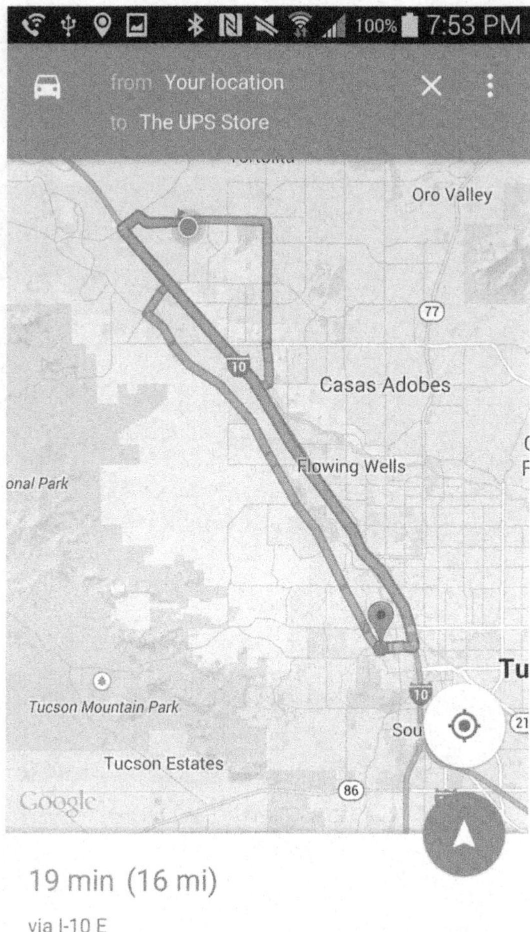

On this preview screen, swipe up the white bottom bar to see text directions without starting navigation. Or, to start navigation, tap .

Showing Current Traffic Conditions

Google collects real-time, live traffic data from DOT sensors installed in roads as well as from other Android users' phones. You can easily overlay this information on a map. To do so, open the menu by tapping on the main Maps screen and then tap "Traffic." (Green = clear, yellow = some traffic, red = congested.) In most cities this data is surprisingly accurate and up-to-date.

Setting Your Home and Work Locations for Easy Directions

Set your home and work addresses by tapping → "Your places" By doing so, you will be able to simply type "home" or "work" as starting or ending points when getting directions rather than typing out your entire address. This is also important for Google Now (p. 174) to function optimally.

Improving Your Location Precision

To find your current location, Maps uses a combination of GPS, cellular, and Wi-Fi data. To make sure Maps is taking full advantage of these resources, tap ≡ → "Settings" → "Location accuracy tips." Follow any instructions that it gives you. This is particularly useful if you spend a lot of time indoors, because GPS is a line-of-sight technology and is not available in many buildings. Cellular and Wi-Fi location data are needed to correctly identify your location when outside of GPS range.

As long as you allowed full location access when first configuring your Galaxy in Chapter 3 (p. 25), your location accuracy should already be optimized. If this is the case, you will receive a message notifying you of that, and you will not need to make any changes to your location settings.

Saving Maps for Offline Use

To save a map for offline use, tap ≡ → "Your places" → "Save a new offline map." Pinch to zoom and pan around the map. When you have selected the desired area, tap "Save." From then on, if you open Maps while you don't have an active data connection, you will still be able to access street-level data for the map region you saved.

Managing Your Schedule with the Calendar App

Samsung includes a custom Calendar app on the Note 5 and S6 Edge+, which I personally prefer to the Google Calendar (available on the Google Play Store and on "pure" Android devices like the Nexus, but not preloaded on the Note 5 / S6 Edge+). Its tabbed interface is very user-friendly and the layout is intuitive. You'll find the Calendar in your app drawer.

Navigating the Interface

Upon opening Calendar for the first time, you'll see the Month view.

To switch to a different view, tap in the upper-left-hand corner of the screen.

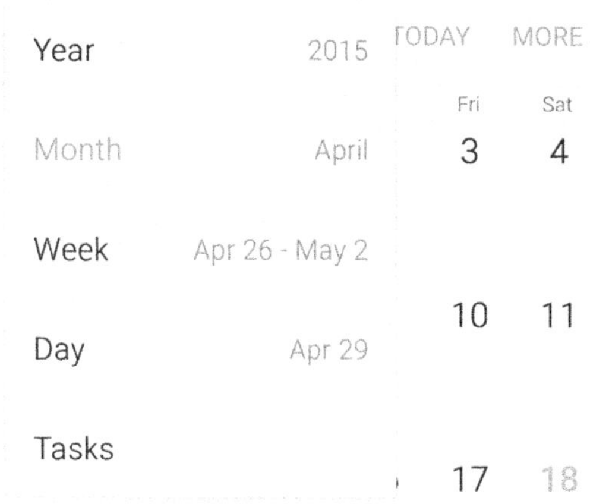

Year 2015 TODAY MORE
Fri Sat
Month April 3 4
Week Apr 26 - May 2
10 11
Day Apr 29
Tasks
17 18

Personally, I find "Week" view to be the most generally useful, although "Month" and "Day" are helpful for zooming in or out of one's schedule. "Year" does not display any events, and is mostly only useful for determining the day of the week for a specific date, or tapping a month to jump to it in the "Month" display.

> ***TIP:*** *Like Gmail and Contacts, the Calendar app automatically synchronizes with your Google account. If you log into your Gmail account on your desktop computer and pull up the calendar, you'll see all of the events in your Calendar App.*

Creating a New Event

To create a new event, tap ⊞.

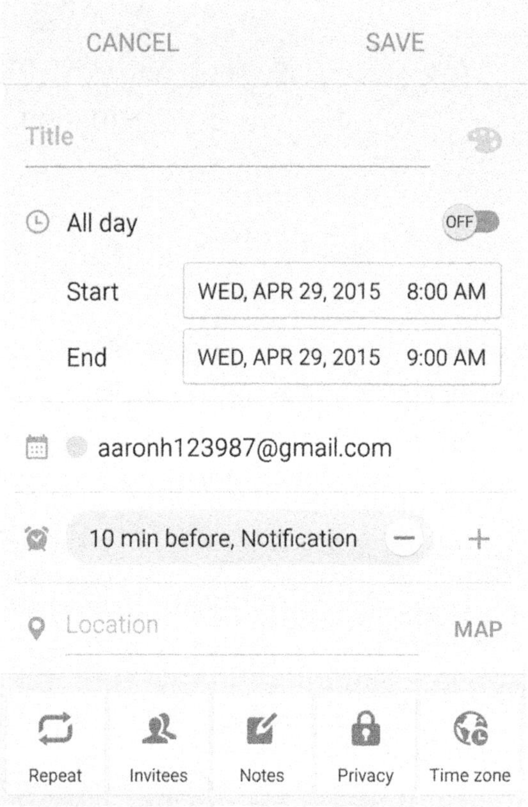

CANCEL SAVE

Title

All day OFF

Start WED, APR 29, 2015 8:00 AM

End WED, APR 29, 2015 9:00 AM

aaronh123987@gmail.com

10 min before, Notification – +

Location MAP

Repeat Invitees Notes Privacy Time zone

Options on this screen include:

- **Title:** Name and color-code the event.
- **All Day:** Set the event for a certain day, but do not give it a specific timeframe. Note that you can have other events overlapping with all day events.
- **Start/End:** Specify the starting and ending times/dates for the event.
- **(Your email address):** Tap to change the calendar to which your event will be saved. Useful if you have multiple Google calendars to separate personal and work tasks, etc. If you don't have multiple calendars but want to set them up, go to https://calendar.google.com on your computer. Look for the "My calendars" box on the left-hand side of the screen, click the down arrow, and then "Create new calendar." Any new calendars you create will automatically be synced to your Calendar app. You can view your calendars on your Galaxy by tapping MORE → "Mange calendars," but you can only edit them from your desktop computer.

- **Reminder:** Set one or more reminders for the event. "Notification" pops up a screen on your Galaxy and sounds an alarm, whereas "Email" just sends you an email. I usually set both types of reminders for important appointments.
- **Location:** Enter a location name or tap MAP to select a location using the Maps app.
- **Repeat:** Set event to repeat every day, week, month, etc. For custom repeat patterns like every other week, or every 20th of the month, tap "Customize."
- **Invitees:** Enter names from your Contacts or email addresses to send email notifications with event details.
- **Notes:** Save miscellaneous text notes related to the event.
- **Privacy:** Specify how the block of time will be displayed on any shared calendars you've joined. For example, you can choose to be shown as "Busy" without revealing any further details about the event.
- **Time Zone:** Specify the time zone for the event. Ensures notifications go off at the correct times even if you're traveling and your Galaxy's clock has been set to a different time zone.

Fill out the necessary information and then tap "Save."

Creating a New Task/To-Do Item

To add a new task, tap ▼ → "Tasks." Tap on the "Enter new task" field and start typing.

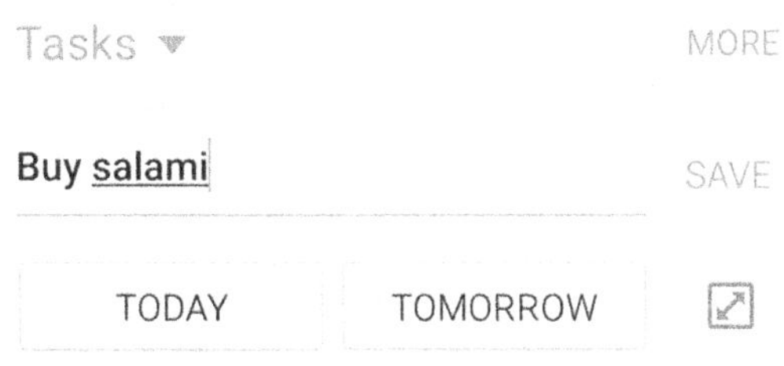

Tap "Today" or "Tomorrow" to quickly set a due date. If you need to set a due date for some other time, tap ⤢. Tap SAVE when you're finished.

Tasks appear on your calendar along with scheduled events, but unlike events, have a checkbox so you can easily mark them as complete.

TIP: *Unfortunately, there is no way to synchronize tasks in the Calendar app with Google Tasks. If you frequently use the task list in your Gmail account and want to sync it with your Galaxy, I highly recommend the third-party GTasks* **(p. 312)** *app.*

Managing and Sharing Events and Tasks

To manage existing calendar events or tasks, tap them once in Month, Week, or Day mode.

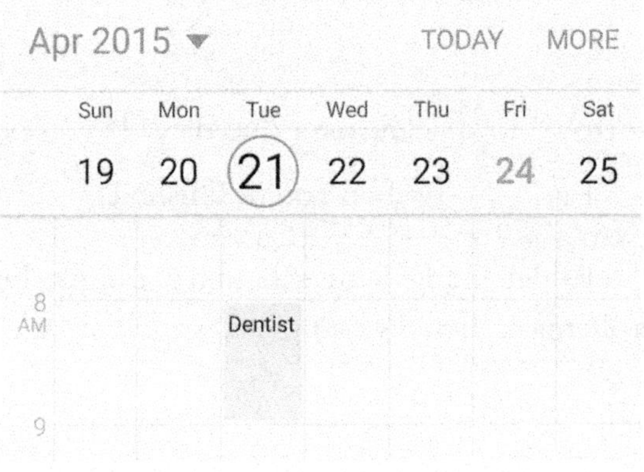

To change event or task details, follow the instructions in the previous section, Creating a New Event (p. 162). You can also share the event by tapping SHARE. Sharing the event as a VCS file will allow the recipient to easily add it to his or her own calendar, whereas sending it as text file will simply send the event information as text in an email.

Searching Events and Tasks

To search your events and tasks, tap MORE → "Search" and enter your search term.

Installing and Uninstalling Apps

Once you've mastered the basics of your Galaxy, you'll want to add new functionality. How? With apps (i.e., programs). Personally, I have apps for banking, for Amazon and eBay, for reading news, for managing my passwords, and much more.

TIP: *Check out Chapter 11 **(p. 306)** for my list of the 50 all-time best Android apps.*

Installing Apps

The best and only official source for new apps is the Google Play Store. You'll find it in your app drawer as the shortcut "Play Store."

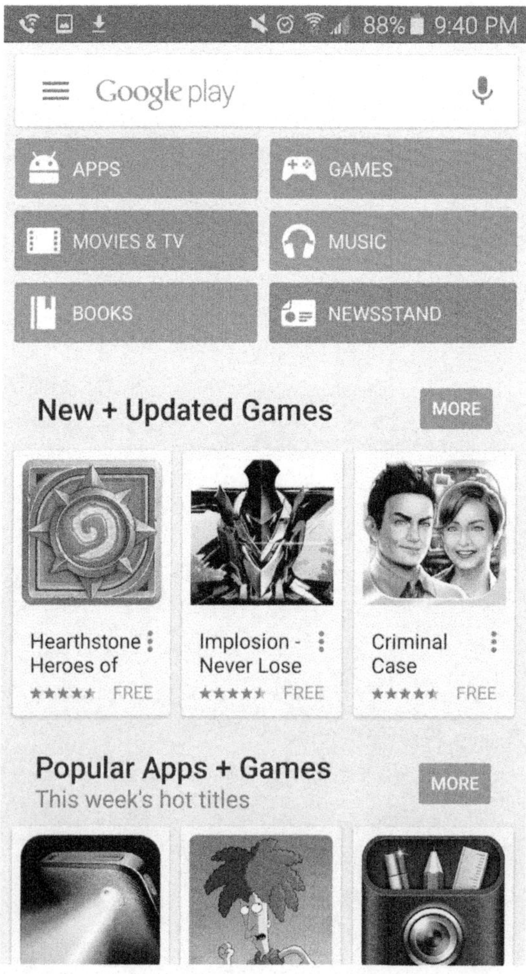

Tap the "Google Play" field to search for and install new apps. If you know the name of the app you want, enter it, or otherwise use keywords (e.g., "shopping list"). Alternatively, explore different categories of apps by tapping the green "Apps" button. You can also tap "Movies & TV," "Music," and so on, to purchase media for your Galaxy. Read more about purchasing media here (p. 185).

You'll find newly installed apps in your app drawer.

Updating Apps

Developers often update their apps, and you'll want to make sure you have the latest versions. In the Play Store, tap ☰ → "Settings" and make sure "Auto-update apps" and "App updates available" are turned on. With these settings enabled, from time to time you'll see automatic update notifications in your notification panel.

To manually check for updates at any time, open the Play Store and tap ☰ → "My apps."

Protecting Yourself from Malware and Viruses

The Google Play Store now has more than 1.5 million apps, and some of these contain malware and viruses that can put your personal data at risk. But you can stay safe as long as you're smart about it. Here's how I recommend protecting yourself.

- First, only install apps found through trusted sources. For example, you can trust apps reviewed on blogs like AndroidCentral.com, as well as those developed by major companies (e.g., Target, Bank of America, etc.). Also, the apps I discuss in Chapter 11 (p. 306) are completely tested and safe. If you're looking for a certain kind of app, run a Google search (e.g., "Android shopping list app") to find apps that are well-reviewed and repeatedly discussed on "best of" lists. Steer clear of apps that you can't find much information about.
- Second, do not download pirated apps. If you're searching Google and you see a paid app being offered for free by a third party, steer clear. Not only is it illegal to download pirated apps, but they also frequently contain malware and viruses, even if the original program is trustworthy.
- Third, pay attention to the number of downloads an app has in the Play Store. In general, apps with hundreds of thousands of downloads or more have been vetted thoroughly enough to be safe. This is not a guarantee, however, and many apps with fewer downloads are also perfectly legitimate.
- Fourth, pay attention to the permissions that an app requires. You'll see this information every time you install an app. Do they make sense given the program's function? For example, if you are downloading a flashlight app that requests full network access, you should be suspicious. I always try to download apps that

require minimal permissions, and permissions that make sense for what the app is supposed to do.

- Fifth, you can use antivirus software such as Lookout, which comes preinstalled on the Note 5 and S6 Edge+. Personally, I maintain that if you take reasonable precautions as described above, you don't need antivirus software. I personally disable Lookout on my Galaxy and feel completely secure in doing so, because I follow all the other guidelines explained above.

Branching Out to the Amazon App Store

Although the Google Play Store is the largest source of new apps, it's not the only source. The second best source of Android apps is the Amazon app store, which is built into the Amazon App (which happens to be preloaded on the Note 5 and S6 Edge+). There are other third-party app stores, but they're generally for niche purposes and are beyond the scope of this discussion.

So, why bother with the Amazon app store? First, it offers a free app every day, which you won't find on the Google Play Store. Second, it sometimes has sales on apps that aren't matched in the Google Play Store.

To download and install apps from Amazon, open the Amazon app and tap ☰ → "Apps & Games."

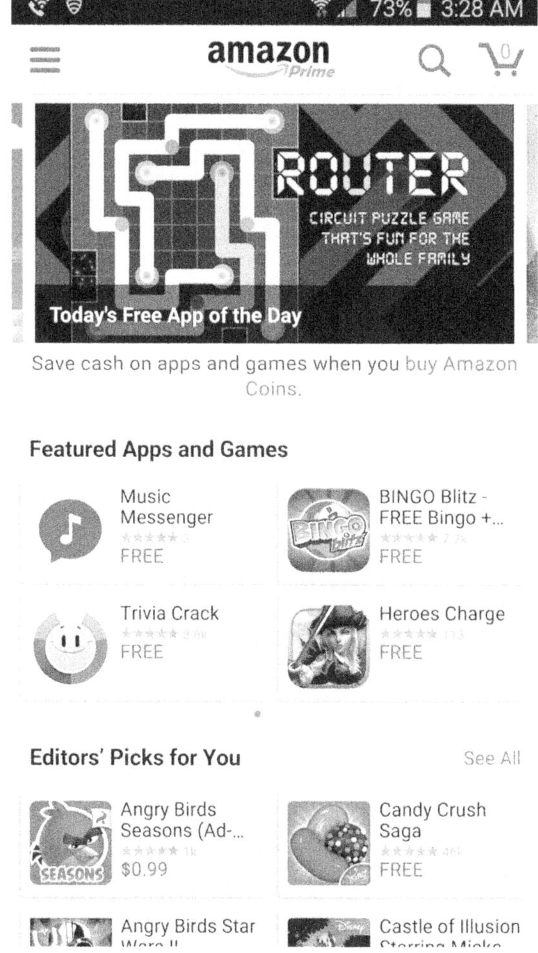

Installing .APK Files Directly from the Internet

You can also install .APK app files directly from the Internet, a technique that sometimes comes in handy. For example, the F-Droid repository, a third-party app store that contains useful software for rooted (p. 281) devices, is only available as an .APK.

https://f-droid.org/

Installing apps from outside the Google Play Store or Amazon app store is slightly more complicated, but it's easy once you have the hang of it. To demonstrate, let's run through an installation of F-Droid.

TIP: *An .APK file is to Android what a .EXE file is to a PC—an executable program (app).*

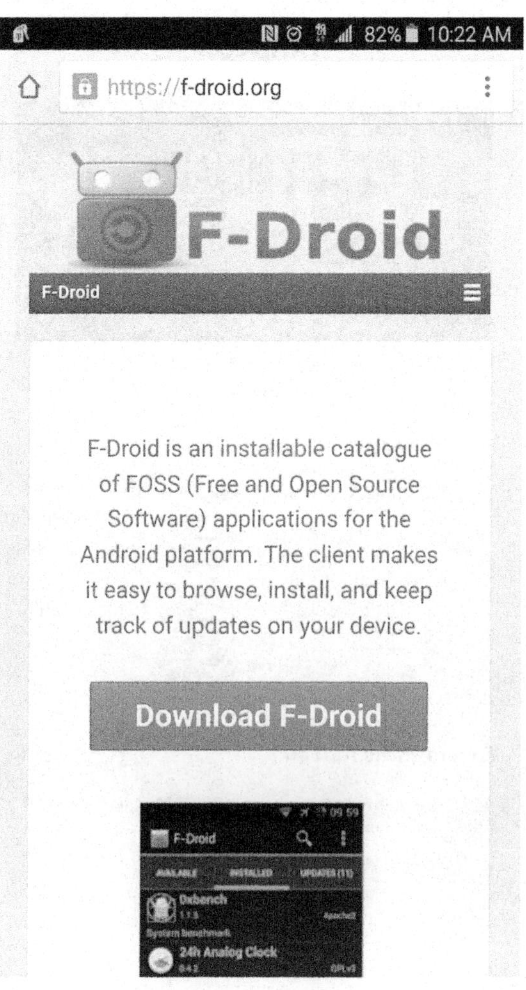

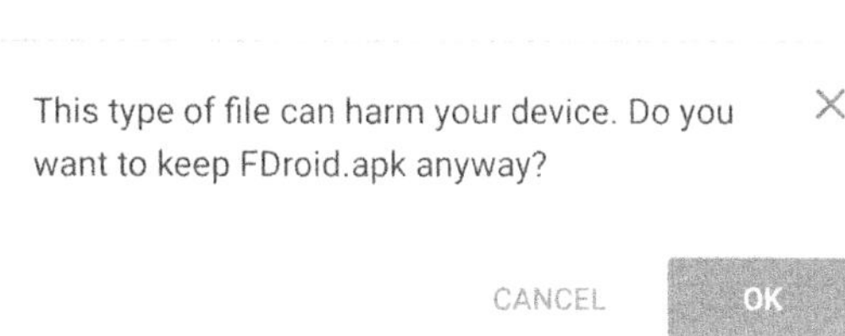

Chrome warns me about downloading apps from outside the Google Play Store. Since I trust the app, I will tap "OK."

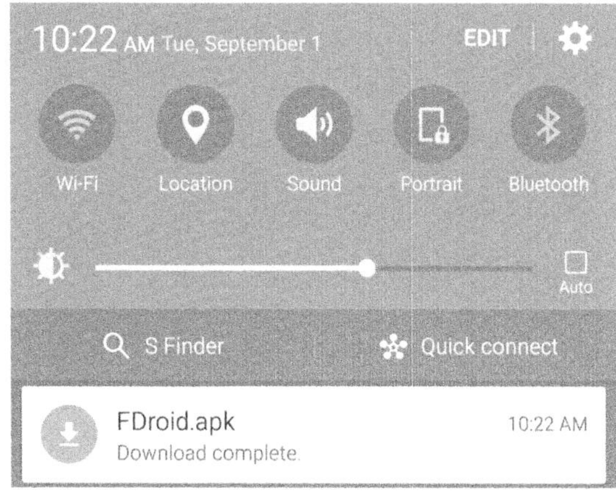

Above, you can see the download is complete. I will tap on the download notification to install the .APK file. When I see the "Open with" dialog, I will tap "Package installer" → "Just once."

Open with

JUST ONCE ALWAYS

Here, I will tap "Settings" to allow my Galaxy to install applications from unknown sources.

Install blocked

For security reasons, your device is currently set to block the installation of apps that were not obtained from Play Store. To change this, go to Settings > Lock screen and security, then turn on Unknown sources.

CANCEL SETTINGS

Unknown sources

Allow installation of apps from sources other than the Play Store.

Other security settings

Change other security settings, such as those for security updates and credential storage.

I have checked "Unknown sources" to allow installation to continue.

Unknown sources

Installing from unknown sources may be harmful to your device and personal data. By tapping OK, you agree that you are solely responsible for any damage to your device or loss of data that may result from using these applications.

☐ Allow this installation only

CANCEL OK

Here, I will tap "OK" to allow installation to continue. I've unchecked the "Allow this installation only" box so I won't be warned again about unknown sources.

Finally, on the following screen, I will tap "Install" to finish installing F-Droid.

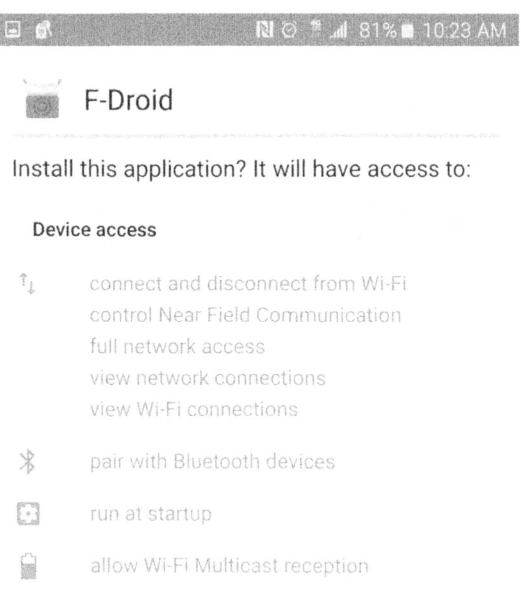

F-Droid will now be available in my app drawer. Any other apps installed from an .APK file will require a similar process.

Uninstalling Apps

To uninstall an app, first open the app drawer. Tap and hold the app's icon, drag it up to the "Uninstall" area, and release. Here, I am uninstalling F-Droid.

Tap "Uninstall" on the confirmation dialog box to complete uninstallation.

Getting a Refund and Trying Paid Apps for Free

The Google Play Store has a two hour grace period for all purchased apps. If you decide you don't want the app within two hours of buying it, go back to its page in the Play Store and tap the "Refund" button. This is a great, low-risk way to evaluate paid apps.

Google Now

What Is Google Now?

Google Now is Google's answer to Apple's Siri—a personal assistant that intelligently interprets your voice commands. However, Google Now also includes a proactive approach to information delivery through its card system, something that Siri lacks. Using the card system, Google Now delivers notifications to you throughout the day that it thinks will be useful, such as traffic information, flight information, nearby events, and so on. Google Now accomplishes this by accessing personal information such as your Gmail inbox, your Google web history, and your location history. The more you use Google Now, the more it learns about you and the smarter it gets.

 ***TIP:*** *Start Google Now by pressing and holding* 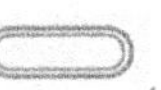.

In total, Google Now has 120+ different cards, some of which include:

- Airbnb
- BookMyShow
- Car rental
- Coinbase
- Concerts
- Currency
- Delivery Hero
- Developing story & breaking news
- Duolingo
- eBay
- ESPNcricinfo
- Event Reminders
- Events
- Fandango
- Flights
- Friends' Birthdays

- Hotels
- Housing
- Instacart
- KAYAK
- Lyft
- Mint
- Movies
- Nearby Attractions
- Nearby events
- Nearby photo spots
- New albums
- New movie
- New TV episodes
- News topics
- Next Appointment
- Packages
- Pandora
- Places
- Public alerts
- Public Transit
- Research topic
- Restaurant Reservations
- Shazam
- Sports
- Stocks
- The Economist
- The Guardian
- Traffic & Transit
- Translation
- TripAdvisor
- TV
- Walgreens
- Waze
- Weather
- Website updates
- What to watch

- Your Birthday
- Zillow
- … and many more.

To summarize, Google Now performs two main functions: (1) proactive information delivery through the card system (information it thinks will be helpful, but that you do not directly request), and (2) reactive information delivery through the voice command system (information that you directly request). If you think about it, this is exactly what you'd want from a personal assistant—things done at your request, or anticipated ahead of time.

Setting up Google Now

The first time you start Google Now, you'll see this screen:

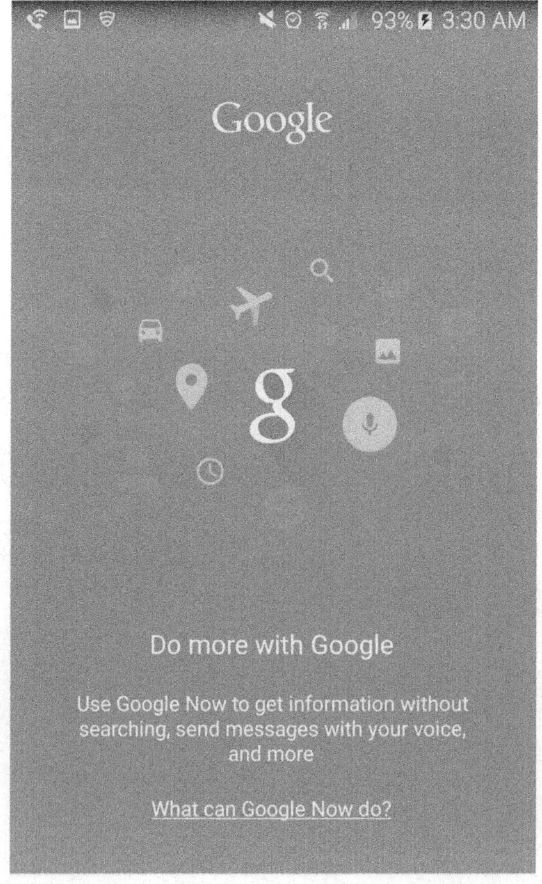

Tap "Get Started," and then "Yes, I'm in" to enable Google Now. From now on, anytime you press and hold [home button icon], you will be taken straight to Google Now's main screen:

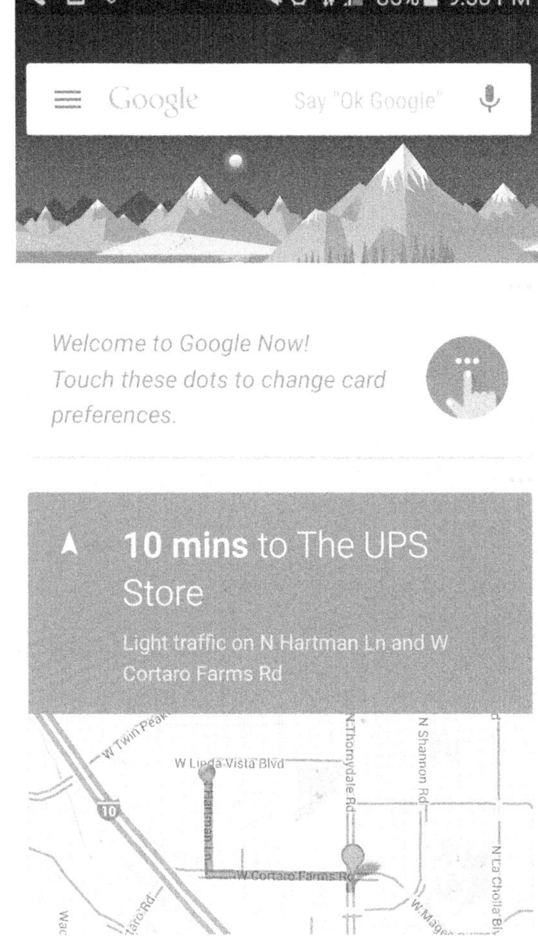

I'll come back to the main Google Now screen in a moment, but first, there are a few settings you need to change to get the most out of Google Now.

- First, make sure Account History is turned on so Google Now can effectively learn your information needs. To do this, tap ☰ → "Settings" → "Accounts & privacy" → "Google Account History" and ensure all the sliders are turned on.
- Second, make sure location precision is as high as possible. Go to system settings → "Privacy and safety" → "Location" and make sure "Locating method" is set to GPS, Wi-Fi, and mobile networks.
- Third go to the Maps app and tap ☰ → "Settings" → "Edit home or work" and set your home and work addresses.

- Finally, return to Google Now's main screen and tap ≡ → "Customize." Work through the categories, answering questions about your information needs. This helps Google Now get up to speed.

Now, you're ready to start using Google Now.

Using Google Now's Card/Notification System

At first, you'll only have a few general cards such as current weather and nearby places. The longer you have Google Now enabled, though, the more it learns about you. It will start to show you more specialized cards and send more relevant notifications to your notification panel. In my experience, it takes a few days to a week for Google Now to really kick into gear.

Even if you don't proactively ask Google Now questions, it still monitors your data in the background and learns about your information needs. For example, if you receive emails with flight reservations or package tracking numbers, Google Now will send you flight information notifications and track your packages automatically. It also monitors your calendar and reminds you about upcoming events.

However, if you *do* ask Google Now a lot of questions, it will learn even more about you. For example, if you run a few searches for your favorite sports team's scores, you'll soon receive a new card with your team's scores.

If you want to stop receiving a certain type of notification—for example, sports scores—open Google Now and find the relevant card. Tap the ••• icon next to it and tell Google Now you're not interested.

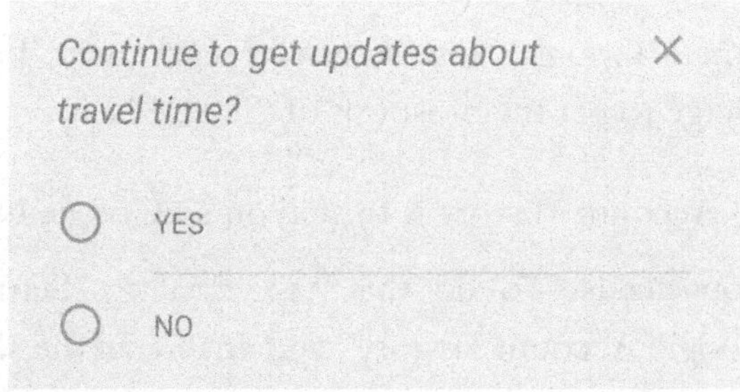

TIP: *Dismissing cards by swiping them left or right does not tell Google that you're disinterested. It simply hides them until the next time they're updated.*

Using Google Now's Voice Command System

Now, let's talk about the voice command system, Google Now's other main feature.

To prepare Google Now for a voice command, press and hold to open Google Now, and then say "OK, Google" out loud. You'll see the following screen, indicating you can proceed with your command or inquiry:

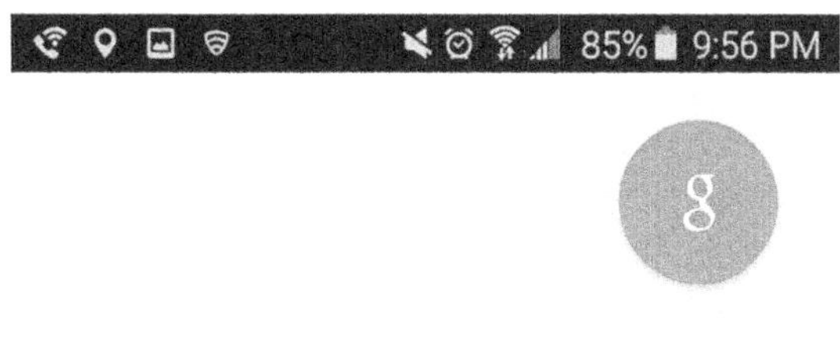

Below are the results of a couple inquiries I spoke to Google Now, to give you an idea of the types of information it can provide.

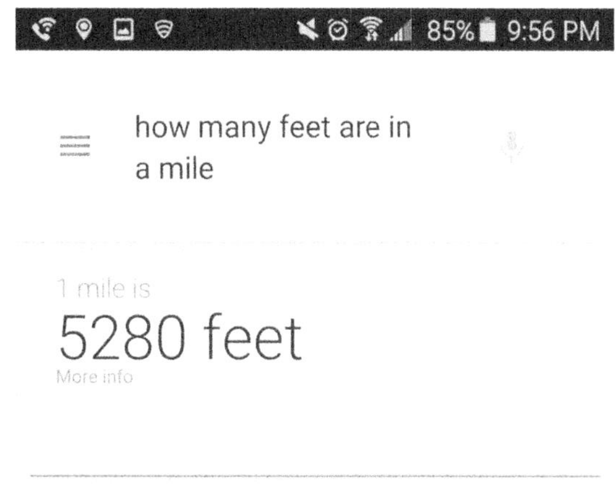

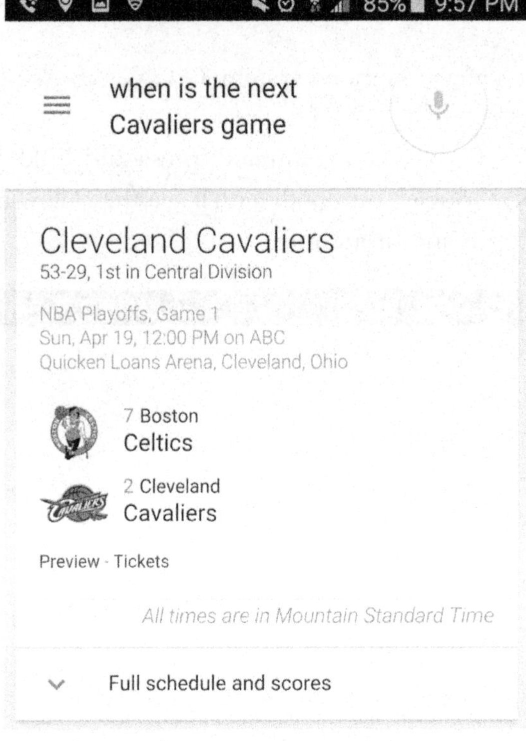

Here is a list of voice commands for you to try. Google is always adding more capabilities, so even if you don't see something on this list, try it.

- "Set an alarm for seven A.M."
- "Wake me up tomorrow at seven."
- "Schedule a meeting at 9 A.M. Thursday morning with John from Microsoft."
- "Will it rain tomorrow?"
- "How many Japanese yen are in three hundred U.S. dollars?"
- "Remind me to buy laundry detergent the next time I'm at Safeway."
- "Send a text message to Craig Johnston saying word up."
- "Driving directions to the nearest Safeway."
- "Call Target."
- "What time is it in London?"
- "Navigate to Yellowstone National Park."
- "Open (app name)."
- "Play (song name)."
- "What am I listening to?" (Google Now will listen through the microphone)
- "Show all hotels near me."

TIP: *On the Note 5 and S6 Edge+, you can enable "OK, Google" voice commands on any screen, including in apps and on the home screen. To do so, tap ≡ → "Settings" → "Voice" → "'Ok Google' Detection" and enable "From any screen."*

Sharing Your Commute

Remember Google Latitude, the web app that let you share your location with friends? Google Now has a similar feature that automatically shares the details of your commute with friends or family. If this sounds like a good idea to you—and I don't blame you if it doesn't—you can enable it by tapping ≡ → "Settings" → "Accounts & privacy" and enabling "Commute sharing". Make sure to specify who you want to share your commute with. They will receive a card on their Google Now main screen containing your commute information.

Privacy Concerns

Using Google Now requires a great deal of trust on your part, because it requires access to so much personal data. My position, however, is that you might as well trust Google. I'm not necessarily saying Google is benevolent—just that their interest is in making money, not being Big Brother. Obviously, you have to make your own decision, and enabling Google Now will allow Google to track and centralize a lot more information about you. Personally, I've made the decision to not worry about it.

Disabling Google Now

If you've had enough of Google Now and want to disable it, tap ≡ → "Settings" → "Accounts & privacy" → "Google Account" to sign out.

S Voice: A Weak Competitor

Samsung packages the Note 5 and S6 Edge+ with its own Google Now competitor called S Voice. It has many of the voice command features of Google Now, but no card system. A year or two ago, I liked S Voice and praised some of its advantages vs. Google Now, especially its voice recognition accuracy. However, as of late 2015, Google Now has pretty thoroughly outpaced S Voice. It doesn't seem like developing S Voice is a priority for Samsung, and it's been de-emphasized on the Note 5 and S6 Edge+ compared to earlier Galaxy models. I suggest sticking with Google Now, but if you want to try S Voice, you can find it in your app drawer.

Viewing and Editing Microsoft Office Documents

The Note 5 and S6 Edge+ come preloaded with the new and official Microsoft Word, Excel, and PowerPoint Android apps. These apps have been a long time coming from Microsoft, and replace the unofficial Office alternatives that Samsung used to include on its devices, such as Hancom Office and Polaris Office.

While it's a matter of opinion whether the official Office for Android apps are as nicely designed and easy to use as their unofficial counterparts, one thing is certain: the official Microsoft apps have a monopoly on file compatibility. Anyone who's ever tried editing an Office document in an alternative office program knows that results vary greatly and document formatting is easily corrupted, and this was certainly true of Hancom, Polaris, etc. The official Office apps, however, have near 100% compatibility, even with complex file layouts. This is incredibly helpful for when you just need to make a quick edit on-the-go and email your document to a colleague.

Let me level with you, though—even though the new Office apps have nearly perfect file compatibility, chances are you're going to be mostly viewing documents, not creating them. No matter how good mobile office suites get, it's just not possible to do serious work on a smartphone screen.

Creating a Microsoft Account

Before you can edit any files in Office, you'll need to create and sign into a Microsoft account. (If you're not signed in, all files will be read-only and you won't be able to make any changes.) You'll be prompted to create an account the first time you open an Office app, but if you skipped the screen, there's an easy fix. Just create a new document as per the instructions below, and look for the yellow bar along the top of the screen:

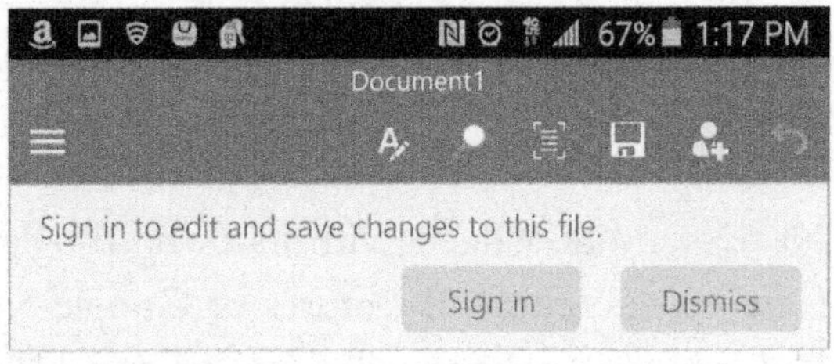

Tap "Sign in" and then follow the prompts to sign in or create a new account.

Creating or Opening Documents

To begin, open the desired app (Word, Excel, or PowerPoint) from the "Microsoft" folder in your app drawer. Then, tap "New" to choose a new document template, or "Open" to edit an existing document. Note that Office integrates with cloud storage apps like Dropbox, Google Drive, and OneDrive, and you can easily open files from these sources after tapping "Open." Recently edited documents appear below "Open" and "New" as shown below.

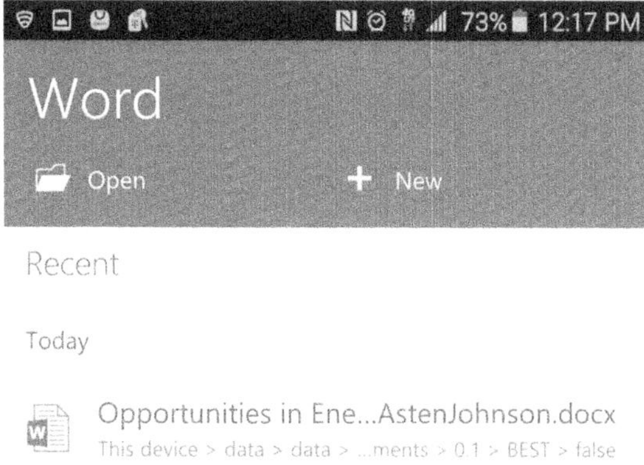

Editing Documents

This is Office's editing screen. The screenshot below is of Microsoft Word, but the controls are the same for Excel and PowerPoint.

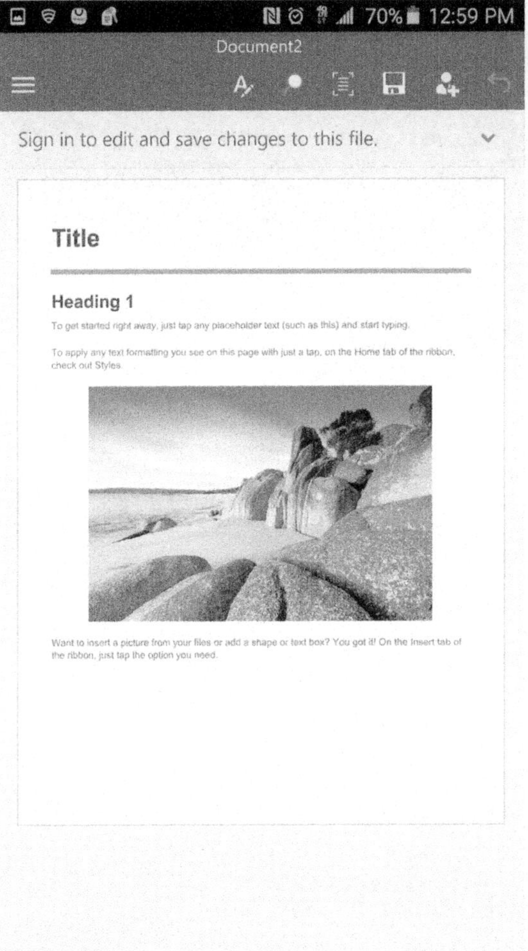

Controls on the editing screen include:

- Tap once anywhere in the document to position the cursor.
- Tap and hold to open a pop-up menu, from which you can choose to cut, copy paste, edit text, etc. **Remember that all files are read-only unless you're signed into a Microsoft account.**
- : Open the menu to save, share, print, etc.
- : Open the text formatting panel.
- : Search for text within file.

- : View document in mobile-reflow style, formatted to fit your Galaxy's screen. Tap again to return to standard view.
- : Save file. You must be signed into a Microsoft account to save files.
- : Share the document using the Share Via tool (p. 91).
- : Undo last change.

Enjoying Movies, Books, Magazines and Other Media on Your Galaxy

> *TIP: The following section is a little more abstract than previous ones. In this section, I'm not going to give you step-by-step directions for using particular media apps. There are so many that it would be impossible. Instead, I'm going to give you the 10,000 foot view, set you on the right path, and leave the details up to you. If you've mastered everything so far, this will be a piece of cake.*

The Note 5 and S6 Edge+ have tremendous potential as entertainment and media consumption devices. But before you can use them that way, you have to decide where that media is going to come from. (It's not going to magically appear by itself.) Broadly, you have two choices: 1) from Google, and 2) not from Google. Which one makes the most sense for you? Let's talk about it.

Google's Media Apps & the Google Play Store

The Note 5 and S6 Edge+ come preloaded with a couple Google media apps: Play Music and Play Movies & TV. (You can also download Play Books, Play Games, and Play Newsstand from the Play Store.) Each of these apps is designed to view media purchased from the Play Store. You see, the Play Store doesn't just contain Android apps, but also books, music, movies, TV shows, and more. Google has huge media catalogs—all of the big-name entertainment you'd expect. It's a simple process: purchase and download media from the Play Store, then view it using the respective Play app. Play Music for music, Play Books for e-books, and so on.

In my opinion, Google Play is an excellent way to get entertainment media for your Galaxy. The prices are affordable, the selection is huge, and the Play Store conveniently consolidates your entire media collection in one spot. Unless you have very unusual and exotic tastes, you'll likely find the books, movies, TV shows, and music you want on Google Play. Want to watch Breaking Bad? Buy episodes in the Play Store and watch them in the Play Movies & TV app. Want to read 1984? Buy it in the Play Store, and read it in the Play Books app. Want to read the New York Times? Buy a subscription in the Play Store and read it with the Play Newsstand app. Want to listen to the Eagles? Buy an Eagles album in the Play Store and listen to it with the Play Music app.

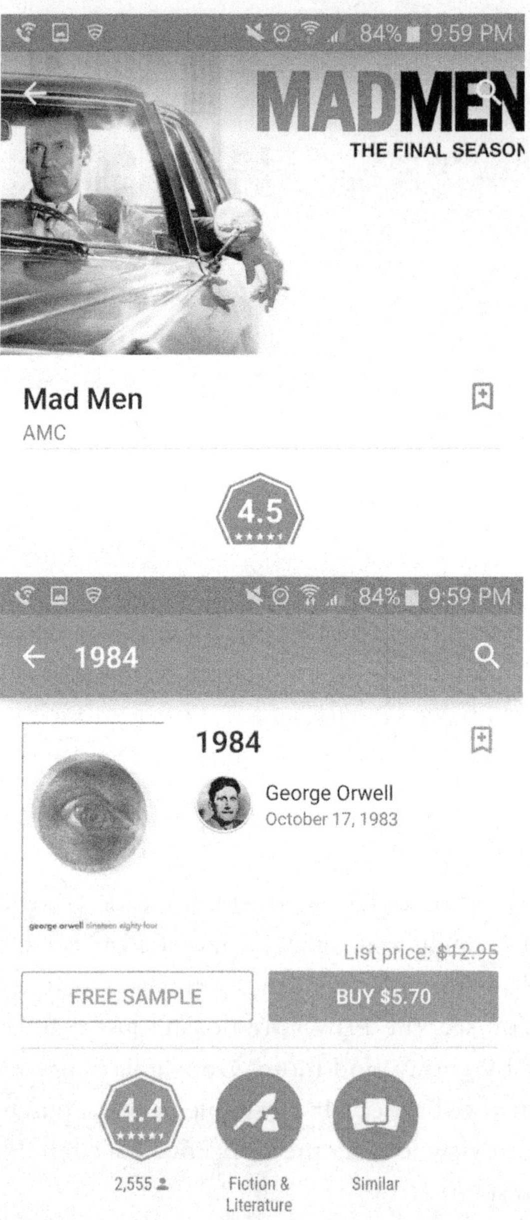

All of these apps are all-in-one packages; you don't need to mess with additional apps to enjoy the media you purchase from Google. If you buy into Google's system like they want you to, you'll be rewarded with a nice and easy experience. Better yet, you can enjoy all your media using your desktop computer too at https://play.google.com/store, as well as any future Android devices you purchase. You're not just getting one-off copies for your Note 5 or S6 Edge+, you're building a permanent collection.

Non-Google Play Media Solutions

So if Google's media ecosystem is so accessible and easy to use, why would you ever need anything else? Well, let's say you already have a Kindle for reading eBooks, and you have a DVD movie collection. In this case, you might *not* want to build a media collection in Google Play because you're already invested in other platforms and it would not make sense to fragment or duplicate your collections. (If you already have a DVD, why would you want to pay twice to buy a digital copy on Google Play?) In this case, you'd probably want to download the free Amazon Kindle app to access your eBook collection, and maybe use a generic third-party video app like MX Player (p. 313) to view ripped DVD files you've copied to your Galaxy via USB (p. 278).

Of course, there are Android apps for almost every media provider out there. Have a Netflix subscription? Download the Netflix (p. 313) app from the Google Play Store, free of charge. Have a HBO GO subscription? There's an app for that, too. Want to get a Pandora (p. 145) subscription instead of purchasing music on Google Play? You're set. Already have a huge library of MP3s? You'll find plenty of great third-party MP3 players on the Google Play Store. Just want to stick to good old free YouTube? Go for it.

Make Your Choice

The bottom line is that the field is wide open in terms of how you want to obtain media and enjoy it on your Galaxy. If you haven't already invested in other platforms, Google Play is a great place to start building a media collection. Google makes it incredibly easy to purchase, organize, and enjoy media on your Galaxy. But if you've already invested in other platforms, you can get the apps you need to enjoy your existing media collections on your Galaxy, regardless of where they came from. Or, if it makes the most sense for you, you certainly can do a combination of the two. For example, there's nothing wrong with subscribing to Netflix and using Google Play to buy movies you can't find on Netflix. You just want to be a little strategic about it, so you don't end up with a media collection that's scattered across a million different platforms.

Chapter 6: The S Pen (Note 5)

The Note 5 is an exceptional device in many ways, from its screen size to its performance. However, its S Pen support truly distinguishes it from the competition. As I discussed in Chapter 2 (p. 21), the S Pen is a revival of the stylus, which was a ubiquitous input device for Palms, Pocket PCs, and other handheld devices before Apple took capacitive (finger-based) touchscreens mainstream with the iPhone.

The S Pen, however, is much more than a plastic stick. It works in conjunction with a Wacom digitizer to allow extremely precise pen input, hovering detection, and thousands of levels of pressure sensitivity. The Wacom technology found in the Note 5 is the same technology used in most professional graphics tablets.

To remove the S Pen from the Note 5, press it in until it clicks and pops out.

> ***WARNING:*** *Although it does not matter whether you insert the S Pen with the main button facing up or down, be VERY CAREFUL not to insert the S Pen backwards, ejection-button-end first. The S Pen will become stuck, and if you forcefully pull it out, you will break the internal mechanism. If your S Pen becomes stuck this way, you'll need to contact a qualified cell phone repair service to have it safely removed.*

Anatomy

There are three main areas of interest on the S Pen: the writing tip, the main button, and the ejection button.

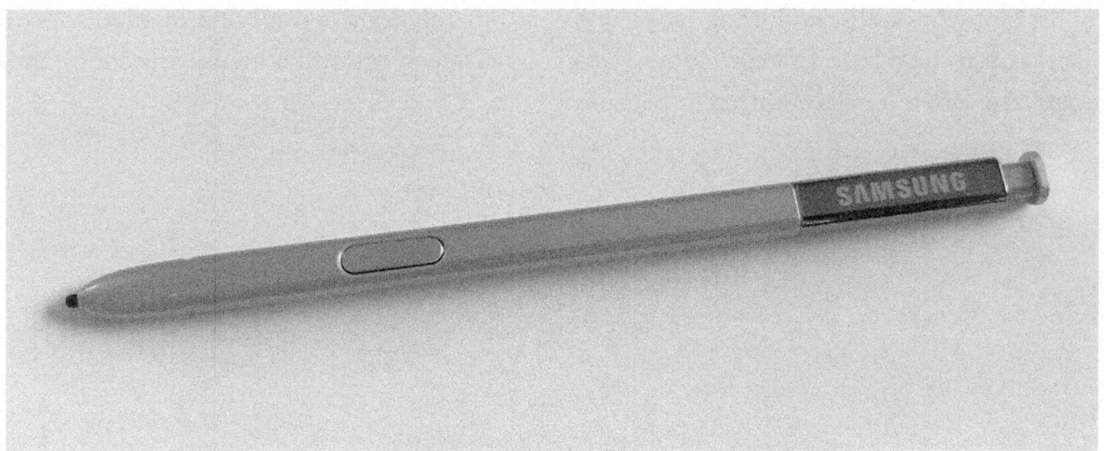

You will notice that the writing tip of the S Pen is very slightly springy; this is the mechanism by which the S Pen senses pressure. Although the S Pen is not extremely fragile, take care not to apply excessive force while writing or you damage the tip.

The main S Pen button performs different functions depending on the circumstance in which it is pressed. I will explain these in detail in this chapter.

The ejection button is a new feature on the Note 5. On previous Notes, one simply pulled the S Pen out with a fingernail.

> ***TIP:*** *Samsung also sells a full-size S Pen with an eraser: (http://www.amazon.com/dp/B009QW3SGQ/). It is essentially a larger version of the stock S Pen, but can be turned upside down and used as an eraser as well. I recommend purchasing one if you plan to use your S Pen extensively.*

Air Command

Before using the S Pen, you need to understand Air Command. Air Command is a quick-access portal to all the S Pen's main features. It opens automatically when you remove the S Pen from its silo, or when you hover the S Pen above the screen and single-press the S Pen button. Air Command looks like this:

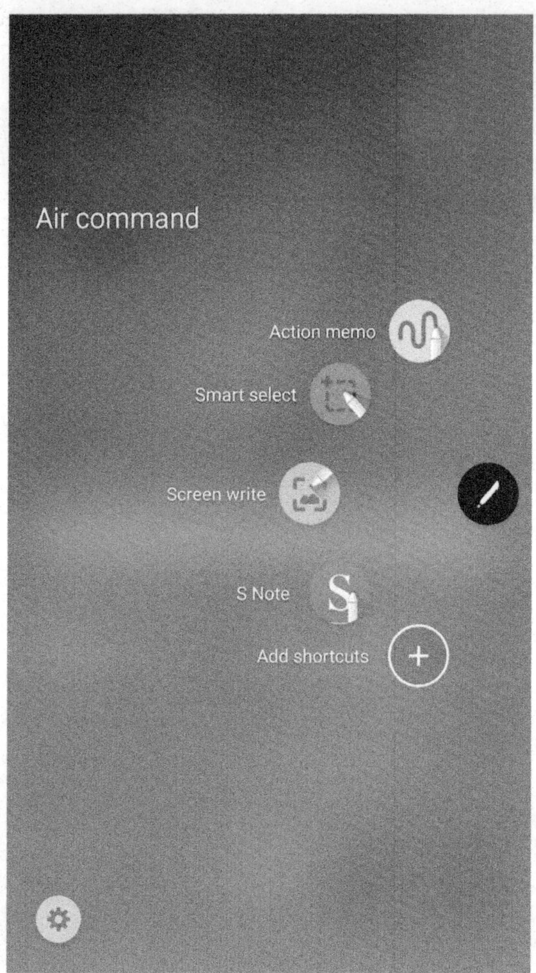

Options include:

- Tap any of the options once with your S Pen to activate them (Action Memo, Smart Select, Screen Write, and S Note). Keep reading for more information about these features.
- Tap "Add shortcuts" to add up to two additional app shortcuts to Air Command—these can be any apps installed on your Note 5—you're not limited to S Pen-related apps.

- Tap ⚙ to see more settings. This is the same as going to system settings → "S Pen" → "Air command."

Action Memo

Action Memo lets you quickly jot a note and then take an action using that note. For example, you can write a name and phone number with the S Pen and then instruct Action Memo to create a new contact based on that information. Or, for example, you can jot an email address and compose a new email to it. Action Memo looks like this:

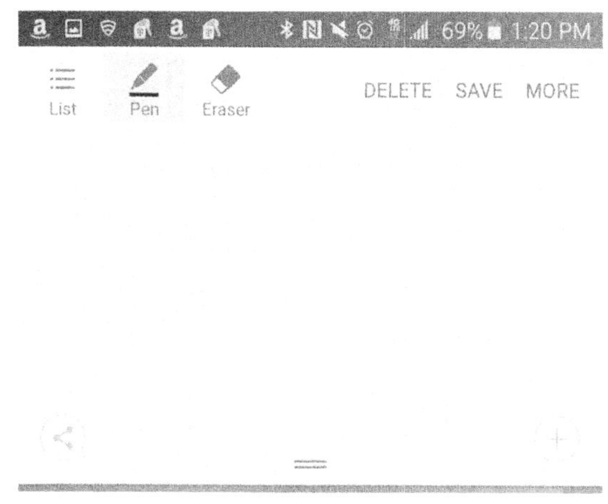

- : View a list of all your Action Memos in the S Note app.
- : Writing mode.
- : Erasing mode. Note that you can also hold the main S Pen button while in writing mode to temporarily activate erasing mode.
- DELETE : Delete and discard the current Action Memo.
- SAVE : Save the current Action Memo into the S Note app and close Action Memo.
- MORE : View more options, including Link to action, Minimize, Set reminder, Edit as S Note file, and Change background color. Keep reading for more information about these options.
- : Share the note with another app, email it to a contact, etc.
- : Adjust note size.
- : Save current Action Memo to S Note, and create a new, blank Action Memo.

TIP: *To quickly create an Action Memo from any screen on your Note 5, double tap the screen with your S Pen while holding down the main S Pen button.*

Link to Action

The key feature of Action Memo is More → "Link to action." Once you've jotted down some information, tap Link to Action to see the following options:

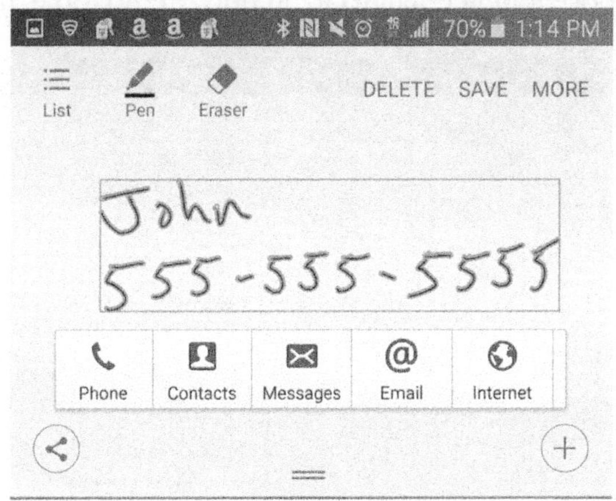

- : If you've written a phone number, dial it.
- : If you've written a name and/or other contact information, create a new contact.
- : If you've written a name or phone number, create a text message to it.
- @: If you've written an email address, compose an email to it.
- : Google the text you've written.
- : Search for the text you've written in Maps.
- : Create a new task with the text you've written.

TIP: *Unfortunately, it's not possible to call a contact already in your Note 5 by writing a name and tapping . Action Memo will say "No phone number detected." The feature only works with numbers.*

Minimize

After writing an Action Memo, tap MORE → "Minimize" to minimize the memo to a tiny floating yellow note. This note will float on top of all apps, not just your home screen. Use Minimize if you need to briefly hide an Action Memo.

Tap the icon to open the memo again, or tap, hold, and drag to move the icon.

Pin to Home Screen

If you want to save your Action Memo for a longer period of time, "Pin to home screen" is a better option than "Minimize." Instead of creating a floating icon that will float on top of all your apps, "Pin to home screen" turns your current Action Memo into a widget which you can move around your home screen at will.

To remove a pinned memo, tap, hold, and drag the memo to the "Remove" icon and release.

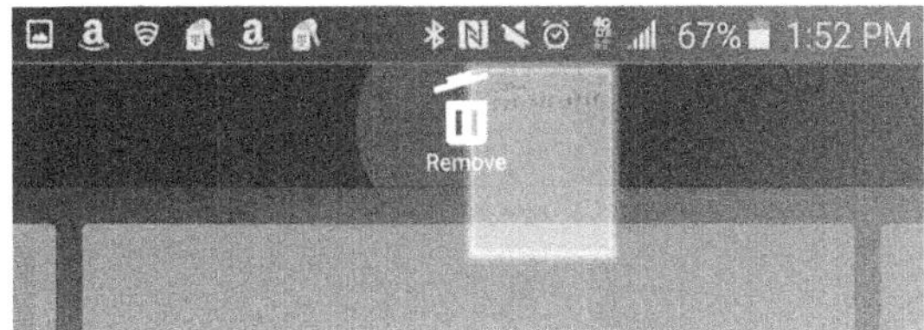

Smart Select & Scrapbook

Smart Select

Smart Select lets you freely clip images and/or text from any screen on your Note 5 and save them into the Scrapbook (p. 195) app or the Gallery. After you start Smart Select from the Air Command menu, just tap and drag the S Pen to select a portion of the screen, and release to capture. Below, I have used Smart Select to select a portion of the Wikipedia article on former U.S. president Franklin Pierce.

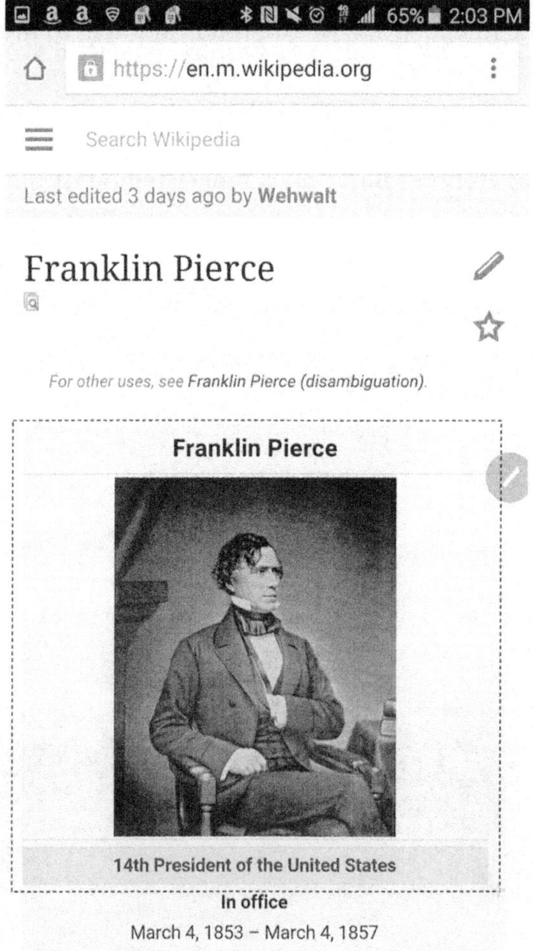

After releasing the S Pen, the selection is clipped and I am taken to a processing queue:

Controls include:

- **Write:** Open the clipped selection in a basic editor, in which you can write and draw on it with the S Pen.
- **Share:** Send the selection to another app using the Share Via tool.
- **Save in Scrapbook:** Send the selection to the Scrapbook, which is found in the "Samsung" folder in the app drawer. See below for more info on the Scrapbook app.
- **Save in Gallery:** Send the selection to your Gallery app, where it'll be stored along with your camera images and other photos.

The Scrapbook

As I've explained, the Scrapbook app works together with Smart Select to save your selections for later viewing or sharing. You'll find it in your app drawer, inside the "Samsung" folder. Below is a screenshot of the main Scrapbook screen.

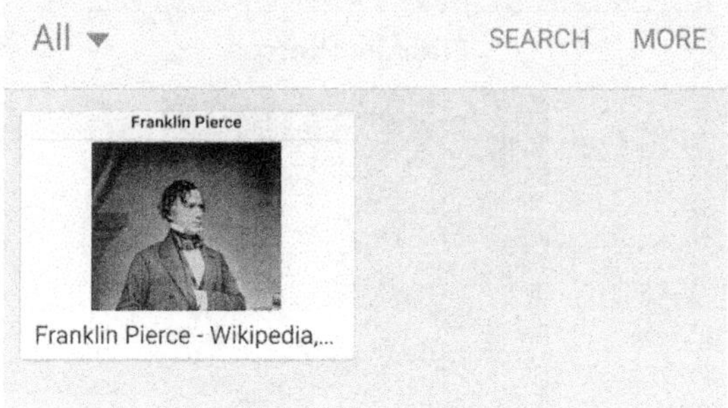

- **Tap a selection** to view it in full-screen mode.
- **Tap and hold a selection** to select it. Once selected, tap MORE to share or duplicate (copy) the selection, or categorize it.
- All ▾: Filter selections by category.
- SEARCH: Search your selections for specific text.
- MORE: View additional options.

Full-screen mode looks like this:

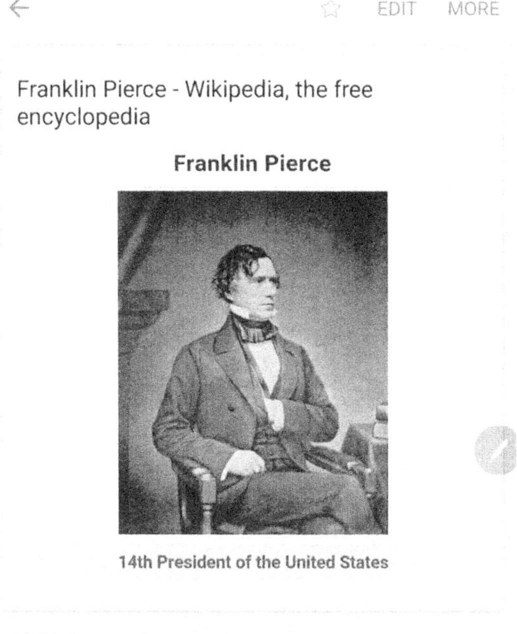

- ←: Back to the main Scrapbook screen.
- ☆: Mark selection as a favorite.
- EDIT : Change the selection's title, add notes, and/or tag it with keywords. Use the SEARCH function to search for specific tags.
- MORE: Delete the selection from the Scrapbook, share it with the Share Via tool, or use a highlighter tool to highlight text in the selection.

Screen Write

Screen Write takes a screenshot of the current screen and immediately opens the screenshot into an image editor where you can draw on and crop the screenshot. Here, I have used Screen Write to take a screenshot of my app drawer:

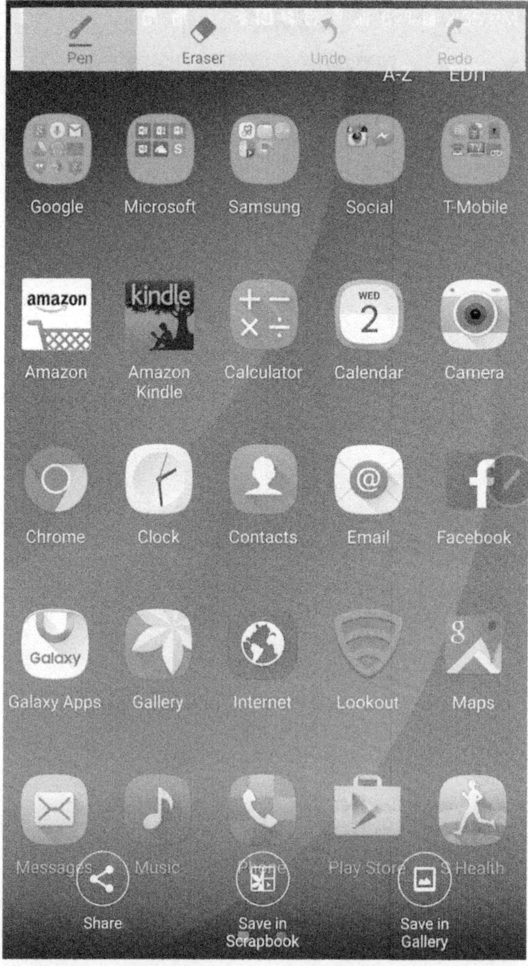

Controls in Screen Write include:

- **Pen:** Tap to select pen thickness, color, etc. Then use the S Pen to write and draw on the screenshot.
- **Eraser:** Enter erasing mode. Once in erasing mode, use the S Pen to erase previously drawn strokes.
- **Undo:** Undo last action.
- **Redo:** Redo last action.
- **Share:** Send annotated screenshot to another app using the Share Via tool.
- **Save in Scrapbook:** Save annotated screenshot to the Scrapbook (p. 195) app.

- **Save in Gallery:** Save annotated screenshot to the Gallery app, alongside your camera photos and other images.

Scroll Capture to Stitch Together Screenshots

Screen Write has a new sub-feature on the Note 5 called Scroll Capture, which lets you automatically stitch together screenshots of anything that's longer than a single screen length. For example, you can use it in a web browser to capture a lengthy web page, or in the Messages app to capture a lengthy conversation thread. To use Scroll Capture, activate Air Command and then Screen Write. You'll see the "Scroll Capture" option in the lower-left-hand corner of the screen:

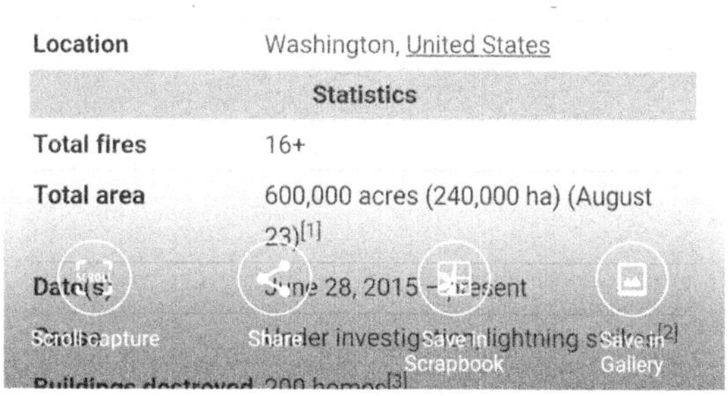

Tap it, and then tap "Capture more" to make the screen scroll and stitch more content onto your screenshot. Keep tapping "Capture more" until you're satisfied, and then tap "Done."

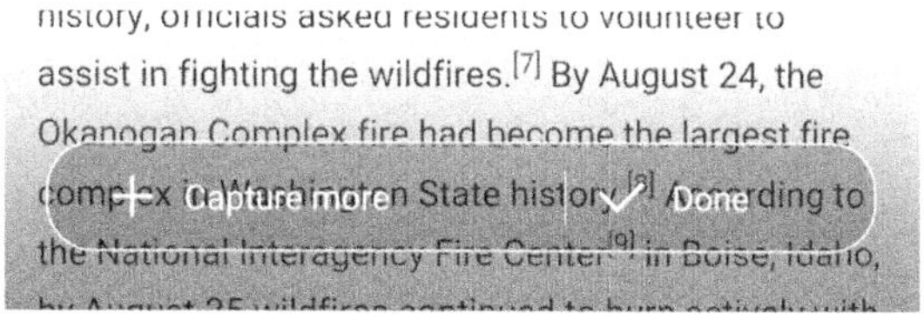

After tapping "Done," you'll be prompted to save the screenshot to the Scrapbook or to your Gallery, allowing you to subsequently share it with your contacts.

Screen Off Memo

Screen Off Memo is exciting new S Pen feature on the Note 5, and is the quickest way to jot down a note. It's activated whenever you remove your S Pen from your Note 5 while the device is asleep, and lets you start writing instantly. There's no need to authenticate yourself or open the S Note app—just pull the Note 5 out of your pocket, eject the S Pen, and start writing. It looks like this:

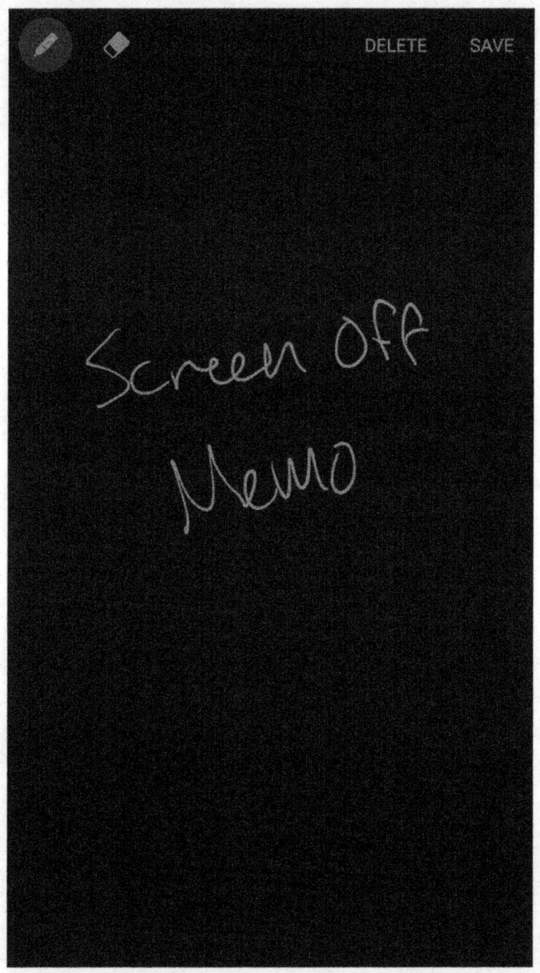

You can tap SAVE to save the memo to S Note and close Screen Off Memo, after which you'll be returned to the device locks screen. However, there's an ever better way to save your Screen Off Memo—just reinsert the S Pen into the Note 5 without tapping SAVE. The note will be automatically saved to S Note, and your Note 5 will go back to sleep again. No need to press the power button at all!

Write on PDF

PDF markup is another new feature of the Note 5's S Pen. You can use your S Pen to write directly on PDF files—very convenient!

When you open a PDF file (from your email, from a web download notification, etc.), you'll see the following prompt at the bottom of your screen. Tap "Write on PDF."

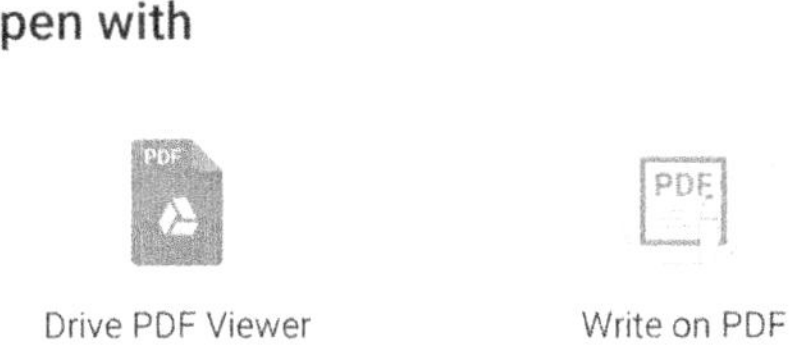

I have found that this prompt sometimes doesn't appear, such as when you open PDF files from the Gmail app. In this case, you will need to save the PDF file to your Note 5, and open it using an app like ES File Explorer (p. 310), which will correctly prompt you to open the file with the Write on PDF tool.

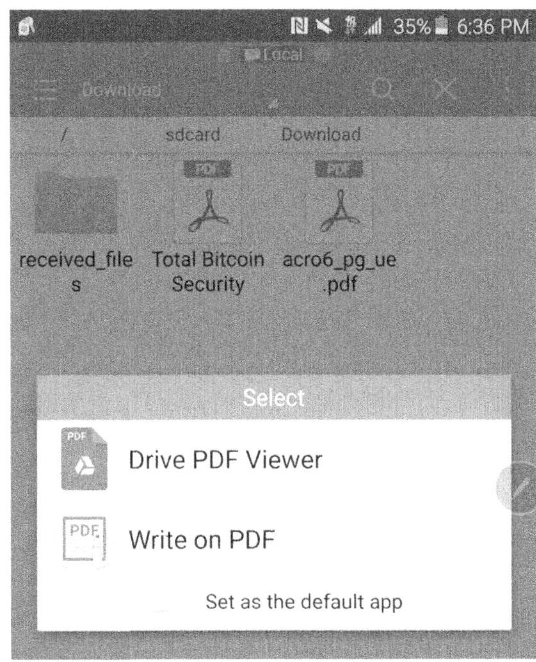

Here is PDF editing in action. Controls are very similar to Edit Mode (p. 207) in S Note.

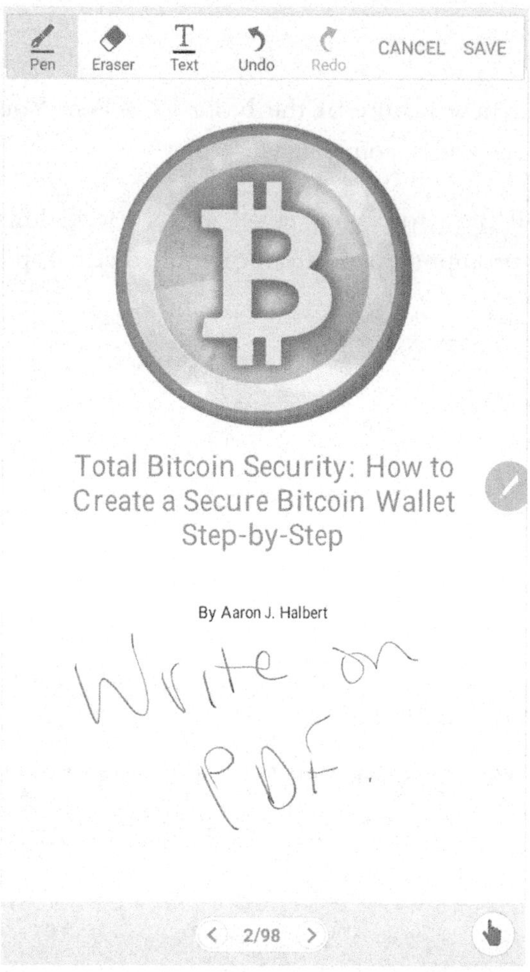

Air View

Air View is an S Pen feature that can be enabled or disabled in system settings → "S Pen" → "Air view." It lets you hover your S Pen above on-screen objects to display additional information about them. Note that Air View is *not* accessed through Air Command (p. 190) like Action Memo, Smart Select, or Screen Write—when enabled, it is always on.

Air View works in many parts of TouchWiz and in most apps preloaded on the Note 5. Here are the four main ways it helps you:

- **Information preview:** Extend text or enlarge picture thumbnails. In this screenshot, I am hovering the S Pen over a thumbnail in the Gallery app to see a larger preview.

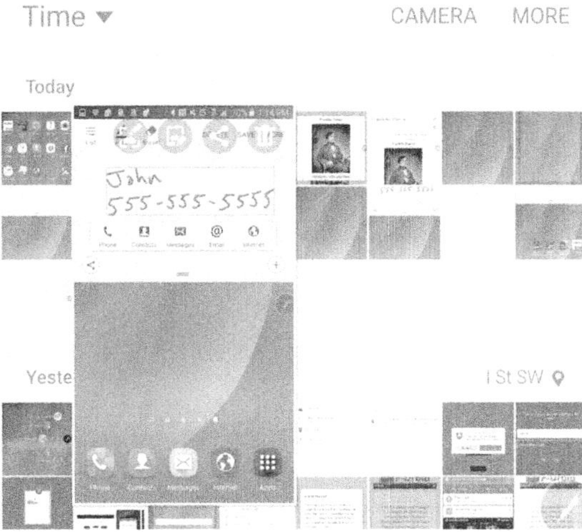

- **Icon labels:** Pop up labels for graphical buttons. In this screenshot, I am hovering the S Pen over the trashcan icon in Scrapbook, and Air View has popped up the "Delete" text to indicate what the icon does.

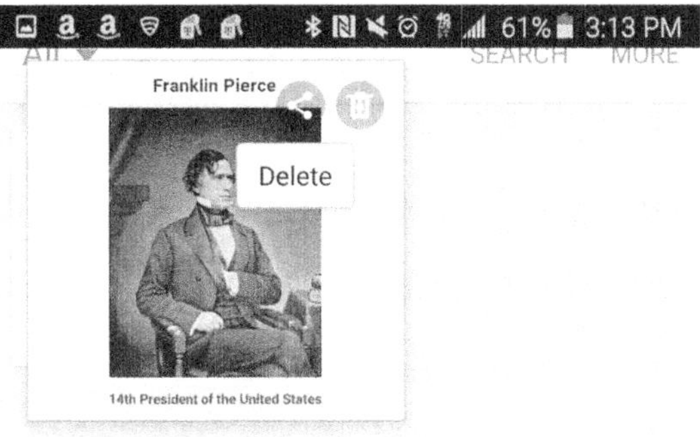

- **List scrolling:** Scroll up or down. In this screenshot, I am hovering the S Pen near the top of the screen, and the system settings are automatically scrolling up without me touching the S Pen to the screen at all.

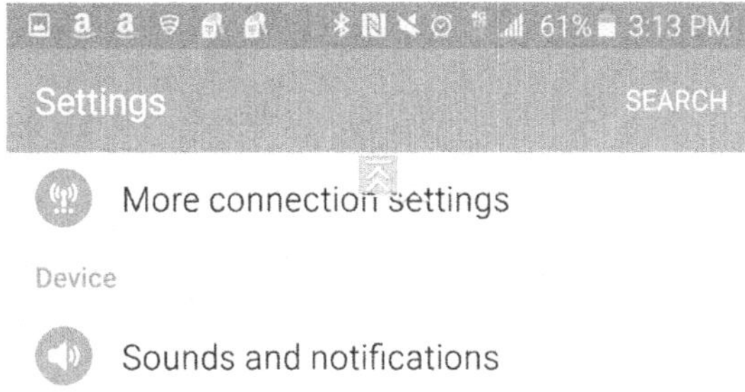

- **Link preview:** Preview web links. In this screenshot, I am hovering the S Pen over the link that my friend Mike texted me, and Air View has popped up text describing the web page to which the link leads.

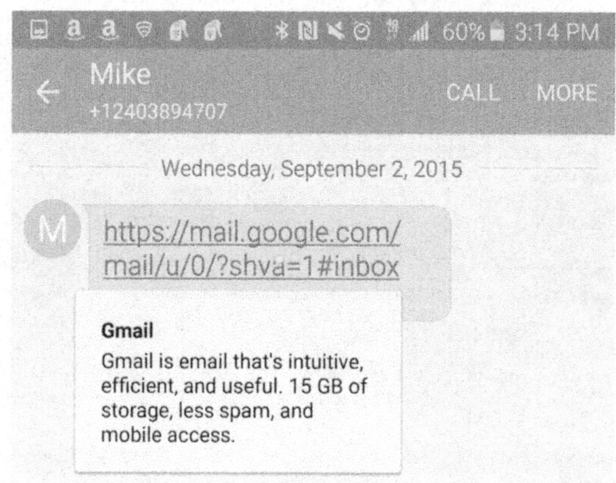

Pen Select

With the Pen Select feature, you can use the S Pen to select text in any app that allows you to do so (e.g., Chrome, Internet, Gmail, and so on. Press and hold the S Pen button, then drag it across text, just like using the left mouse button to select text on a computer. In the below screenshot, I have selected a line of text in Chrome using this method.

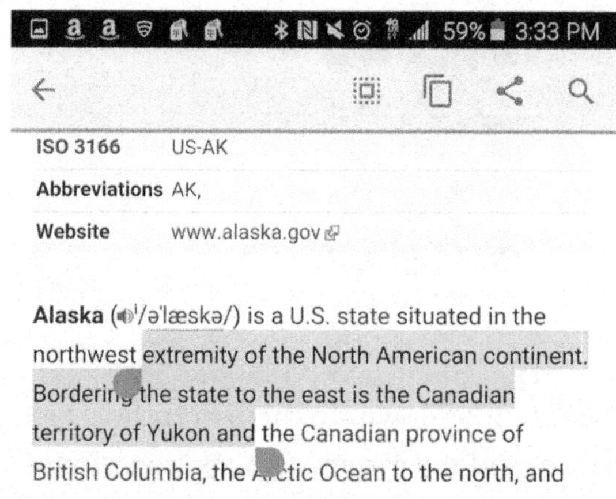

S Note

S Note is a note-taking app designed for use with the S Pen. Use it to write, draw, or sketch anything you want to record for later. Conveniently, S Note ignores all input from your fingers/hands and only records input from the S Pen, so you can rest your hand against your device while doodling in S Note.

Main Screen

The main S Note screen looks like this:

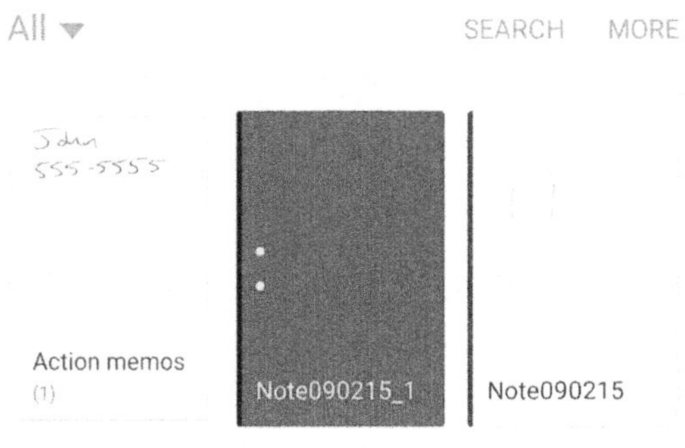

From this screen, tap any note to open it in View Mode **(p. 206)**. Other controls include:

- All ▾: **Filter your notes by category.**
- SEARCH: **Search your notes.**

- MORE: **Access additional options**, including note sharing with the Share Via tool, category management, additional S Note feature pack downloads, and more.
- +: **Create a new note.**

View Mode

View Mode lets you read a note without making any changes to it. Here's a note in View mode:

1/1

Controls in View mode include:

- ←: **Return to the main S Note screen.**
- EDIT: **Open the current note in Edit Mode (p. 207).**
- SHARE: **Share the current note.**

- MORE: **Additional options including delete page, manage pages, and tag notes.**
- < : **Previous page.**
- > : **Next page.**
- 1/1: **Page indicator.**

If the controls are hidden in view mode, just tap the screen with your finger to reveal them. Tap ⮌ to return to the main S Note screen (p. 205).

Edit Mode

Here's a note in Edit Mode:

Controls in Edit Mode include:

- : **Pen tool.** Use this tool to doodle and sketch freely. Tap it again while it's already selected to choose the type of pen (regular pen, pencil, brush, etc.), color, and thickness.
- : **Eraser tool.** Use this tool to erase. Tap it again to reveal two options: "Erase by stroke" and "Erase touched area." When "Erase by stroke" is selected, the eraser erases the entirety of any continuous stroke by simply touching it. When "Erase touched area" is selected, the eraser acts more like a normal eraser, removing only the portions of the ink that it overlaps. "Erase all" erases everything on the current page.
- T : **Text tool.** Use this tool to type regular characters using the on-screen keyboard. Tap it again while it's already selected to choose the font, size, formatting, and color.
- : **Undo last action.**
- : **Redo last action.**
- SAVE: **Save the note and switch to View Mode (p. 206).**
- MORE: **Menu.**
  - **Insert:** Insert images, voice recordings, Scrapbook selections, and more.
  - **Selection mode:** Temporarily switches out of Pen/Eraser/Text mode, and lets you use the S Pen to draw a selection around objects in your note. Once you have selected objects, you'll see a popup window with options including Layout (bring selected object in front of other objects, or send it behind other objects), Cut, Copy, and Delete.
  - **Add page:** Same as tapping +.
  - **Manage pages:** See an overview of all pages in the current note.
  - **Background settings:** Select a color and/or style for the note background, such as college ruled, grid, etc.
  - **Tags:** Tag the current note with keywords, to make it easier to find with the Search function.
- : **Favorite pens.** Once you've created a pen style you really like, tap this icon and then "Add favorite pens" to save it for future use. Tap this icon anytime to save additional favorite pens, or to choose from your previously saved favorites.
- : **Previous page.** Same as swiping left to right with your finger.
- : **Next page.** Same as swiping right to left with your finger.
- 1/1 : **Page indicator.** Does the same thing as MORE → "Manage pages."
- + : **Create new page in current note.**

You can also zoom in and out in Edit Mode by pinching with two fingers. Tap SAVE to save and switch back to View Mode (p. 206) or ⮌ to return to the main S Note screen (p. 205).

Downloading More Features

Samsung offers several free downloads that add functionality to S Note. These include:

- **Extension pack:** Extended toolbar, handwriting recognition, magnified notes, recorded sketches, and more.
- **Easy chart:** Create and insert charts in your notes.
- **Idea Sketch:** New tools to create line art.
- **S Note widget:** Add an S Note widget to your home screen.

Handwriting Recognition Mode

Instead of using an on-screen keyboard to input text, you can use your S Pen in handwriting recognition mode. This option is available anywhere keyboard input is possible. To enable it, tap and hold 🎤 and then tap T/ on the Samsung keyboard. The keyboard will be replaced by this panel:

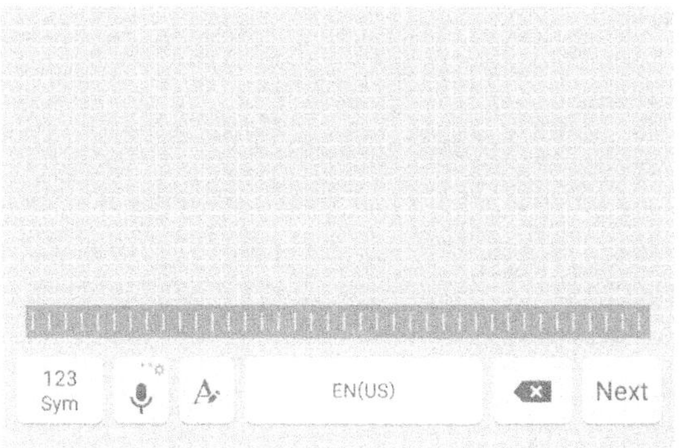

Write along the thin white line inside the gray grid, and your writing will be automatically recognized and entered into the current text field:

To scroll back and correct previously entered text, place your S Pen on the dark gray area with white dashes, and drag left and right. Tap between letters to place the cursor, enabling you to use the space and backspace keys at the bottom of the screen. To correct a single letter in a word, simply write the new letter over the old one, or to delete an entire word, cross it out from left to right. Read about additional S Pen gestures here (p. 212).

In my opinion, Handwriting Recognition Mode isn't the most useful feature of the S Pen. I think you'll find it's faster and easier to use the on-screen keyboard in most cases. The S Pen really shines not for handwriting recognition, but for free-form sketching, jotting, and drawing in S Note (p. 205).

> ***TIP:*** *If you do prefer Handwriting Recognition Mode, however, you'll want to set it up as your default input method so it automatically pops up instead of the Samsung keyboard. To do so, go to system settings → "Language and input" → "Samsung keyboard" → enable "Pen detection."*

Using the S Pen with the Menu and Back Buttons

While we're discussing the S Pen, I want to point out a hidden feature: you can tap the and buttons using the S Pen. This feature is very convenient when using the S Pen as your main mode of navigation around the Note 5. Unfortunately, tapping with the S Pen does nothing (unless you tap it hard enough to physically press the button, which I don't recommend—you can damage the S Pen's tip this way).

Quickly Entering Text with Direct Pen Input

In some apps such as Messages, Contacts, and Calendar, you can use a feature called Direct Pen Input to enter a short amount of text. Honestly, Direct Pen Input doesn't do anything that Handwriting Recognition Mode (p. 209) doesn't already do, but sometimes it's a little faster. Either way, you should know about it so you know what it is if you see it.

You can use Direct Pen Input any time you see this "T" icon when hovering your S Pen over a text field:

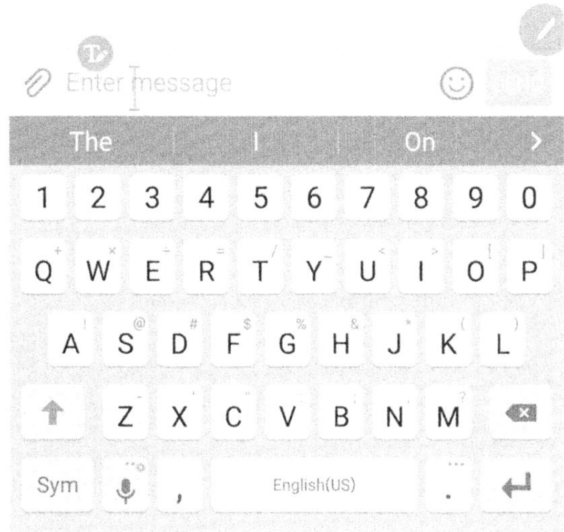

Tap the "T" with your S Pen to open the Direct Pen Input panel:

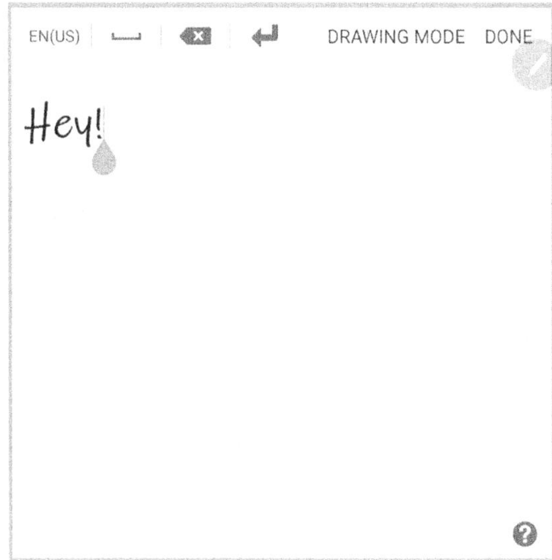

Write in the panel with your S Pen to have your handwriting automatically recognized and translated to text. You can use the S Pen gestures described below to make corrections to your input.

S Pen Gesture Guide

If you plan to use the S Pen for handwriting recognition, you should know the correction gestures:

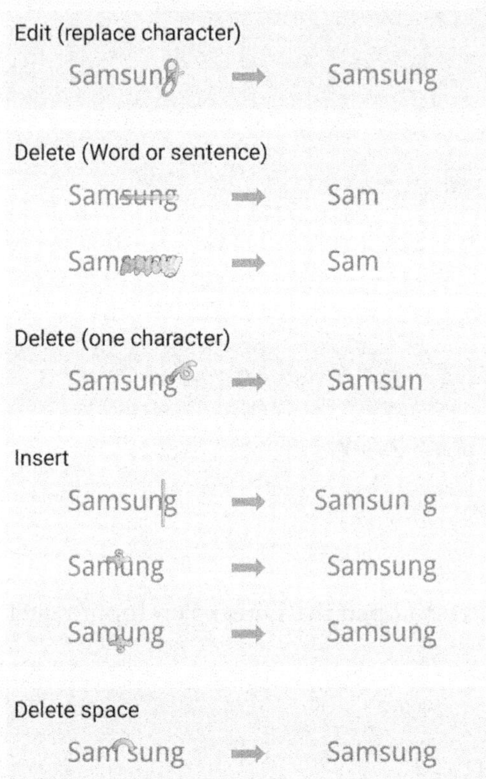

Enabling S Pen Alerts to Avoid Losing Your S Pen

Want your Note 5 to sound an alert if you try to walk away with your S Pen detached? Go to system settings → "S Pen" and enable "S Pen alerts."

Chapter 7: The Edge Screen (S6 Edge+)

The S6 Edge+ lacks the S Pen features found on the Note 5, but adds a unique feature of its own: a sleeker, more modern design with a screen that curves on the left and right edges.

The S6 Edge+ is about two things: design and functionality. Aesthetically, it's new and exciting—it looks different than all the other phones on the market. Functionally, it adds several features related to its curved screen. In this chapter, I discuss these Edge-specific features.

Edge Lighting

With Edge Lighting enabled, the curved edges of the S6 Edge+'s display light up to get your attention when you receive a call or notification. It's primarily meant to be used with the device face down on a table—thanks to the screen's curves, you can see the light peeking out from the edge of the device. In this way, Edge Lighting is a discrete way to monitor your phone while it's sitting on the table at dinner, at meetings, etc. Edge Lighting even works when the S6 Edge+ is completely muted, so it'll illuminate without intrusively beeping or vibrating.

To enable Edge Lighting, go to system settings → "Edge screen" → "Edge lighting" and turn the slider on. You can also enable "Quick reply" here, which lets you reject incoming calls and send a predefined text message to the caller by tapping and holding the heart rate sensor for two seconds while the device is face-down.

To choose the types of notifications for which Edge Lighting will activate, tap ⮌ to return to the "Edge screen" settings page and then go to "Select notifications." You can choose to receive Edge Lighting notifications for missed calls, text messages, and emails.

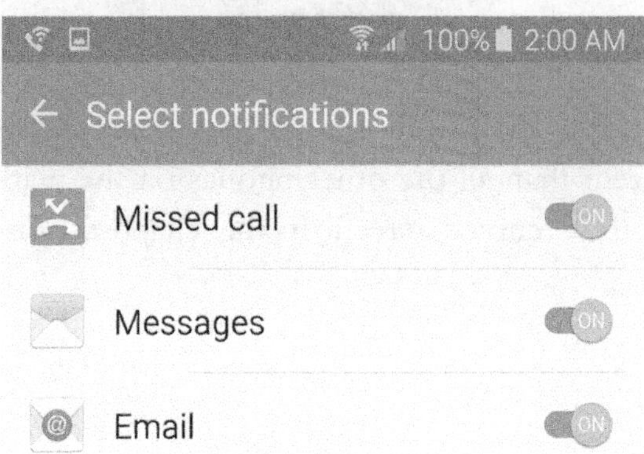

If you've set up People Edge (see below), the color of Edge Lighting will match the contact's designated color.

People Edge

People Edge lets you specify up to 5 of your most important contacts and associate them with custom colors. These colors are used when you receive Edge Lighting notifications and People Edge tab notifications (more on these soon).

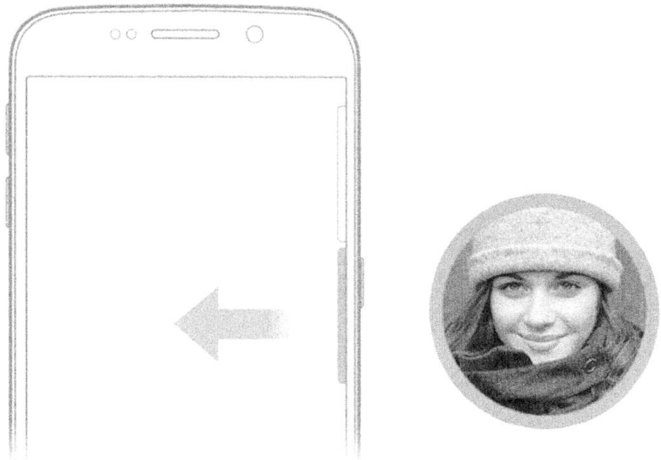

To enable People Edge, go to system settings → "Edge screen" → "People edge" and turn the slider on. Now, you'll have a thin, translucent tab on the edge of your screen, as pictured below. This is called a People Edge Tab.

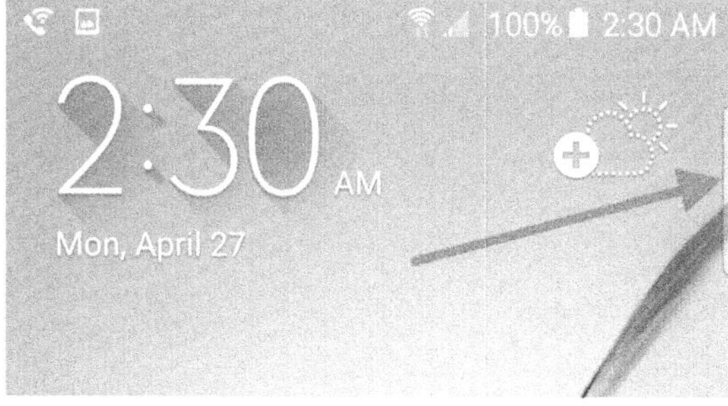

Swipe it toward the center of the screen to view your People Edge contacts:

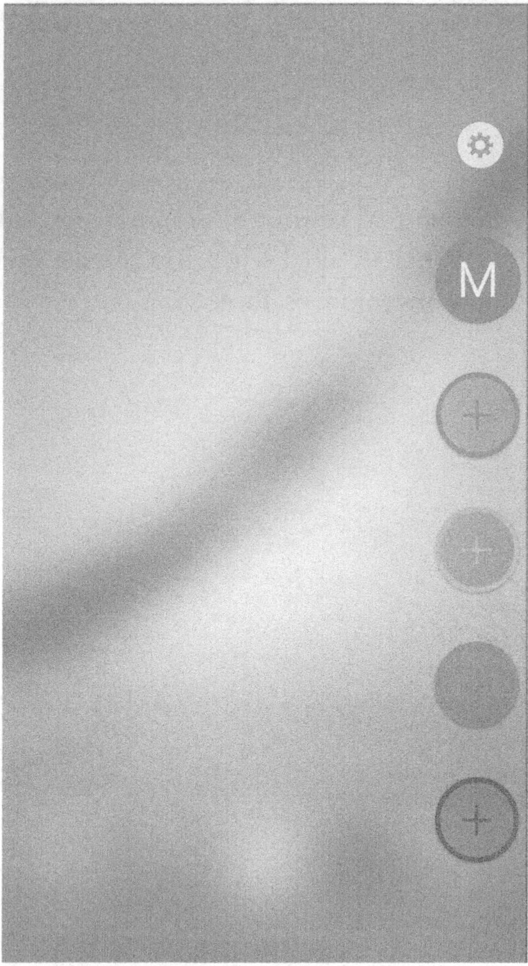

- Tap a "+" to add a contact to People Edge if you haven't already added 5 contacts.
- Tap ⚙ to access People Edge settings.
- Tap a contact to call or text message him or her:

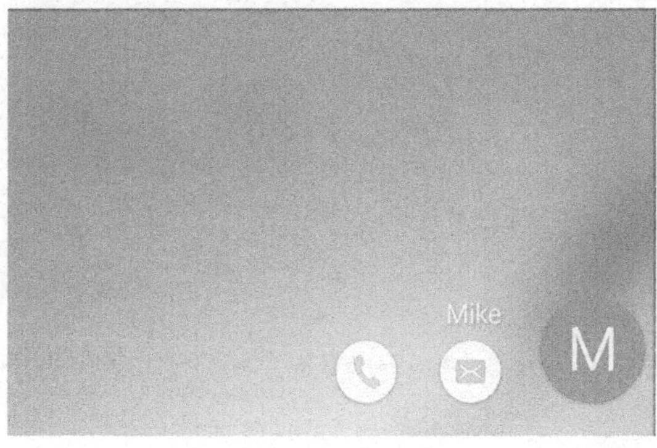

Tab Notifications

When you've a missed call or text message from a People Edge contact, you'll see an additional colored tab along the right-hand edge of the screen (the People Edge color you assigned to that contact):

Swipe it left to view the notification and call or text message the contact.

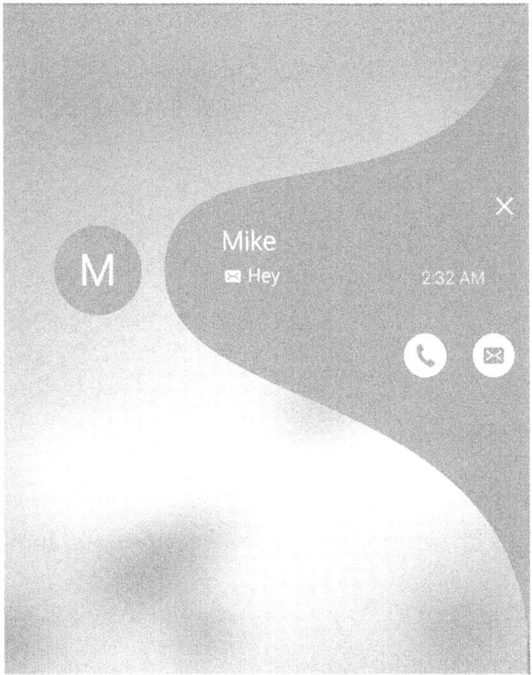

Apps Edge

After you've swiped the People Edge Tab to reveal your People Edge Contacts, swipe left or right on those contacts to switch to Apps Edge:

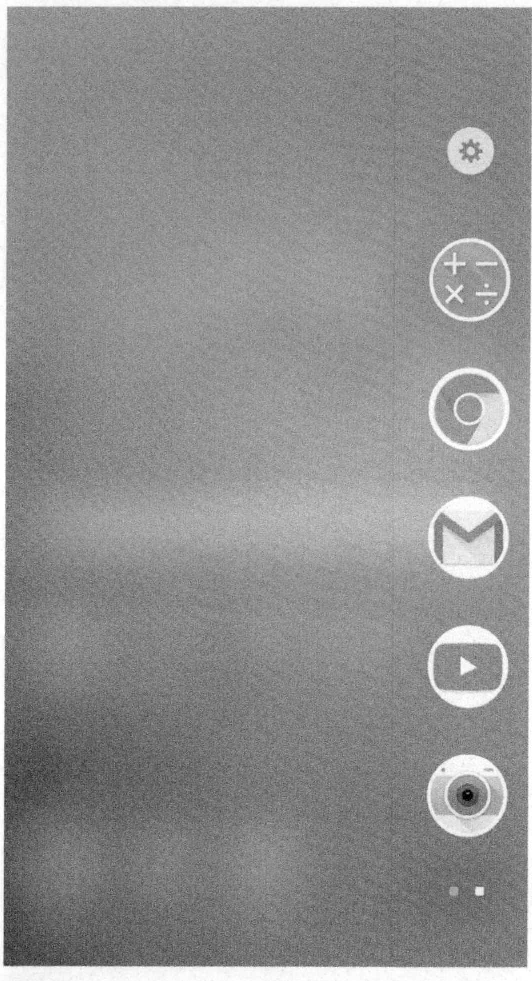

Just like People Edge is a way to quickly call or text your five most important contacts, Apps Edge is a way to quickly open your five most important apps.

- Tap a "+" to add an app to Apps Edge if you haven't already added 5 apps.
- Tap to access Apps Edge settings.
- Tap an app to open it.

Information Stream

Information Stream lets you view high-priority information on the edge of your screen while the S6 Edge+ is asleep. To activate Information Stream while the screen is off, quickly swipe your finger **left-right-left** or **right-left-right** parallel along the edge (i.e., swipe one direction and then quickly back the other way). Then, swipe **up and down** perpendicular to the edge to switch between the different streams.

To enable Information Stream, go to system settings → "Edge screen" → "Information stream" and turn the slider on. Tap "Manage feeds" to enable or disable the available streams. Tap and to enable or disable streams, or to customize a stream. You can also swipe to the right and tap "Download feeds" to get additional streams from the Samsung app store.

Night Clock

Night Clock lets the S6 Edge+ display the time and date along the edge screen while the device is asleep. Caveat: the maximum duration for Night Clock is 12 hours, so unfortunately you cannot use it to have an always-on clock.

To enable Night Clock, go to system settings → "Edge screen" → "Night clock" and turn the slider on. Set the start and end times.

Changing the Edge Screen Position

To change the side of the screen used for Edge features, as well as to adjust the vertical position of the Edge Screen tab, go to system settings → "Edge screen" → "Edge screen position."

Chapter 8: Intermediate Tips & Tricks

Congratulations! By now, you should be getting very comfortable with your Galaxy. You've learned how to perform all its basic functions, and now it's time to discuss some intermediate-level tips and tricks.

Multitasking with Multi Window

Multi Window lets you open two apps at the same time. It's not compatible with all apps, but is compatible with most of the apps preloaded on the Note 5 / S6 Edge+.

Split Screen View

To launch Split Screen View, tap and hold ⧉ Below, I've launched Split Screen View while in the Gmail app. As you can see, the bottom half of the screen is prompting me to open a second app.

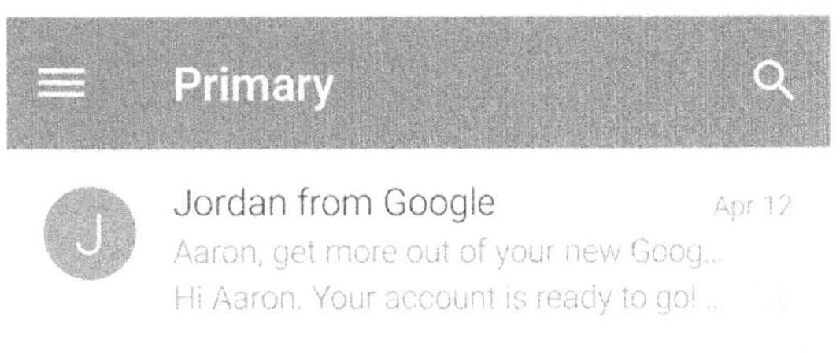

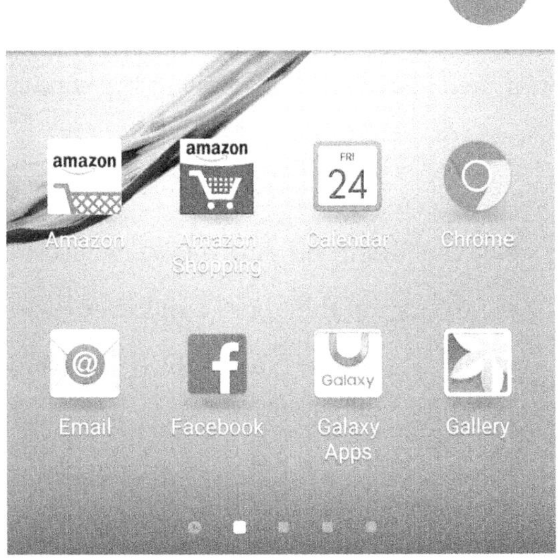

Here, I've chosen Amazon as the second app.

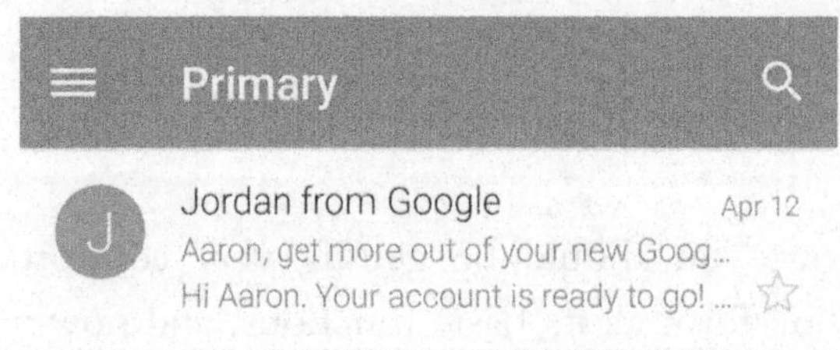

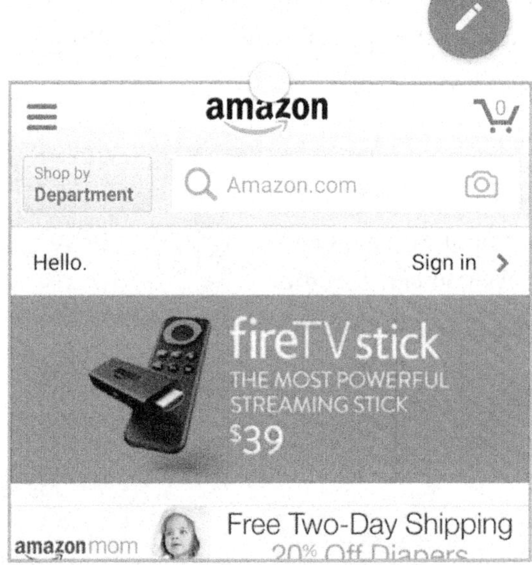

From here, tap the white circle in the center of the screen to access more options:

- Tap the upper or lower app to select it. A blue border indicates which app is selected.
- Tap, hold, and drag the white circle to resize the upper and lower apps.
- : Swap the upper and lower apps.
- : Activate Drag & Drop mode, which lets you drag text or an image from one app to the other.
- : Minimize the selected app into a button.
- : Make the selected app full screen and close the non-selected app.
- X: Close the selected app and make the non-selected app full screen.

Buttons and Pop-Up View

Tapping [icon] turns the selected app into a button. Here, I've turned the Gmail app into a button:

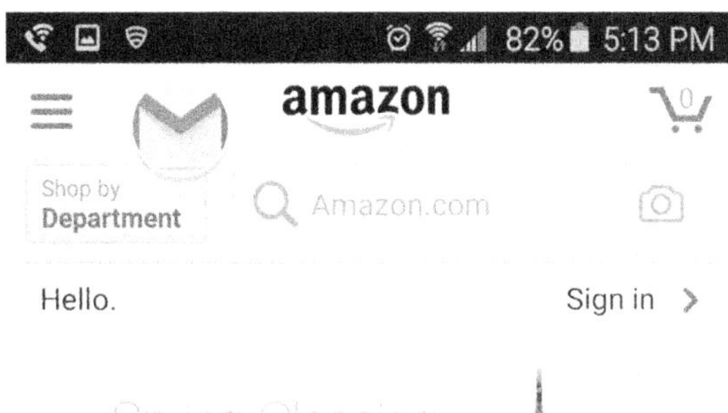

Buttons persist on all screens, including the home screen:

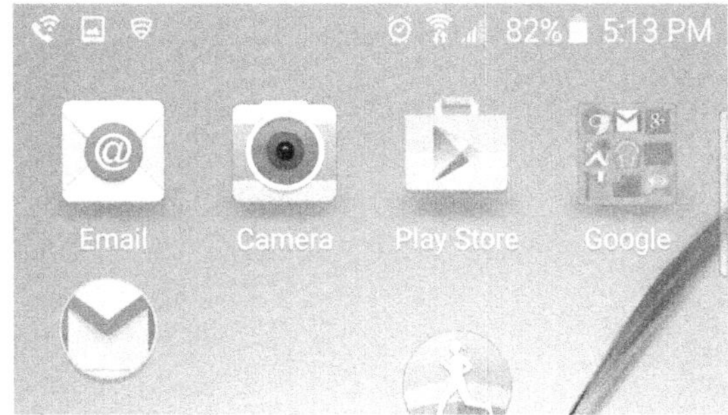

Tap, hold, and drag buttons to relocate them. Single-tap a button to open it in Pop-Up View:

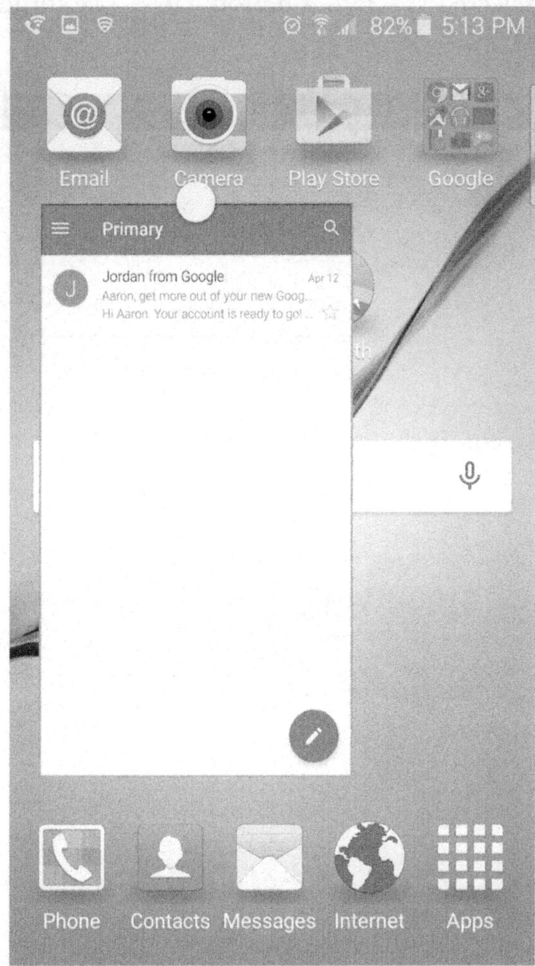

From here, tap the white circle at the top of the pop-up to access more options:

- Tap, hold, and drag the white circle to move the pop-up.
- : Activate Drag & Drop mode, which lets you drag text or an image from one app to another.
- : Minimize the pop-up into a button again.
- : Make the pop-up full screen.
- X or : Close the pop-up.
- : Return to the home screen and minimize all pop-ups into buttons.

You can have multiple buttons and/or pop-ups active at once:

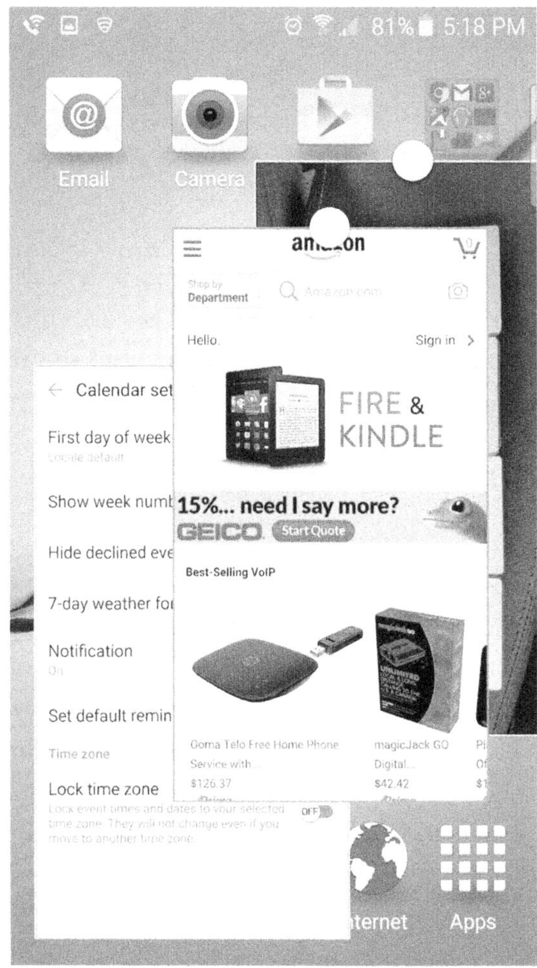

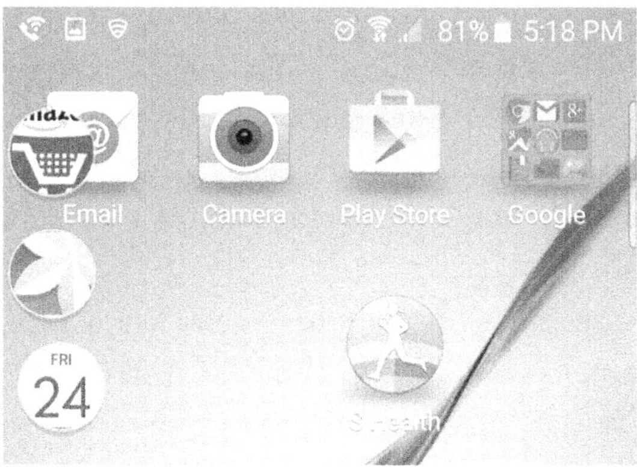

TIP: There are a few other useful Multi Window tricks to know. First, you can also open apps in Split Screen View by tapping → . Second, you can swipe from the very top right or top left corner

of the screen down to the center of the screen to convert an open app into a pop-up. Third, you can quickly open a recent app in Pop-Up View by tapping ▭ and then tapping and holding a recent app.

Securing Your Data

Enabling a Lock Screen

A lock screen keeps your Galaxy safe from unauthorized access. When enabled, your Galaxy will lock itself after a specified duration when it's asleep. Next time it's woken, it'll require authentication before the lock screen can be cleared and the device can be used. A lock screen prevents anyone from accessing your data if you lose your device.

To set up a lock screen, go to system settings → "Lock screen and security." Available locking methods include:

- **Swipe:** This is a zero-security option that only prevents accidental operation in your pocket. On some older Samsung Galaxy phones, you could add widgets to the swipe lock screen, but this feature is absent on the Note 5 / S6 Edge+. In general I suggest you avoid the swipe setting. You probably have a great deal of sensitive information on your device, and if you don't have security measures in place, you will open yourself up to identity theft and other crimes should you lose it. Using a lock screen with a fingerprint, PIN, password, or other feature is worth the minor inconvenience of having to enter it when you power on your Galaxy.
- **Pattern:** This option lets you unlock your Galaxy by drawing a pattern on a 3x3 grid (with a PIN backup). I suggest a PIN or password instead. It's fairly easy to defeat pattern security by tracing smudges on the screen.
- **PIN:** This unlock option secures your lock screen with a minimum 4-digit numerical PIN code. There is no maximum PIN length. A PIN is much faster and easier to type than a password on a keyboard, especially when using one hand. Before I started using fingerprint recognition, I used a six-digit PIN code on my Android devices.
- **Password:** A password works almost exactly like a PIN, but can include letters and special characters in addition to numbers. A password can be more secure than a PIN code but slower and more difficult to type each time you wake your Galaxy.
- **Fingerprint:** Your Galaxy's home button doubles as a fingerprint reader, and this option allows you to unlock your device by tapping and holding your finger on it. Personally, this is the option I use. I formerly preferred PIN security but fingerprint recognition is faster, accurate, and very secure.

- **None:** The final option in this menu is to use no lock screen whatsoever. Although this setting is convenient, I suggest carefully thinking through the consequences of losing your phone before using it.

In addition to choosing a locking method, I suggest putting a "Reward If Found" message in the "Owner Information" field (available in system settings → "Lock screen and security" → "Show information"), with a phone number to call. This information will be prominently displayed on your lock screen. Also, make sure to set the locking delay and choose whether to lock instantly with the power key in system settings → "Lock screen and security" → "Secure lock settings" (only visible if you've set a locking method). Personally, I set a 5 second delay with power key locking disabled. That way, if I accidentally hit the power button, I can turn my Galaxy on again without having to re-authenticate myself.

Making Unlocking Easy with Smart Lock

Android 5.0 Lollipop has a new feature called Smart Lock that can automatically unlock your Galaxy under approved conditions. For example, you can set your device to stay unlocked while you're at a certain address or connected to a certain Wi-Fi network or Bluetooth device. I have my Galaxy set to stay unlocked as long as it's at my house, connected to my car's Bluetooth stereo, or connected to my Pebble watch.

To set up Smart Lock, go to system settings → "Lock screen and security" → "Secure lock settings" → "Smart Lock." Add trusted devices or trusted places and save your settings. You can also set up trusted voices or on-body detection, but in my opinion these features are much more gimmicky than trusted devices and trusted places.

> *TIP: At the time of writing, some users were reporting problems using trusted places. If you find that your Galaxy is not staying unlocked while in your trusted places, try using trusted devices instead.*

Encrypting Your Data

If you have very sensitive data on your Galaxy, consider encrypting it. To do so, go to system settings → "Lock screen and security" → "Other security settings" → "Encrypt device." This process may take 1-2 hours, so make sure to plug in your phone first. With your information encrypted, even a computer forensics laboratory will be unable to read information on your Galaxy without your authorization. Contrary to popular belief, encrypting your data will *not* significantly slow it down or increase drain on battery life.

Locating, Locking, and Remotely Wiping Your Galaxy

Google offers a convenient and free remote locate/wipe service called "Android Device Manager." To use it effectively, you'll need to ensure your locating method is set to "GPS, Wi-Fi, and mobile networks" in system settings → "Privacy and safety" → "Location."

> ***TIP:*** *This feature works well and is totally free. However, I personally use a third-party security app called Cerberus* ***(p. 308)*** *that has even more options. Cerberus requires a one-time fee of a few dollars, but in my opinion it is well worth it.*

To locate your Galaxy, login to your Gmail account on your desktop computer and go to the link below. Click the gear icon in the upper-right-hand corner of the screen, and click "Android Device Manager."

https://play.google.com/store

My orders
Settings
Android Device Manager

Google will automatically locate your Galaxy and report its location on a map within a few seconds.

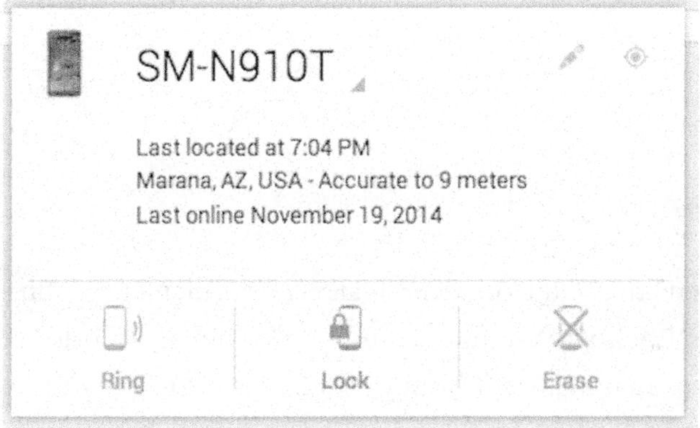

Google can locate your phone very precisely using a combination of GPS, cellular, and Wi-Fi signals (within 9 meters in the above case). Tap "Ring" to have your Galaxy ring at full volume for 5 minutes to help you find it, "Lock" to enable the lock screen with a new password, and "Erase" to wipe all data.

> *TIP: If you see "Setup Lock & Erase" instead of "Lock" and "Erase," click it and follow the instructions to enable Android Device Manager for your Galaxy. It is VERY important to make sure this feature is set up ahead of time, because there's no way to enable it after your device is lost or stolen. If you lose your phone and you haven't set up this feature ahead of time, you're out of luck.*

Hiding and Securing Files with Private Mode

Private Mode lets you encrypt and hide files that you don't want anyone to accidentally see. It works in only a few select apps: Gallery, Video, Music, Voice Recorder, My Files, Internet, and S Note.

To use it, swipe down the notification panel and enable "Private mode." If you don't see it, tap EDIT to add it to your toggles.

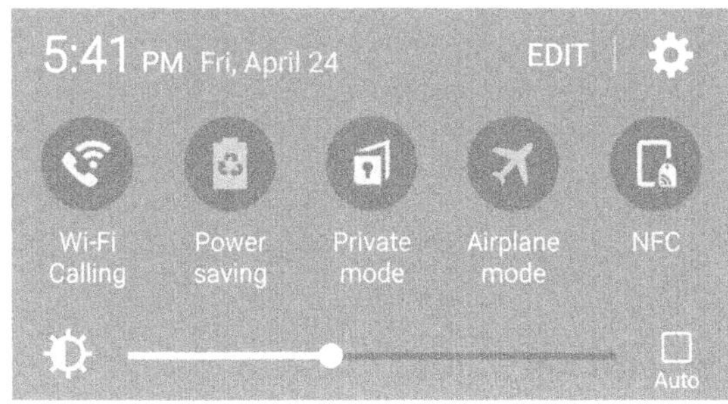

The first time you enable Private Mode, you'll have to tap through the tutorial screens and configure an unlock method (it can be different than the method you use to unlock your Galaxy). I suggest fingerprint mode or a PIN for a good balance of convenience and security.

Now, in the apps mentioned above, any time you're viewing media and you tap a "More" menu, you will see the option "Move to Private." When you move a file to private storage, it will be shown as long as Private Mode is enabled, but will completely disappear when Private Mode is disabled, like it never existed.

To view all the files in Private storage, open the app "My Files," swipe down, and tap "Private."

My Files SEARCH MORE

Images 555MB

Videos 38.28MB

Audio 28.74MB

Documents 0.00B

Download history 30.26MB

Local storage

Device storage

Private

Cloud storage

Google Drive
Not signed in.

STORAGE USAGE

Remember—you have to turn off the Private Mode toggle button when you're done viewing your private content. If you forget to turn it off, your private files will be displayed along with all the others.

TIP: *Enable "Auto off" in Private Mode settings to disable Private Mode any time the screen turns off. That way, if you forget to disable Private Mode, your Galaxy will take care of it for you.*

Pinning Screens to Protect Your Privacy

Android 5.0 Lollipop has a new feature that lets you lock ("pin") an app to the screen, so that nothing outside of that app can be accessed. Use this feature if you need to hand off your phone to someone who you don't want snooping around your personal information.

To pin a screen, first make sure Pinning is enabled in system settings → "Lock screen and security" → "Other security settings" → "Pin windows." Then, to pin an app, open it, tap → .

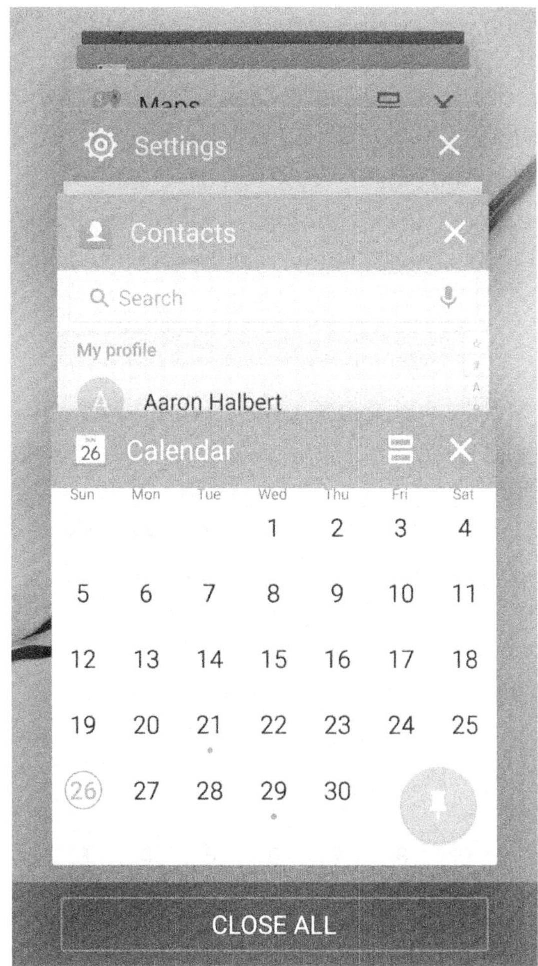

To unpin a screen, tap and hold and at the same time.

Android Beam, Wi-Fi Direct, NFC, WTF?!?

The Note 5 / S6 Edge+ include several wireless features, and it can be very hard to disentangle them. Each of these features is slightly different, so what exactly does each one do?

Let's start with NFC. NFC stands for "Near-Field Communications" and is a fairly new feature in Android smartphones. NFC is basically synonymous with RFID, which you've probably heard of before. RFID tags are tiny chips that can store data but do not require batteries. They're frequently used for passports, inventory tracking in stores, subway passes, and tap-to-pay debit and credit cards. So how does your Galaxy use its NFC chip?

The first way is through the protocol called "Android Beam," found under the "NFC and payment" menu in system settings. It's used for sending links, images, contacts, and other content to and from other Android devices that have Android Beam. Data transfer is not actually accomplished through NFC, though—rather, the NFC chips 'handshake' with each other, establishing a Bluetooth connection between the two Android Beam-enabled devices.

In general, you can expect Android Beam to work with stock apps such as the Gallery, Internet, Contacts, and Music. To use it, enable Android Beam in system settings → "NFC and payment" → "Android Beam." Ensure it's also enabled on the receiving device. Then, open the song/contact/photo/etc. you wish to share in its respective app, and place your Galaxy back-to-back with the receiving device. When prompted, tap the content you wish to share and then pull the devices apart to initiate data transfer.

The Note 5 / S6 Edge+ also use NFC technology to read and write NFC tags, which automate software actions in conjunction with the Samsung TecTiles app (p. 291). Additionally, with Google Wallet (p. 247) or Samsung Pay (p. 248), you can use your Galaxy's NFC chip at tap-to-pay terminals just like a tap-to-pay credit card, starting in September 2015.

Wi-Fi Direct, another wireless protocol you may see in your Galaxy's menus, establishes a direct device-to-device Wi-Fi connection between two Android devices to transfer large files quickly. It uses Wi-Fi instead of Bluetooth for *much* higher data transfer speeds than Android Beam, but has a slightly more complicated setup process.

To use this feature, use any app's Share Via (p. 91) tool to share a file via Wi-Fi Direct.

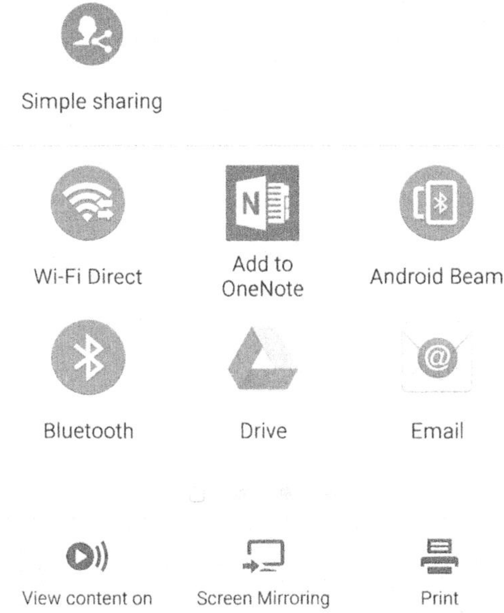

After tapping Wi-Fi Direct on the Share Via screen, you'll be prompted to connect to the receiving device, and when successful, the file will automatically be transferred. Note that older Android devices may not support Wi-Fi Direct, and even if they do, transfers may not be successful. Wi-Fi Direct is finicky.

If you have trouble with Wi-Fi Direct, I suggest checking out SuperBeam (p. 318) (free on the Google Play Store) as a Wi-Fi Direct alternative. SuperBeam is a third-party Wi-Fi beaming app that can send any file to any other Android device that's running SuperBeam, and it doesn't require the receiving device to have Wi-Fi Direct support. It works very reliably and I highly recommend it if you can't get Wi-Fi Direct to work through the Share Via screen.

Pairing with a Bluetooth Device Such as a Headset or Car Stereo

Whereas Wi-Fi is used to wirelessly connect to the Internet, Bluetooth is used for connecting to accessories such as car stereos, headsets, keyboards & mice, and other mobile devices. Connecting to a Bluetooth device is called "pairing." To pair a device with your Galaxy, make sure Bluetooth is turned on in the notification panel, and then go to system settings → "Bluetooth."

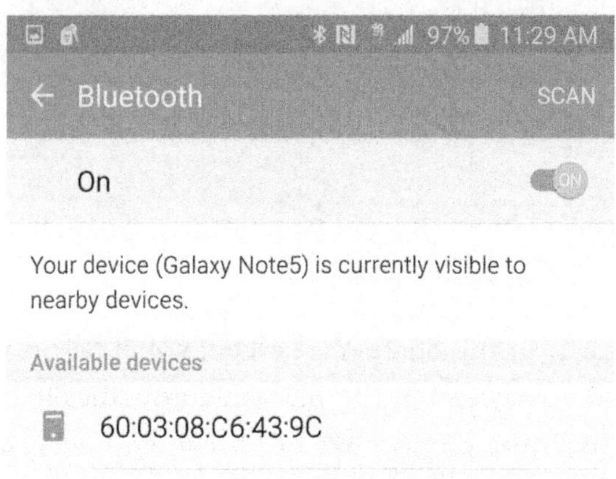

You'll see devices available for pairing under "Available devices." If you don't see the device you want to connect to, it's most likely because the other device has not been made discoverable. Consult the device's instruction manual for instructions on doing so (may be called "pairing mode" or something similar).

Tap SCAN if necessary to re-scan for devices. Once you see the device you want to connect to, tap it and follow the prompts to pair the devices. You will have to confirm a PIN code on both devices to establish a connection.

Once paired with Bluetooth speakers, your Galaxy will automatically play through them when you're in range and Bluetooth is on. To switch back to the internal speakers, swipe down the notification panel and turn Bluetooth off. For headsets, switch to them while in-call by tapping the "Bluetooth" button, or by using controls on the headset itself.

Setting Up a Wi-Fi Hotspot and Tethering Your Computer

Your Galaxy's tethering/hotspot feature allows you to share your cellular Internet connection with another device such as a laptop, a desktop, or even another Android device. It makes your Galaxy act as a Wi-Fi router.

Note that your hotspot feature may not work if it's not included in your service plan. All major U.S. carriers bill wireless hotspots as an add-on that generally runs between $20-30 per month.

To turn on the hotspot, go to system settings → "Mobile HotSpot and Tethering." Depending on your carrier, this option may have a slightly different name but will still be found in system settings.

After enabling the mobile hotspot, you will be prompted to enter a name (SSID) for your network, select a security protocol (choose WPA2 PSK), and specify a password. You may also see settings that let you hide the SSID, adjust the transmit power, and so on. Do not change these from their defaults unless you have a specific reason to do so.

After you have created a Wi-Fi network using your wireless hotspot feature, connect to it from your laptop or other device just as you would connect to your home network. If you have trouble connecting, reset your Galaxy by holding the power button and tapping "Restart," and restart the other device as well before trying again.

TIP: By rooting *(p. 281)* *your Galaxy, you can enable Wi-Fi tethering without paying extra fees.*

USB Tethering

It's also possible to tether your Galaxy's connection via USB instead of Wi-Fi, if you wish. In general, this is less convenient than using Wi-Fi tethering and is only advantageous in very select cases. Nevertheless, you have the option. To tether via USB, connect your Galaxy to your computer using the included USB cable. Go to system settings → "Mobile HotSpot and Tethering" (or similar—exact name may depend on carrier) and enable "USB tethering." On Windows 7, Windows 8, and Linux, your computer will automatically connect to the Internet when you plug in your Galaxy via USB. If you have Windows XP or another OS, you may need to take extra steps to get USB tethering working. USB tethering does not work at all on Mac OSX, although there is a third-party driver called HoRNDIS to work around this limitation. http://joshuawise.com/horndis

Get further information about USB tethering here:

http://android.com/tether

Preventing Extra Charges by Capping Your Data Usage

If you have a limited amount of data on your cell plan, you can set a hard limit to ensure your Galaxy doesn't rack up overage charges. To set it, go to system settings → "Data usage" and turn on "Set mobile data limit."

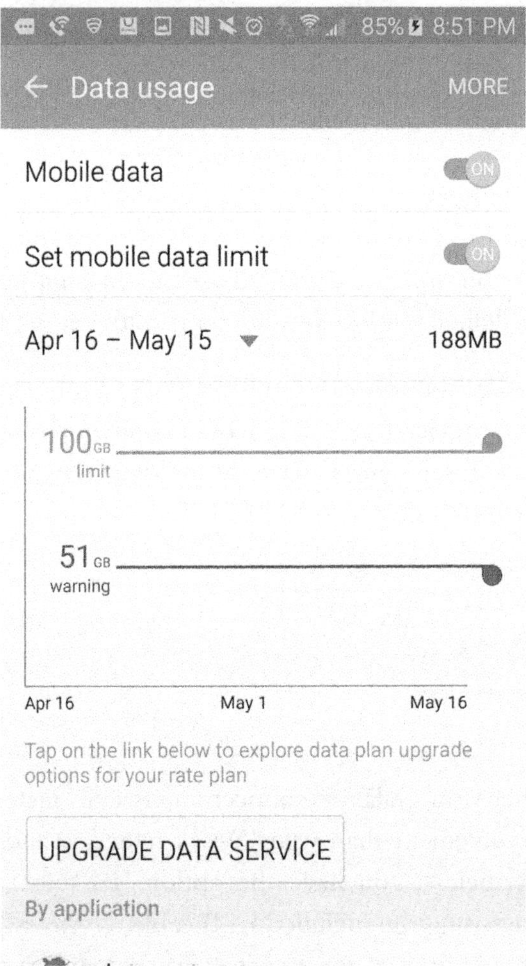

Set the data usage cycle to match your billing cycle, and then adjust the red slider up and down to specify the maximum amount of cellular data your Galaxy is allowed to use during that period. Adjust the black slider to set a warning level. Upon reaching the warning level, you will get a notification in the notification panel, and upon reaching the hard limit, your Galaxy will shut off cellular data completely. Of course, you can always return to this screen and uncheck "Set mobile data limit" if you need to.

TIP: If the sliders appear to be stuck, it's likely because you need to decrease the "warning" level below 100 GB before enabling "Set mobile data limit." 100 GB is the maximum value on the chart, and if your warning level is set to 100 GB, you won't be able to adjust the mobile data limit below (or above) that level.

Mirroring Your Galaxy's Screen on Another Display with SideSync

Samsung has created a new, free software tool for the Note 5 and S6 Edge+ called SideSync, which lets you mirror your Galaxy's display on a computer screen or an Android tablet's screen.

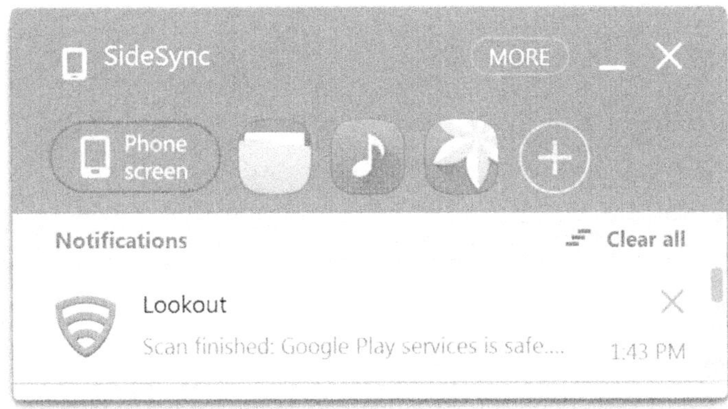

Your Galaxy has the SideSync app preinstalled, but you will need to install SideSync on the partner device. If the partner device is an Android tablet, download SideSync from the Google Play Store. If the partner device is a computer, download SideSync from the following URL. At the time of writing, SideSync was available for Windows only.

http://www.samsung.com/us/sidesync/

Once SideSync is installed on the partner device, start SideSync on both sides and follow the instructions provided. Note that while SideSync claims to be able to connect to your computer via Wi-Fi, I found wireless connectivity to be flaky, whereas USB was very reliable. I recommend using USB if mirroring your display on your Windows PC.

Disabling Annoying Sounds and Vibrations

By default, TouchWiz makes a lot of blips and bloops. For those of us who relish peace and quiet, it's easy to disable them. Go to system settings → "Sounds and notifications" → "Ringtones and sounds." Disable some or all of the following:

- Touch sounds
- Dialing keypad tone
- Screen lock sounds
- Keyboard sound

Personally, I also change my default notification sound from "Whisper" to "Beep Once" (Tap "Default notification sound" → "Media Storage" → "OK" → "Beep Once" →). I find "Beep Once" more professional and less intrusive than the default notification sound.

Customizing the Notification Panel Toggle Buttons

Customize the toggle buttons displayed in the notification panel by swiping down the notification panel and tapping EDIT Tap, hold, and drag the toggle buttons to rearrange them. Releasing a toggle button over another toggle button on this screen will cause the two toggle buttons to swap places. Note that only the first 10 toggle buttons, highlighted in light blue, will be available in the notification panel. (Swipe the toggle buttons in the notification panel right to see toggles 6-10).

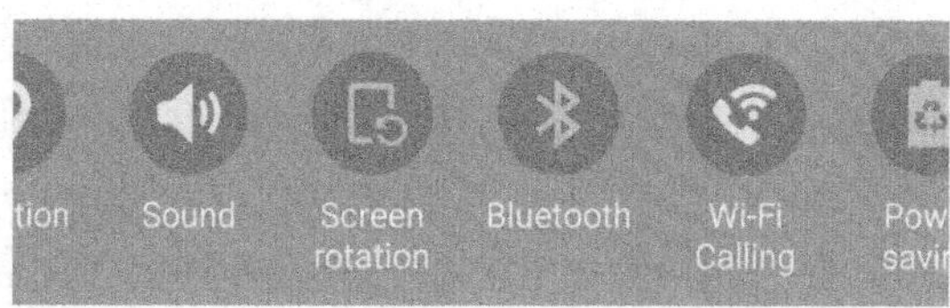

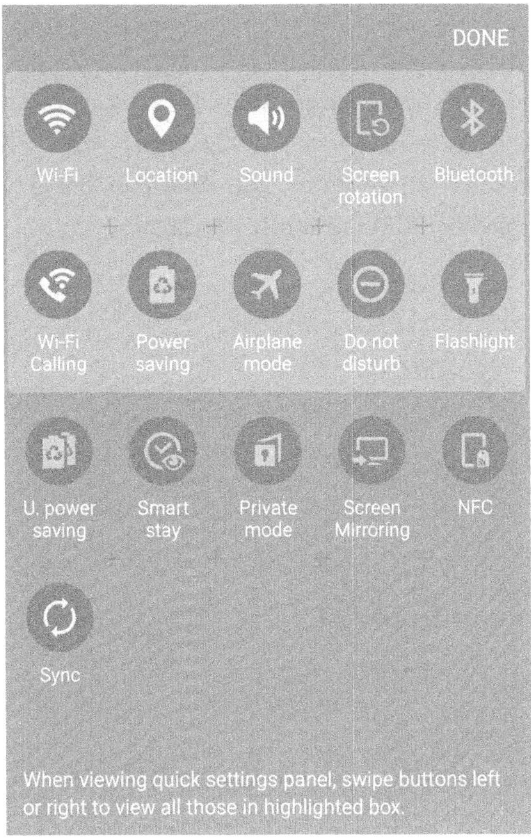

Be sure to tap DONE when finished, or your changes will not be saved.

Vision Accessibility Settings for Users Hard of Seeing

Voice Assistant is the main feature of the Note 5 / S6 Edge+ for users who are hard of seeing. Enable it in system settings → "Accessibility" → "Vision" → "Voice Assistant."

When it is enabled, the entire TouchWiz experience changes. To use the device with Voice Assistant enabled, drag your finger around the display to make the device select different elements and speak a description of them to you. For example, it will highlight buttons, menu items, and so on. Once you have successfully selected a screen element, double-tap anywhere on the screen to activate it (equivalent to a single tap under normal circumstances). Scrolling is accomplished by swiping with two fingers at once. Similarly, pull down the notification panel by using two fingers.

The Note 5 / S6 Edge+ have several other vision accessibility settings. From system settings → "Accessibility" → "Vision," you can also adjust the system font size, magnification gestures (discussed below), colors, and more.

Zooming In on Any Screen

Your Galaxy has a very cool zoom feature that allows you to triple tap on any screen to zoom in. Enable it in system settings → "Accessibility" → "Vision" → "Magnification gestures." Triple-tap anywhere to zoom in, and then pan using two fingers. You can also triple-tap and hold the third tap to temporarily zoom in.

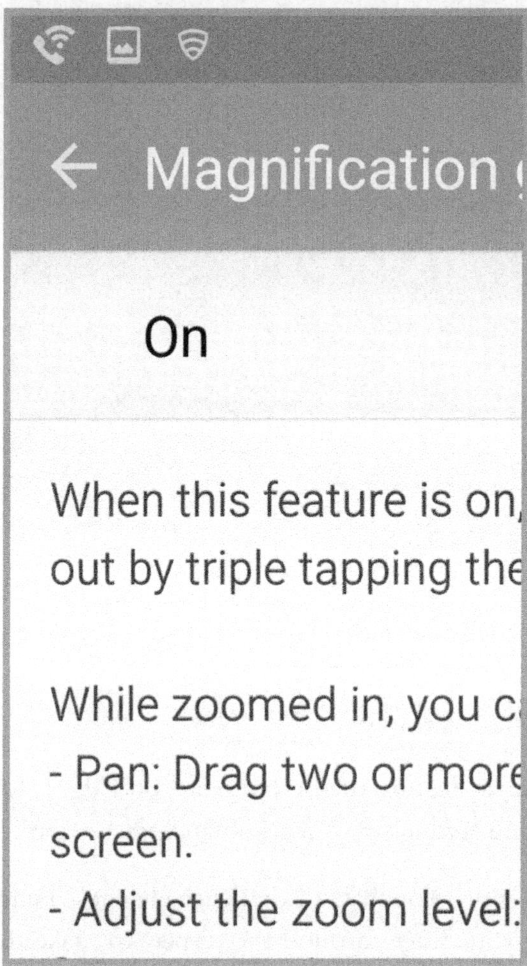

Alternatively, you can enable the Magnifier Window, which provides a loupe-like window you can move around the screen:

Enable the Magnifier Window in system settings → "Accessibility" → "Vision."

Adjusting Colors to Improve Screen Readability and Visibility

Do you find your Galaxy's screen too low-contrast and hard to read? Samsung has a built-in color adjustment feature to calibrate the display for your eyes. To use it, go to system settings → "Accessibility" → "Vision" → "Color adjustment."

Blocking Unwanted Calls

To block a number from calling you, open a call from that number in the "Logs" tab of the Phone app and tap MORE → "Block number." Your device will no longer ring when you receive a call from that number.

To manage your reject list or to block a number you haven't already received a call from, open the Phone app and tap MORE → "Settings" → "Call blocking" → "Block list."

Configuring Hands-Free Options and Voice Commands

The Note 5 / S6 Edge+ have a number of hands-free options that are useful if you drive a lot or otherwise have your hands full.

Answering Calls Easily with the Home Button or Voice Commands

This is a cool feature that makes it easier to answer phone calls that you *do* want. Open the Phone app and go to MORE → "Settings" → Answering and ending calls" and enable "Pressing the Home key" and/or "Using voice commands." With these features enabled, answer calls by pressing or saying "Answer" out loud." To reject a call, say "Reject" out loud.

Going Hands-Free with Car Mode

Car Mode is a special hands-free mode optimized for driving. It gives you a simplified home screen containing only options for placing calls, sending text messages, starting navigation, and playing music. Better yet, you can use all the features of Car Mode with your voice. It looks like this:

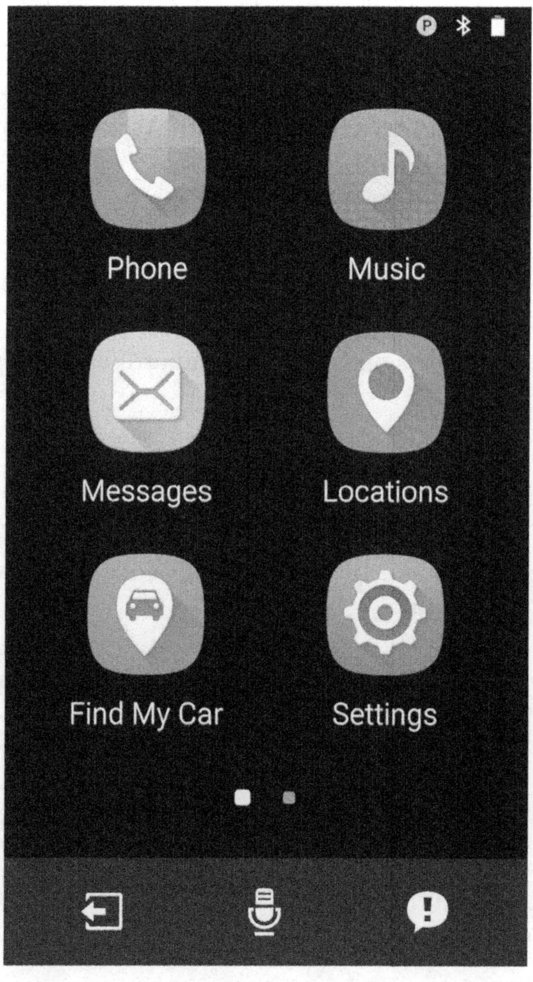

To use Car Mode, download and install Car Mode from the "Galaxy Apps" store in your app drawer. After you've installed Car Mode, you'll see it in your app drawer as well.

The first time you enter Car Mode, you'll have to accept several legal disclaimers and configure a wake-up command if you have not already done so. Just follow the prompts and answer the questions you are asked. If your car stereo supports Bluetooth, follow the instructions to pair your Galaxy with your car.

Once you've configured Car Mode and you see the main screen, just say your wake-up command out loud, wait for the tone, and then speak a command. For example:

- "Call John on mobile."
- "Send a text message to Mike."
- "Play Daft Punk."
- "Navigate to Target."

When you receive an incoming call in Car Mode, say "Accept" or "Reject' out loud to answer or decline the call.

Shrinking the Screen for One-Handed Operation

The Note 5 and S6 Edge+ have a convenient one-handed mode that shrinks down the screen to make it more thumb-friendly:

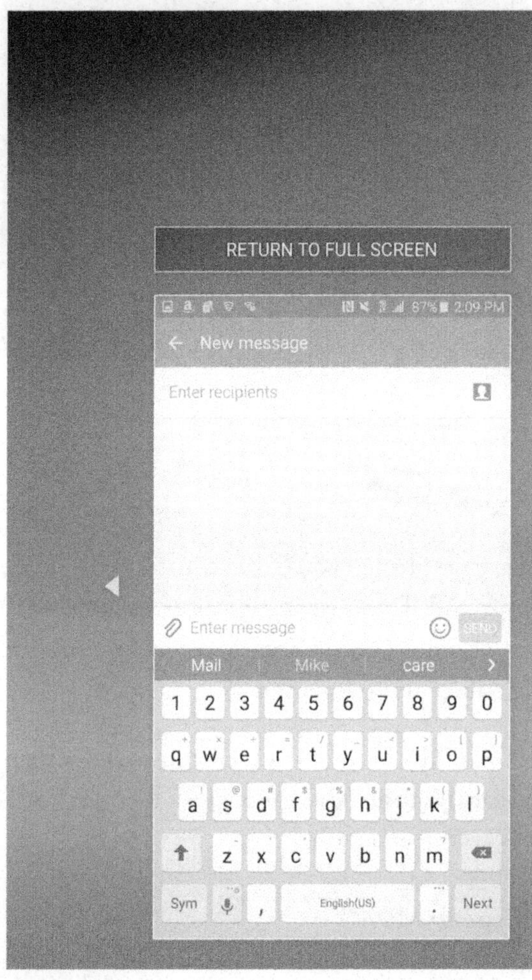

To enable this mode, go to system settings → "Display" → "One-handed operation" and turn on "Reduce screen size." Then, just triple-press to enter or exit one-handed operation at any time.

If you'd like to shrink the Samsung keyboard only, enable "One-handed input" in system settings → "Display" → "One-handed operation." Note that this mode doesn't have a quick-access shortcut like triple tapping . It can only be enabled or disabled from this menu.

87% 2:09 PM
New message
Enter recipients

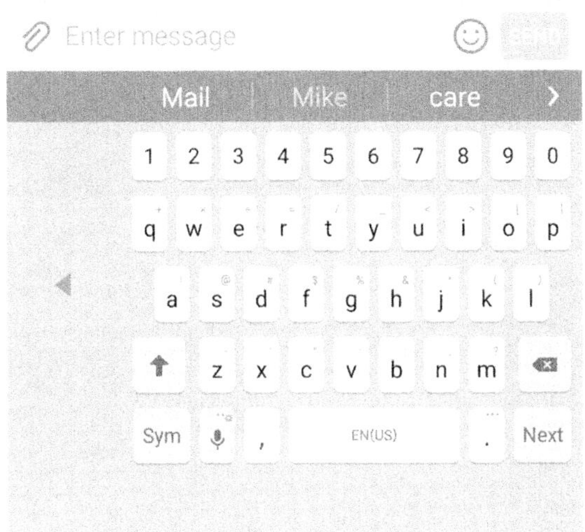
Enter message
Mail
Mike
care
1 2 3 4 5 6 7 8 9 0
q w e r t y u i o p
a s d f g h j k l
z x c v b n m
Sym
EN(US)
Next

Enabling the Assistant Menu for Easier Button Access

The Assistant Menu is a movable button (tap, hold, and drag) that provides easy access to common shortcuts such as home, back, recent apps, volume, lock screen, screen capture, and much more. Enable it in system settings → "Accessibility" → "Dexterity and interaction" → "Assistant menu." Be sure to investigate all the settings available for the Assistant Menu, including Assistant Plus, which adds app-specific shortcuts to the Assistant Menu.

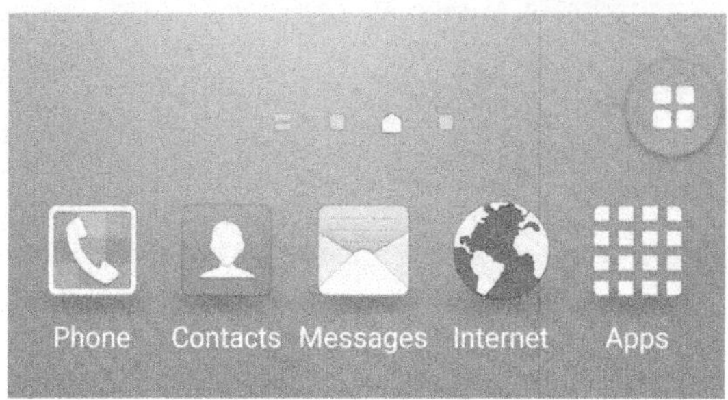

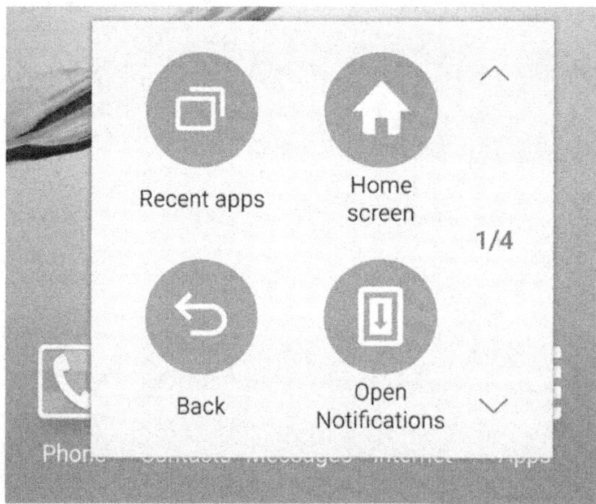

Configuring Motion Shortcuts

The Note 5 / S6 Edge+ support some useful motion controls like automatically calling an on-screen contact by raising the device to your ear (Direct Call), or silencing it by placing it face down on a surface (Mute). To enable these and other motions, go to system settings → "Motions and gestures."

Keeping the Screen On by Monitoring Your Face

The Note 5 / S6 Edge+ have an experimental feature called Smart Stay that uses the front camera to observe your face and keep the screen on as long as you're looking at it. I think this feature is a curiosity more than anything else, but it's still interesting to try out, and may be a sign of things to come in future devices. Turn it on in system settings → "Display" → "Smart stay."

Tapping to Pay with Google Wallet

Your Galaxy contains an NFC (near-field communications) chip that uses RFID technology. This chip is compatible with tap-to-pay terminals found at establishments like 7-11, CVS, Walgreens, McDonalds, Subway, and more. With Google's free Wallet app, you can import your existing credit and debit cards and use your Galaxy to tap and pay with them.

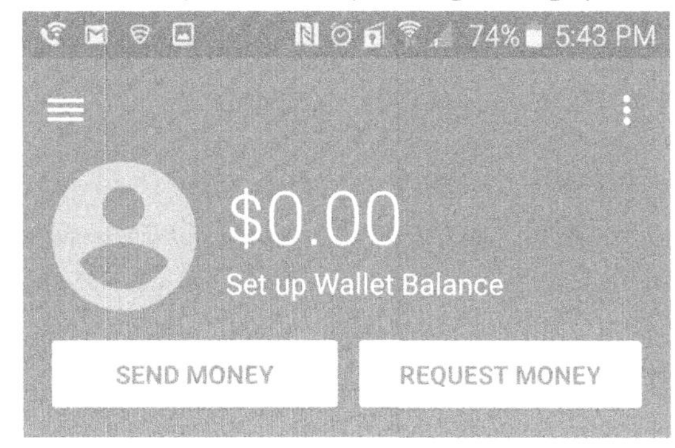

First, enable NFC in system settings → "NFC and payment."

Second, open the Google Play Store, search for "Google Wallet," and install the app. Open it from your app drawer, tap through the introductory screens, and enter the requested information. You will have to create a PIN code for the Wallet app, so pick something you'll be sure to remember. You'll be taken to the main Google Wallet screen.

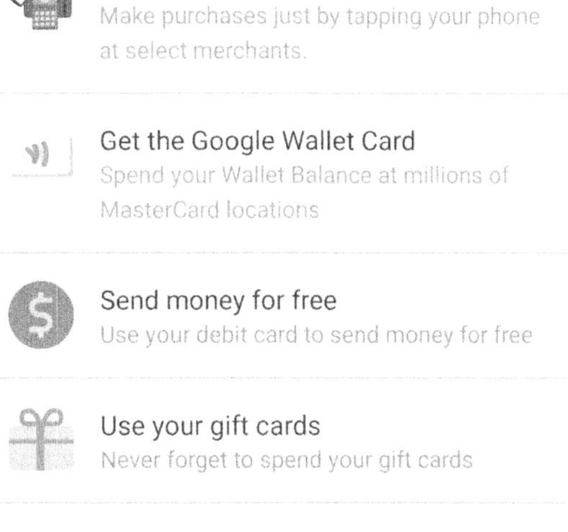

Tap "Set up tap and pay." If you don't see this option, double check that NFC is enabled in the notification panel. Accept the terms of the agreement. You will be asked to input your card details. Do so, or alternatively, tap "Scan your card" to import the details using your Galaxy's camera. (You have to line up the edges of the card exactly with the on-screen outline, or it won't work.)

After you have entered your details, tap "Save" at the bottom of the screen. You can then customize your card's name and appearance in the Google Wallet app.

Done! Now, as long as your NFC toggle is enabled, you can tap to pay at any compatible terminal. You don't need to open the Google Wallet app—just wake the device, touch it to the terminal, and enter your PIN code when prompted. Right now there's a limited selection of retailers that accept tap-to-pay payments, but it's becoming more common all the time. To find retailers near you, visit the following link:

> *http://www.mastercard.us/cardholder-services/paypass-locator.html*
>
> *(Short URL: http://goo.gl/xHYlwi)*

Tapping to Pay with Samsung Pay

Samsung Pay is one of the Note 5 / S6 Edge+'s main selling points, but at the time of writing (August 2015), Samsung Pay is not yet operational. It's expected to come online on September 28, 2015. If you're reading this any time after the 28th—good news! Samsung Pay should already be working.

What is Samsung Pay? It's similar to Google Wallet in that it's a tap-to-pay system that will work at all tap-to-pay terminals like those found at gas stations, McDonalds, etc. However, it adds one key feature that Google Wallet does not support—it'll also work with ANY credit/debit card terminal that takes a card swipe. Samsung Pay taps into the Note 5 / S6 Edge+'s built-in LoopPay technology to let you wirelessly trigger any magnetic card terminal just by holding your device next to it. Pretty sweet!

On September 28, Samsung will push notifications to all compatible Galaxy devices, and the Samsung Pay app in your app drawer will become functional. Check the official Samsung Pay web site for more information and usage instructions:

> *http://www.samsung.com/us/samsung-pay/*

Until Samsung Pay is released, I suggest using Google Wallet (p. 247).

> ***TIP:*** *Both Samsung Pay and Google Wallet are more secure than traditional credit card payments. Both services mask your real credit card number when you make a payment. The merchant never sees or records your credit card number—only a one-time "token" that authorizes the transaction and then becomes useless. This is a really great side benefit of using tap-to-pay payment systems that a lot of people don't realize!*

Downloading Files Super-Fast with Download Booster

Download Booster combines your Wi-Fi and 4G LTE connections to download files larger than 30 MB super-fast. However, in the United States, Sprint and AT&T have blocked this feature. The only major U.S. carriers that have left it intact are T-Mobile and Verizon.

To use Download Booster, go to system settings → "More connection settings" → "Download booster." When you are in range of both Wi-Fi and 4G LTE and you're downloading a file larger than 30 MB, you'll see Download Booster kick in:

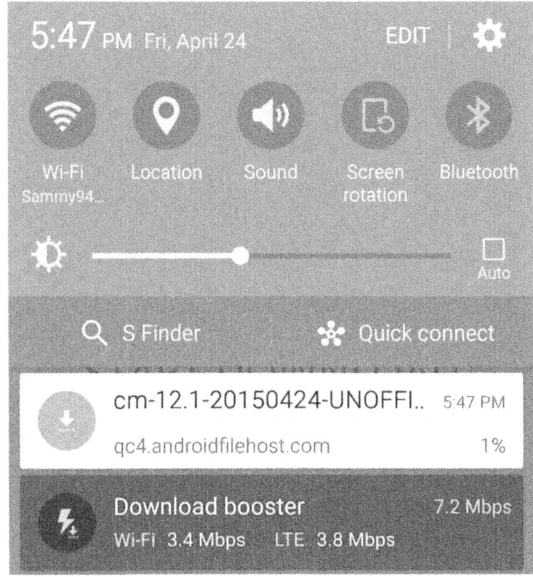

Note that Download Booster only works with file downloads in the Internet browser, Chrome, YouTube, the Play Store, and a select few other apps. If you try to use it with a third-party app, it may not work.

Finally, if you have a limited data plan, keep an eye on your usage or consider setting download limits to avoid expensive overage charges.

Using Quick Connect Mode to Share Media with Nearby Devices

The Galaxy Note and Galaxy S lines have slowly but steadily accumulated a vast selection of media sharing modes. If you've owned a Samsung phone before, you probably remember things like Group Play, AllShare Cast, DLNA, and other vaguely named media sharing tools.

Well, Samsung finally realized that these options had gotten out of control and no one understood what they were for or how to use them. So, they consolidated all of these features into Quick Connect Mode. This mode allows your Galaxy to connect and share media with other nearby Galaxy devices, smart TVs, game consoles, video dongles, Galaxy Gear smart watches, and so on. For compatible media devices, Quick Connect will guide you through the process and make it easy to share your photos, videos, or other files.

Access Quick Connect mode by swiping down the notification panel and tapping "Quick Connect." (Verizon users: find "Quick Connect" in the notification panel's EDIT area.)

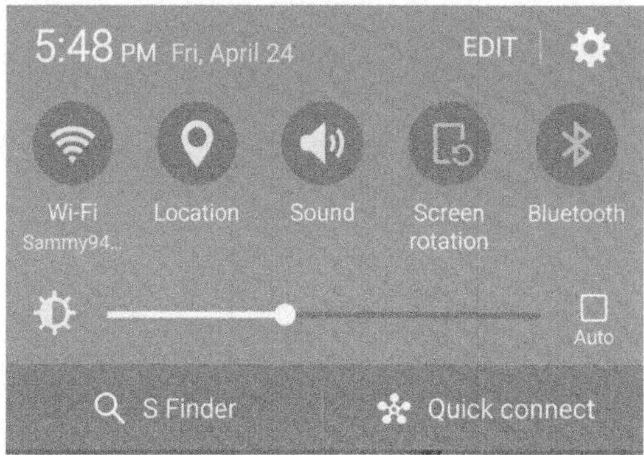

Your Galaxy will automatically detect nearby media devices and tell you what media sharing actions you can take with each device. To get started, just tap a device and follow the prompts. You may need to put other devices in their "sharing" or "discoverable" modes for your Galaxy to detect and connect to them.

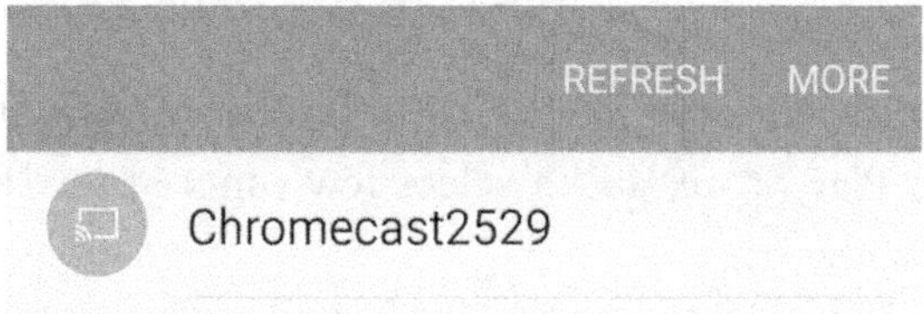

Searching Your Galaxy Using S Finder

S Finder is a search engine that searches (almost) all the data on your Galaxy. Let's say you want to find everything pertaining to your friend Mike Lee. Without S Finder, you would have to open each app individually to search for information. For example, searching for "Mike Lee" in the Phone app would turn up Mike's contact information but not any text messages or e-mails in which he participated. S Finder solves this problem by providing a centralized search function for multiple apps. It can definitely come in handy, but has at least one major limitation: it doesn't support searching your Gmail inbox. And of course, there's no guarantee it'll work with data from third-party apps. But for searching through stock apps, it's quite effective.

Access S Finder by swiping down the notification panel and tapping "S Finder." (Verizon users: find S Finder in the notification panel's EDIT area.)

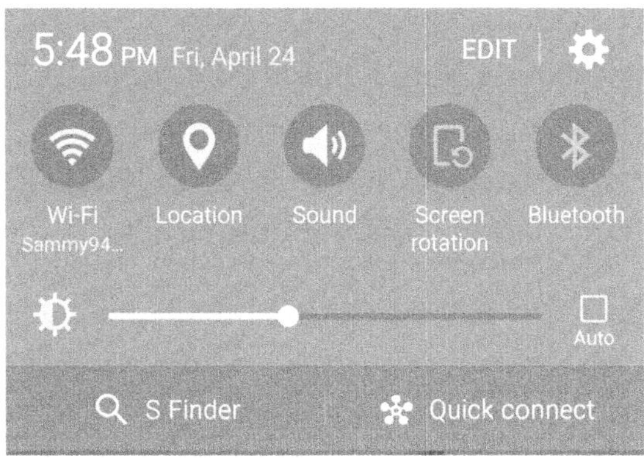

Claiming Your Free Gifts from Samsung

Samsung has partnered with several third-party companies to offer free apps and subscriptions with the Note 5 / S6 Edge+. These include:

- **ArtRage (Note 5 only):** Paint and draw as you would on real paper with a toolbox packed with realistic painting tools such as oils and watercolors.
- **Driver Speedboat Paradise:** Take to the water with thrilling high-octane boat races through exotic locales with a free speedboat in the game.
- **The Economist:** Stay informed on international news from this weekly publication with a 6-month subscription (valued at $64).
- **Empire Four Kingdoms:** Build, trade and conquer in a world with millions of players. Raise your banners now with a starter package.
- **The Guardian:** Get premium content from breaking news to commentary with an ad-free subscription for 6 months (valued at $24).
- **Hearthstone Heroes of Warcraft:** Jump into the action with 3 card packs and 1 exclusive card back for the hit strategy card game from Blizzard Entertainment.
- **Kindle for Samsung:** Look forward to reading an eBook for free every month through Samsung Book Deals (valued at $50).
- **komoot:** Go hiking or bicycling in the great outdoors with 3 regional bundles which include topographic maps, real-time navigation and more.
- **Lifesum:** Achieve your goals with 6-month free Gold subscription which includes personalized guides to dieting, exercise, and more.

- **NY Times - Latest News:** Stay on top of the headlines with a 6-month subscription (3 months in the US and Canada).
- **OneDrive:** Share files and photos across all your devices with an extra 100 GB of storage space for 2 years (valued at $48).
- **Scribd:** Get 3 months of unlimited access (valued at $27) to a library of 1 million eBooks and audiobooks.
- **SketchBook for Galaxy (Note 5 only):** All features and brushes are unlocked in this great app for anyone who loves to paint and draw.
- **TripAdvisor:** Take 15% off your total (up to $100) the next time you book a tour through TripAdvisor. Offer is valid for one purchase.

To take advantage of these free promotions, find the home screen with the Galaxy Gifts widget and tap it. Download any apps you want, and upon installing them, you will receive your free gifts or instructions on how to redeem them. If you previously removed this widget, see instructions on adding widgets (p. 68) to re-add it to one of your home screens.

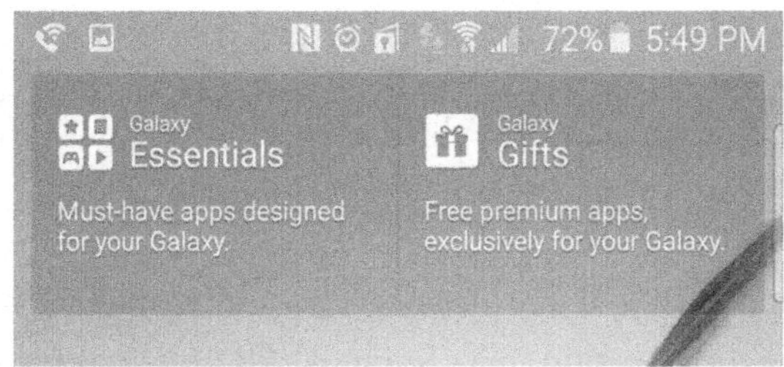

Keeping Your Device Awake While Charging

The longest available screen timeout setting on the Note 5 / S6 Edge+ is 10 minutes. Sometimes this isn't enough. For example, when I'm using a calculator app on my phone, I don't want it to sleep at all.

Fortunately, there's a way to accomplish this. Go to system settings → "About device." Swipe down until you see "Build number." Repeatedly tap this box. You will see a message that you are about to become a developer. Keep going until Developer Mode is activated.

Now, tap ⮌. You will see a new option in system settings called "Developer options." Tap this, and then check "Stay awake." Done! As long as your device is plugged in and charging, it won't go to sleep.

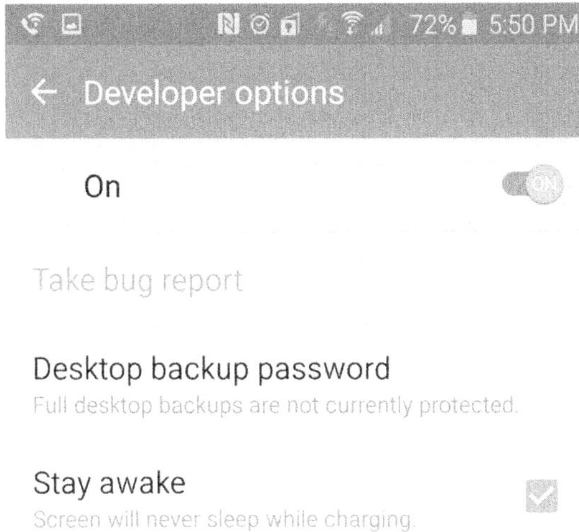

Taking Screenshots

Want to take screenshots like the ones included in this book? Just press and hold the ⬭ and power buttons together for approximately one second until the screen flashes. Your screenshot will be saved in your Gallery with the rest of your photos.

Maintaining Peace of Mind with Do Not Disturb Mode

Do Not Disturb mode lets you set quiet hours during which your Galaxy will not display or sound notifications.

Access it by going to system settings → "Sounds and notifications" → "Do not disturb." Enable it by tapping "Turn on now."

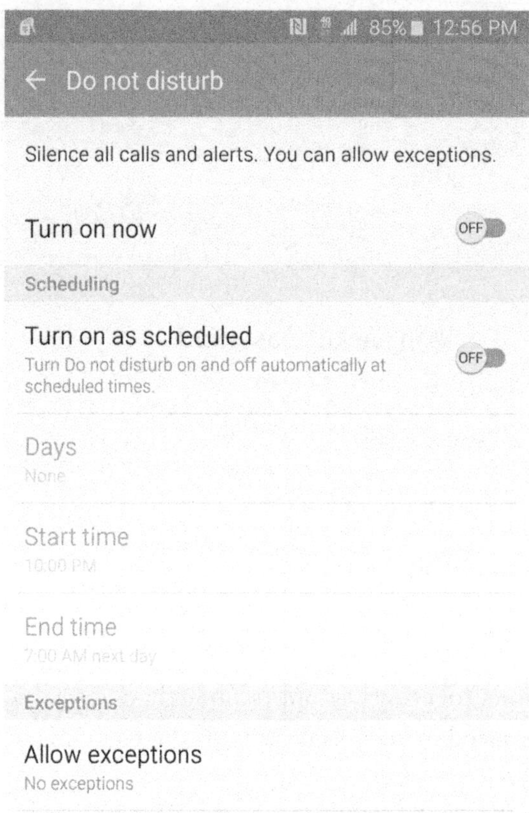

To schedule quiet hours, enable "Turn on as scheduled" and specify a schedule using the "Days," "Start time," and "End time" options. To selectively block notifications, either by notification type or by contact, tap "Allow exceptions." You can selectively block calls, notifications, alarms, text messages, events and reminders, or any combination of those things. Tap "Calls and/or messages from" to set exceptions by contact (for example, your spouse or kids).

Conserving Battery Power with the Power Saving Modes

The Note 5 / S6 Edge+ have two power saving modes: regular Power Saving Mode and Ultra Power Saving Mode. Regular Power Saving Mode works by dimming the screen, restricting CPU performance, shutting off the touch key backlights, and making a few other adjustments. Turn it on by swiping down the notification panel and enabling "Power saving." If you don't see it, tap EDIT to add it to your toggles.

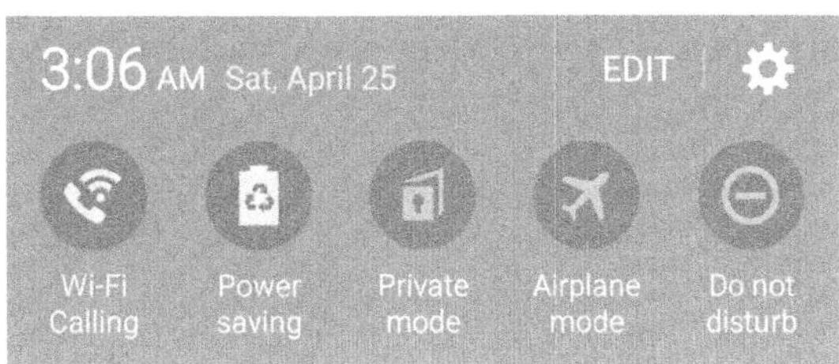

Ultra Power Saving Mode takes things even further. In addition to forcing grayscale mode, dimming the backlight, and restricting CPU performance, it deactivates Wi-Fi and Bluetooth, deactivates mobile data while the screen is off, and limits you to a few select apps. You'll only want to use Ultra Power Saving Mode if you absolutely need to conserve your battery power down to the last drop. It's similar to the power conservation features of Emergency Mode (p. 273) but without the safety features.

Turn it on by swiping down the notification panel and enabling "U. power saving." If you don't see it, tap EDIT to add it to your toggles.

Accessing Kids Mode

Kids Mode lets you set up a "sandbox" environment for young kids. It contains various fun apps and games that entertain your kids without letting them screw up your phone.

You must download Kids Mode before you can use it. To do so, go to your app drawer and open the Galaxy Apps store. Search for and download Kids Mode and follow the prompts to install the app.

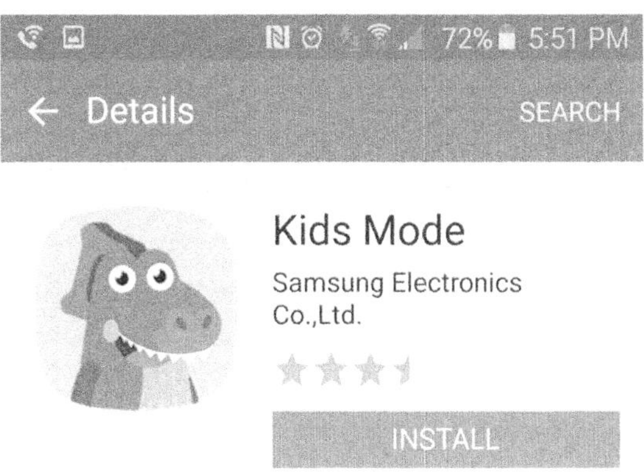

After installation, the Kids Mode app will appear in your app drawer. Tap it to launch Kids Mode.

When you first launch Kids Mode, you will need to set a PIN used for disabling Kids Mode in the future and enter your child's name and date of birth. You will also be prompted to select which, if any, third-party apps and contacts will be allowed in Kids Mode.

The three buttons at the bottom of the screen go to parental control, play zone (for kids), and close Kids Mode, respectively.

If you forget your PIN code while Kids Mode is engaged, you will need to remove the battery from your Galaxy to exit Kids Mode.

Using Your Galaxy as a Magnifying Glass

Your Galaxy comes with a widget that lets you use the camera and flash LED as an illuminated magnifying lens, and the feature works quite well. To use it, go to the home screen and add a widget (p. 68). Swipe right to the Magnifier widget, and tap and hold it to add it.

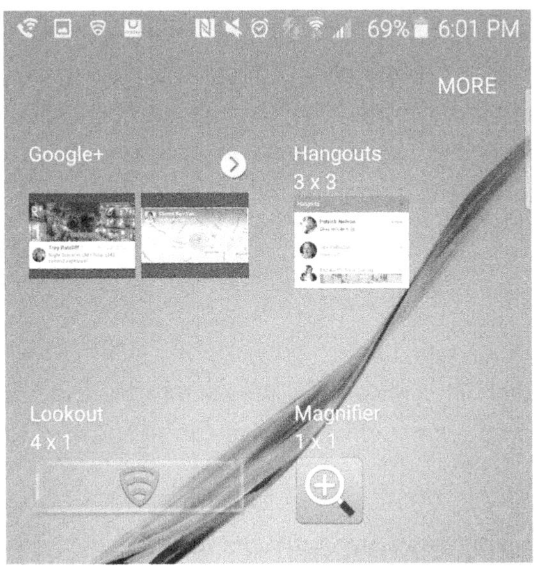

After placing the Magnifier widget on a home screen, just tap to launch it.

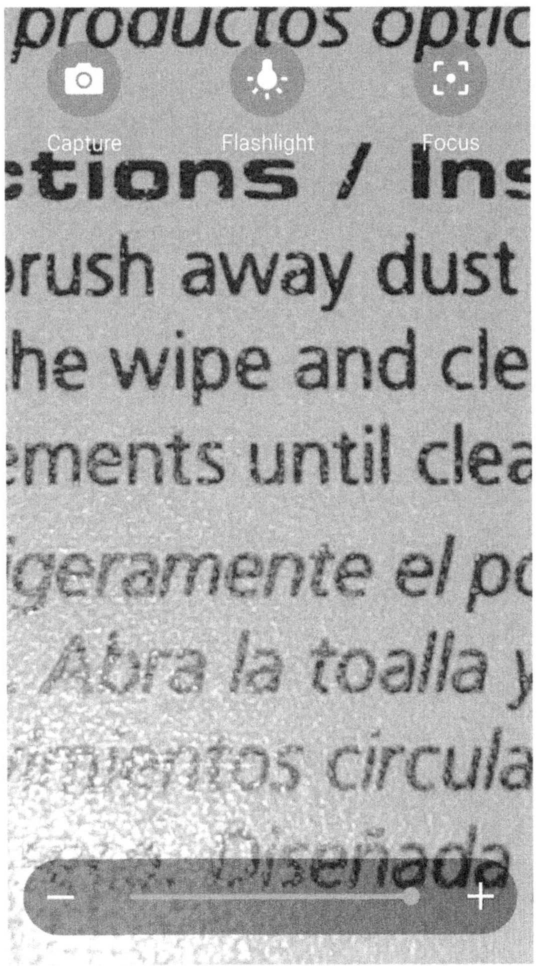

Tap anywhere on the screen or tap the "Focus" button to autofocus the image. If the camera refuses to focus, increase the distance between your Galaxy and the object you are trying to focus on. Adjust the zoom level with the slider on the bottom of the screen or by pinching in and out, and turn on illumination and/or capture a photograph using the buttons at the top of the screen.

S Health: Managing Your Diet, Exercise, and Fitness

S Health is Samsung's entry into the growing mobile health & fitness market. It's an app designed to help you track all aspects of your exercise and diet and is compatible with a huge selection of fitness accessories like the Samsung Gear Fit, various Fitbit devices, and more.

In my opinion, if your goal is to get into shape or lose weight, you should consult a professional or at least do your own research instead of completely relying on an app made by Samsung. Safely and effectively improving your health and fitness requires knowledge, not just a smartphone app. However, S Health is a fine assistant if you're only interested in tracking calories and basic health stats as part of a broader fitness program.

Note that S Health is not really a "coach"—instead, think of it as a very high-tech logbook.

The first time you open S Health, you'll have to consent to the terms of use. You'll also receive a notification in your notification panel asking you to sync S Health with your Samsung account, if you're logged into one. Tap the notification to do so. You'll want your fitness data to be backed up to the cloud so you don't lose it if you lose your Galaxy.

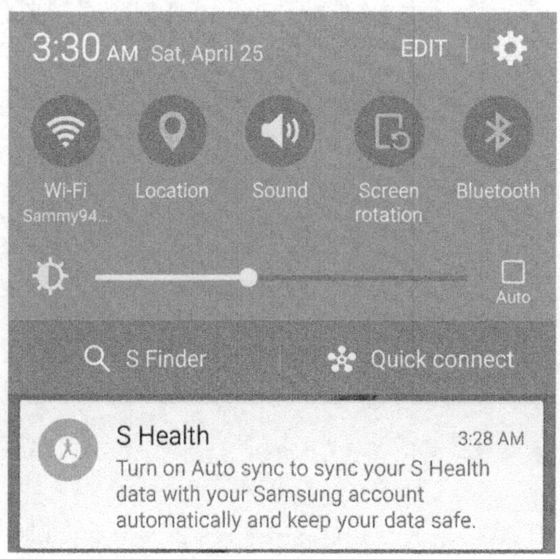

The main S Health screen looks like this:

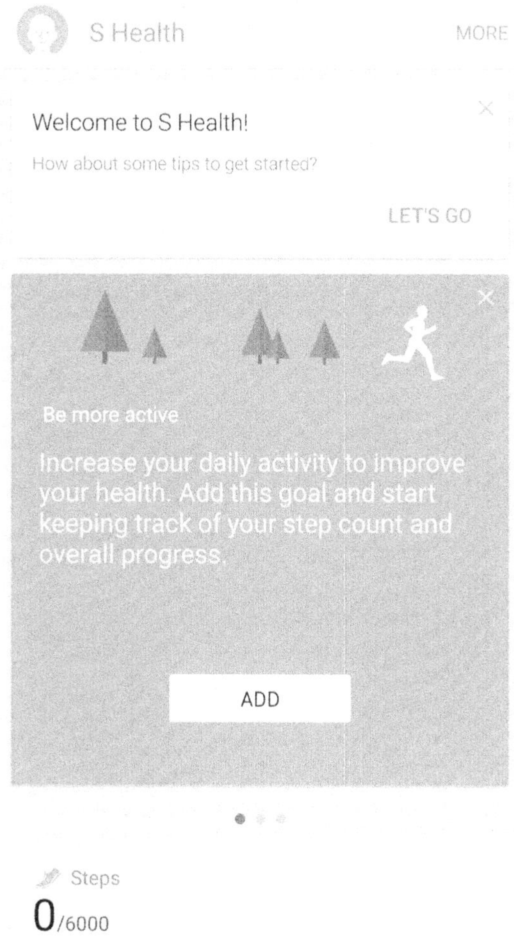

The first thing you'll want to do is tap S Health → EDIT to access "My page" and customize your profile, including gender, age, weight, height, etc. S Health requires this information to perform accurately interpret fitness data like steps taken, calories, etc.

After you've set up your profile, return to the main S Health screen and scroll down to view more tiles. Tiles are the main engine of S Health. Use them to record and monitor all your health data.

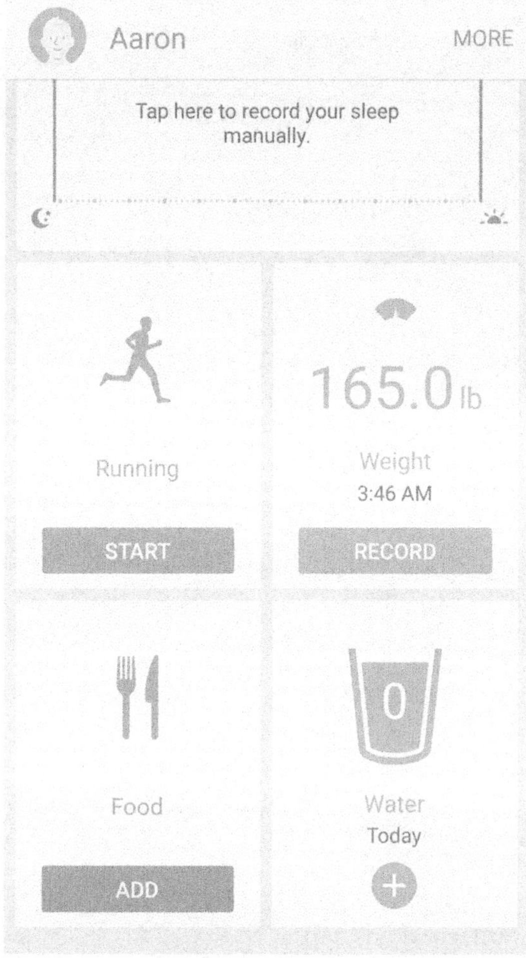

Tap a tile to input and track data. To add or remove tiles, tap MORE → "Manage items." Available tiles include:

Trackers

- Steps (pedometer; works even while S Health is closed and the device is asleep)
- Walking
- Running
- Cycling
- Hiking
- Sports
- Food

- Water
- Caffeine
- Weight
- Sleep
- Heart rate
- SpO2 (oxygen level)
- Stress
- Blood glucose
- Blood pressure

Goals

- Be more active
- Eat healthier
- Feel more rested

Programs

- Baby steps to 5K
- Run 5K
- First attempt at 10K
- Run 10K

Overall, the key to using S Health is to be diligent in inputting information. The more data S Health gathers about you, the better it can help you manage your goals and help you understand the progression of your fitness over time.

In my opinion, S Health's main strength is its ability to store your health data and visually display it with logs and charts. S Health's running programs and goals are less compelling; you're probably better off doing your own research when setting fitness goals. But for tracking information while pursuing your goals, S Health excels.

Measuring Your Heart Rate

To take a quick heart rate measurement, enable the "Heart rate" tile in MORE → "Manage items" and tap MEASURE. Place the tip of your index finger lightly on the sensor next to the rear camera lens. Hold still until your heart rate has been successfully measured. If the measurement fails, it's probably because you were pressing too hard. Try again with the tip of your finger softly resting on the sensor.

Tracking Your Steps with the Pedometer

S Health's built-in pedometer ("Steps" tile) tracks your steps even when S Health is not running and your Galaxy is asleep. No setup is necessary; after you've launched S Health for the first time, the pedometer will automatically start tracking your steps. You can optionally set a step target by tapping MORE → "Set target," but this isn't necessary to simply track your steps. Return to the "Steps" tile at any time to view your count.

Connecting Compatible Accessories

If you have a companion device (e.g., a running watch) that's compatible with S Health, you can configure it to wirelessly sync its data with S Health. To view a list of compatible devices, go to the main S Health screen and tap MORE → "Accessories." To connect an accessory, tap its name in the "Accessories" list and then tap REGISTER to begin the pairing process.

Printing with Google Cloud Print

Google Cloud Print is relatively new software from Google that makes it easy to print documents from your Galaxy.

First, you'll need to set up your printer with Google Cloud Print. On your desktop computer, go to the link below. If your printer connects to your computer via USB, click the "Add Classic Printer" button and follow the instructions. If your printer has Wi-Fi or is connected to the Internet via an Ethernet cable, click the "Add Cloud Ready Printer" button instead. After you've configured your printer this way, you'll be able to print to it over the Internet at any time using your Galaxy.

http://www.google.com/landing/cloudprint/

After your printer is configured, open the Google Play Store on your Galaxy and search for "Cloud Print." Download and install the app.

Once installed, you'll receive a notification in your notification panel. Tap it to enable the Cloud Print service. If you don't see the notification, instead go to system settings → "More connection settings" → "Printing" → "Cloud Print" and enable Cloud Print. If you've already set up your printer using your computer, you'll see its name on this screen. This means you're ready to print.

Now, in any app that has a print function (like Microsoft Office (p. 182)), you'll be able to wirelessly print using your printer via Cloud Print. Additionally, you can print anything that you can share with the Share Via (p. 91) tool. To do so, tap "Print" on the Share Via screen → 🖶.

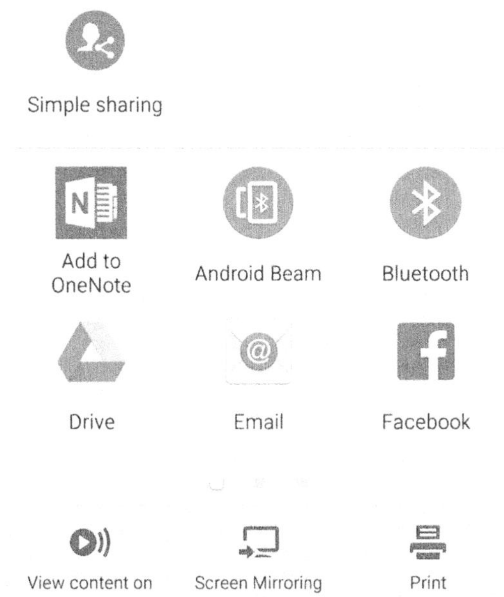

TIP: *You can also print using the pre-installed Samsung Print Service, but only if you have a networked printer. I personally prefer using Google Cloud Print since it can be used with any printer and has an easy setup process. If you'd like to use the Samsung Print Service instead, add your printer by going to system settings → "More connection settings" → "Printing" → "Samsung Print Service Plugin" →* MORE *→ "Add printer" →* ADD PRINTER*. You'll need to know your printer's local IP address, which you can get from your router's configuration screen.*

Disabling Briefing to Speed Up Your Galaxy

The Note 5 / S6 Edge+ come preloaded with Flipboard Briefing, a social media and news aggregator app accessed by swiping left from the main home screen. Briefing is pretty, but it's not as functional as many 3rd party apps like GReader (p. 311) and Pulse from the Google Play Store. Plus, it's too easy to accidentally start Briefing by accident.

If you don't use Briefing, disable it to avoid accidental launches and to slightly speed up your device. Tap to go to the home screen, and then tap and hold an empty space on the home screen to open the home screen menu. Swipe left to the Briefing page and uncheck the box.

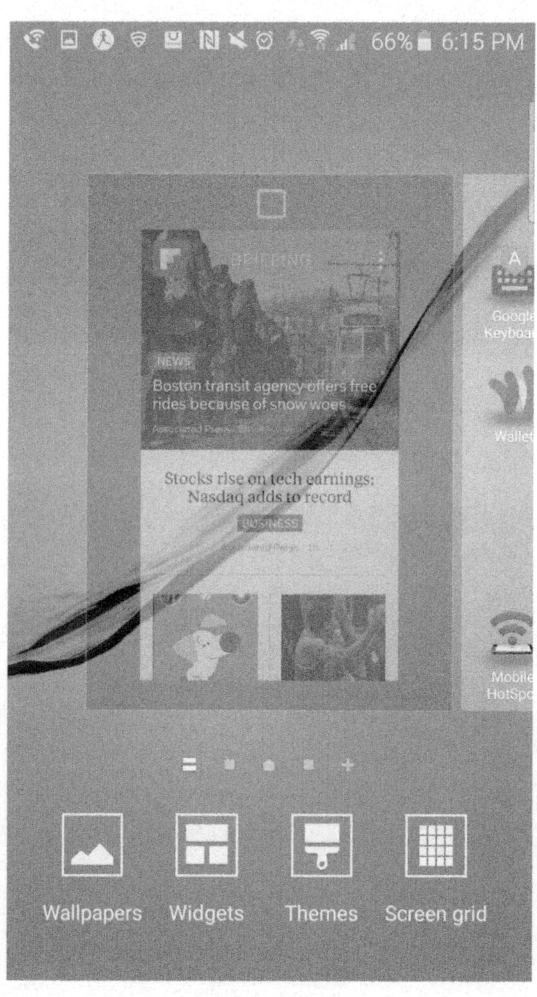

Taking Advantage of Cloud Storage with Google Drive

This tip will not only power up your Galaxy, but also your computing in general. In fact, it's one of my top tech tips of all time.

What is cloud storage? It's hard disk space that's on a remote server instead of your computer's internal hard drive. Common cloud storage services include Dropbox, Google Drive, OneDrive, and more. When you install a cloud storage utility on your computer, it creates a new folder that works like any other folder, except the files you save in it are automatically and instantaneously backed up to the remote server I mentioned.

What are the advantages?

- If your computer crashes or is lost or stolen, any files saved to your cloud storage folder will be **safely backed up** to the cloud. You won't lose your data.
- You can install a cloud storage utility on multiple computers to easily **synchronize your files** between them. Say you install a cloud storage utility on both your home and work computers. Any time you save a file to the cloud storage folder on your home computer, it will instantly be synchronized to your work computer—and vice versa. No more need to carry USB drives back and forth.
- **Every version of every file is backed up.** Did you accidentally corrupt a document and save over it? No problem—you can easily roll back to a previous version.
- If you need a file while you're away from your computer, you can login to the service's website and **download** the necessary file with an Internet browser.
- If you **upgrade your computer**, you won't have to worry about transferring your data. Just install the cloud storage utility on your new computer, and it will automatically download all your files to your new hard drive.
- Finally, every major cloud storage service offers an **Android app**, so you can access your files from your Galaxy on-the-go. In conjunction with apps like Microsoft Office (p. 182), you can easily view and edit your documents from your device.

Personally, I keep all of my work and personal files in my cloud storage folder, and I suggest you do, too. It'll make your life a lot easier, and at some point, is guaranteed to save you from disaster.

I used to use Dropbox because it was more polished than Google Drive, but now I recommend Google Drive. Drive gives you more free storage space than Dropbox (15 GB vs. 2 GB), has more affordable paid tiers (100 GB for $1.99/month), and integrates nicely with Gmail and other Google services. To get started, download the desktop utility from the following link and download the Android app from the Google Play Store.

https://www.google.com/drive/download/

TIP: Your Galaxy comes with the OneDrive app, which is Microsoft's competitor to Google Drive and Dropbox. If you're willing to try OneDrive, you can get 100 GB of storage for free through the Galaxy Gifts *(p. 251)* *program.*

Detecting Crying Babies and Ringing Doorbells

Here's a weird one: a feature to detect crying babies or ringing doorbells. I know, it's a bit…oddly specific, and of questionable usefulness. But if, say, your job requires you to work from home and wear headphones all day, maybe you'll find it useful?

Go to system settings → "Accessibility" → "Hearing" → "Sound detectors." The doorbell detector requires you to record samples of your doorbell ringing before you can use it, but the baby crying detector does not.

Changing the System Font

Want to personalize your Galaxy with a custom font? Go to system settings → "Display" → "Font." A custom font applies to all system menus, the home screen, the app drawer, most apps, and more.

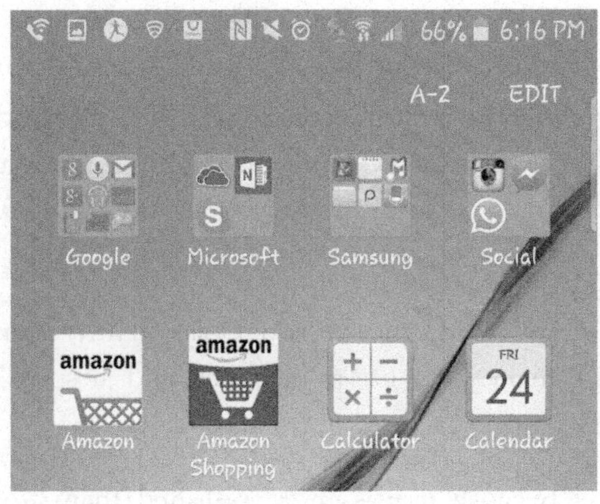

Disabling Useless Apps for Good

Ever heard the term "bloatware?" It refers to preloaded software that you don't want. Although the Note 5 and S6 Edge+ don't have as much bloatware as some older Samsung phones have had (Galaxy S4, I'm looking at you), there are some apps that you might not want on your device, like Milk and Instagram.

You can't completely uninstall these apps since they're in the device's ROM (read-only memory), but you can permanently disable them so they don't appear in your app drawer and consume system resources. To do so, go to the app drawer and tap EDIT. Tap the red minus sign on any app you want to disable and confirm when prompted. Tap DONE to exit this mode.

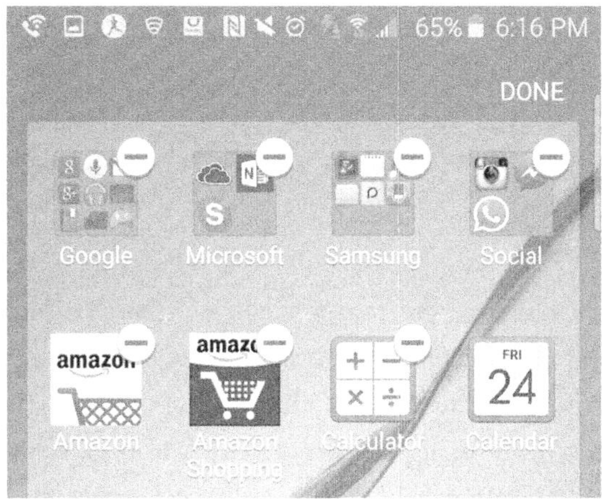

Using the Camera Flash as a Flashlight

Your Galaxy has a built-in toggle button that lets you use the camera's LED flash as a flashlight. Use this feature by swiping down the notification panel and enabling "Flashlight." If you don't see it, tap EDIT to add it to your toggles.

TIP: Try the TeslaLED (p. 319) app for a brighter flashlight, plus additional options like a strobe and Morse code. You can't place

TeslaLED in your toggle buttons like you can with Flashlight, but it does come with *widgets (p. 63)* *you can place on your home screen.*

Speeding Up the Home Button by Disabling Camera Quick Launch

By default, double-tapping launches the Camera app (in about 0.7 seconds!). This means that whenever you tap the button once to go to the home screen, there is a slight delay while the system waits for a second press. If you don't care about launching the camera with the home button, you can turn off this shortcut and make single presses of the home button register faster. To do so, open the Camera app and tap → . Disable "Quick launch." You'll notice the home button is snappier with this setting disabled. Personally, I think the slight sluggishness is worth the convenience of being able to open the Camera app so quickly; it lets me get a lot more shots I would otherwise miss.

Getting 4 Hours of Juice in 10 Minutes with Adaptive Fast Charging

The Note 5 / S6 Edge+ have a new feature called Adaptive Fast Charging that lets you charge your battery faster than ever before. Samsung claims that your Galaxy can operate for up to 4 hours after just 10 minutes of charging. To take advantage of Adaptive Fast Charging, just make sure you're using the power brick that came with your device, plugged into a regular AC outlet. Adaptive Fast Charging won't work if you use a different power brick or a USB port. Also, the device's screen must be off for Adaptive Fast Charging to kick in.

TIP: *Any third party charging accessory that conforms to the Quick Charge 2.0 standard will work with Adaptive Fast Charging. Look for this designation when buying aftermarket chargers.*

Troubleshooting Apps by Clearing App Cache and Data

If one of your apps is acting buggy, the first line of defense is restarting your Galaxy. If restarting does not fix the problem, though, the next step is clearing app and cache data. Go to system settings → "Applications" → "Application manager." Swipe right to the "All" tab. Scroll down and tap on the app that's misbehaving. Tap "Clear cache" and "Clear data." This will reset the app to its original state. In general, this doesn't delete data like notes, contacts, or pictures—just settings and configuration information.

Restarting Your Device Automatically with Auto Restart

The Note 5 / S6 Edge+ have a new feature to help you keep your device running smoothly at all times—Auto Restart. This feature lets you schedule regular device restarts so everything is always nice and fresh. I strongly recommend enabling this feature, because regularly restarting your Android is one of the best ways to prevent buggy behavior.

To set up Auto Restart, go to system settings → "Backup and reset" → "Auto restart." Note that this feature may not be available if you have a carrier-branded phone—it's generally only enabled on unlocked and international devices.

Setting Up Blackberry-Like Text Shortcuts

How many of us used Blackberries before Android hit the scene? Blackberries had a lot of very cool keyboard shortcuts and tricks to master. Samsung has included one very Blackberry-like feature in the Samsung keyboard: Text Shortcuts. With Text Shortcuts, you can program your Galaxy to automatically convert abbreviations into longer words or phrases. For example, you can program it to change "bc" to "because," "wrt" to "with regards to," or "em" to your email address. Hot Keys can save a lot of typing for your most-used words or phrases.

To enable Hot Keys, go to system settings → "Language and input" → "Samsung keyboard" → "Text shortcuts."

Powering Up Your Selfies with Wide-Angle Group Shots

If you're not already familiar with the term "selfie," it refers to a self-shot portrait. Almost all newer smartphones have a front camera specifically for taking selfies, but the Note 5 / S6 Edge+ have a special feature for group selfies. It's called wide-angle selfie mode, which is basically a panorama mode for the front camera, allowing you to capture more people in a group. To use it, open the camera app and tap [camera switch icon] to switch to front camera mode. Then, tap MODE → "Wide selfie" and follow the instructions.

Customizing the Lock Screen

After you've set a lock screen (p. 226) to protect your personal information, you can customize it to show useful information while your Galaxy is locked. To do so, go to system settings → "Lock screen and security" → "Show information" (only visible if you have a lock screen enabled). Personally, I like to put my email address in "Owner information" so if my phone is ever lost, there's at least a chance it'll find its way back to me.

TIP: On some older Samsung phones, it was possible to add widgets to the lock screen. Unfortunately, this feature has been removed from the Note 5 / S6 Edge+. If you must have a particular feature on your lock screen, your best bet is to try finding a third party lock screen replacement app on the Google Play Store that has the feature you need.

Customizing Quick Settings to Speed Up Settings Access

The Note 5 / S6 Edge+'s settings menu is long and not particularly easy to navigate. If you find yourself always scrolling around the page in search of a particular category, consider adding it to your Quick Settings. To do so, go to system settings → EDIT. Place a checkmark next to your most frequently used settings pages to pin them to the top of the settings page for easier access.

Pinpointing Battery Drain

Normal battery use is 2-3% per hour while asleep and around 10% or more per hour while awake, depending on what task you're doing. If your Galaxy is consuming significantly more battery power than this, you might have a rogue app that's sucking down your juice. To pinpoint the source of the drain, go to system settings → "Battery" and examine the "Abnormal battery usage" section for any apps that are consuming a significant percentage of battery power. Uninstall or disable (p. 267) these apps.

TIP: If nothing looks out of the ordinary in the Battery settings but you're still experiencing drain, try installing BetterBatteryStats from the Google Play Store. This app examines battery drain at a much deeper level and is useful for particularly tricky sources of battery drain. Search Google for more information on using BetterBatteryStats.

Waking Up Your Galaxy with the Wave of a Hand

The "Gesture wake up" feature lets you wake your Galaxy by waving your hand over it instead of pressing the power button. Gesture wake up uses a sensor next to the front camera, so the device must be screen-up for it to work.

To enable Air Wake Up, go to system settings → "Accessibility" → "Dexterity and interaction" → "Gesture wake up."

Recording Interviews with the Bidirectional Voice Recorder

The Voice Recorder app is capable of recording from both the top and bottom microphones, which makes it especially useful for recording interviews or conversations between two people. Voice Recorder has a special "interview" mode for exactly this purpose.

To use it, open the Voice Recorder app and tap ▼ → "Interview." Record using the ● button.

All About Notifications

Never Miss a Notification with Smart Alert

How often do you pick up your phone throughout the day to check the LED light for notifications? I know I do it all the time. The Note 5 / S6 Edge+ have a special feature that makes your device vibrate when you pick it up and there are new notifications. This helps ensure you don't miss any notifications as you check throughout the day. To turn Smart Alert on, go to system settings → "Motions and gestures" and enable "Smart alert."

Using the Camera Flash for Notifications

The iPhone has offered flash notifications for a while, and Android has only recently caught up. With flash notifications, your camera flash will blink to provide a much more visible signal than the usual dim blue LED. Of course, remember that you'll only be able to see the flash blink if the device is face down. To enable this feature, go to system settings → "Accessibility" → "Hearing" and enable "Flash notification."

Getting Repeat Reminders for Missed Notifications

By default, notifications make a sound the first time they appear in your notification panel, but never again. If you want to receipt repeat reminders (e.g., every 5 minutes) for unacknowledged notifications, go to system settings → "Accessibility" → "Notification reminder."

Configuring Lock Screen Notifications and App-Specific Notifications

Android 5.0 Lollipop has some new notification control settings. First, you can control if and how notifications are shown on your lock screen in system settings → "Lock screen and security" → "Notifications" (only visible if you have a lock screen enabled). "Show content" will show all notifications while your device is locked. "Hide content" will still show all notifications, but hide sensitive details like the actual text of text messages or the contents of email. "Do not show notifications" will prevent your device from displaying any notifications at all on your lock screen.

Second, you can tailor notifications on a per-app basis. You can block all notifications, set an app's notifications as priority so they always appear at the top of your notification panel, and choose whether to hide that app's notifications on the lock screen.

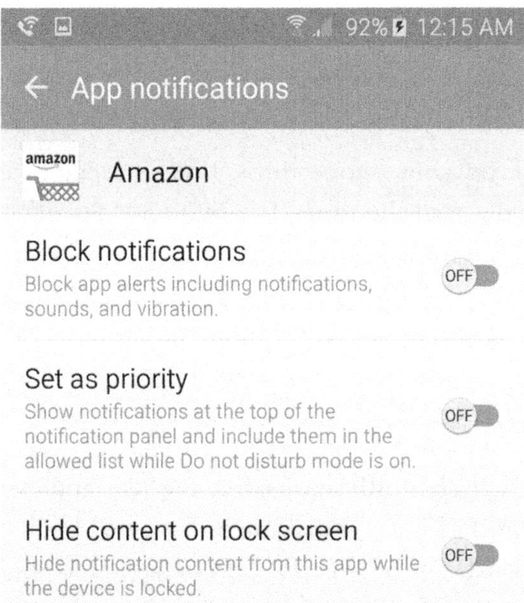

Find these options in system settings → "Sounds and notifications" → "App notifications."

Connecting Your Galaxy to Your Car Using MirrorLink

MirrorLink is a new feature for connecting your Android device to a MirrorLink-enabled vehicle. It allows you to control your phone and access its apps and media using your car's infotainment system (i.e., its dashboard/steering wheel buttons).

Today, pretty much every vehicle and car stereo manufacturer has a different protocol for interfacing with your phone; sure, they all use Bluetooth, but the details are very different.

MirrorLink aims to standardize this process and provide new functionality, like accessing your Maps app with your car's controls.

If your car supports MirrorLink, it will automatically detect your Note 5 / S6 Edge+ when you plug it in via USB. If it doesn't immediately detect your device, make sure that MirrorLink is enabled in system settings → "More connection settings" → "MirrorLink." Consult your car's instruction manual for details on operating your Galaxy with the car's built-in controls.

Simplifying Gestures with Single Tap Mode

Single tap mode changes several tap-and-drag gestures to single taps, including dismissing alarms & events and answering and rejecting calls. Enable it in system settings → "Accessibility."

Securing Internet Passwords with the Fingerprint Scanner

If you use the built-in Internet app as your browser, you can save and secure your passwords in it using the fingerprint sensor. First, make sure "Save sign-in info" is checked in Internet → MORE → "Settings" → "Privacy." Then, go to system settings → "Lock screen and security" → "Fingerprints" and enable "Web sign-in." Follow the instructions to save and secure your website logins with your fingerprint.

> ***TIP:*** *Although it is convenient to use the fingerprint sensor to store your login information in Internet, the downside is that your login information can't be easily backed up or shared with your computer. If you want a comprehensive desktop and mobile password manager, I strongly suggest looking into Lastpass* ***(p. 312)****. The trade-off, however, is that Lastpass can't be secured with the fingerprint sensor!*

Configuring SOS Messages and Using Emergency Mode

The Note 5 / S6 Edge+ have a mode called Emergency Mode, which disables all non-essential features, extends battery life as much as possible, and gives you a simplified control panel. Turn it on by pressing and holding the power button, then tapping "Emergency mode." Use it if you're in a bad situation and you need your battery to last as long as possible, or if you just need easy access to a flashlight and an alarm.

You can also configure an SOS message, which can be dispatched at any time by triple-pressing the power button.

To configure an SOS message, go to system settings → "Privacy and safety" → "Send SOS messages." Switch this feature on and configure settings as desired.

Now, any time you triple-press the power button—even with the device asleep and locked—it will take pictures with the front and back cameras, and text them along with a sound recording and your current GPS location to your emergency contact(s). The device will quickly vibrate 3 times to confirm the command has been processed. If it does not vibrate, the message has not been sent, and you must try again.

Simulating a Battery Pull to Reset Your Galaxy

Sometimes, when an Android device gets completely locked up, you need to pull the battery to restart it. However, the Note 5 / S6 Edge+'s battery is sealed inside and cannot be removed. There's a trick, though: press and hold the power button for 7 seconds to simulate a battery pull. It'll power off the device no matter how frozen its software is.

Making Your Galaxy Like New with a Factory Reset

Sometimes you need to wipe your device completely—to sell it, or because it's gotten buggy and you want a fresh start. To factory reset your Galaxy, go to system settings → "Backup and reset" → "Factory data reset." Be warned that this permanently erases everything on your device. Make sure you've backed up all the files you need using your apps' cloud backup features, or by copying them to your computer via USB (p. 278).

> ***TIP:*** *A factory reset does not render data completely unrecoverable, much like formatting a hard drive or SSD in your computer does not permanently wipe data. With the proper tools and dedication, it is still theoretically possible for someone to recover data on a factory reset phone. If you want to make sure your data is completely unrecoverable, you need to encrypt* *(p. 227)* *your data before factory resetting.*

Keeping Tabs on Your Galaxy's Health with Smart Manager

The Note 5 / S6 Edge+ include a new app called "Smart Manager" that lets you easily monitor battery life (including estimated time remaining), storage capacity, RAM usage, and device security. It can help you identify and delete large files in your internal storage, in the event you're running out of space. It also has a convenient "Clean All" button that deletes all caches and temporary files to keep your Galaxy running smoothly. It's not necessary to monitor Smart Manager all the time, but use it if you're experiencing unusual battery drain or if you need to free up extra storage space.

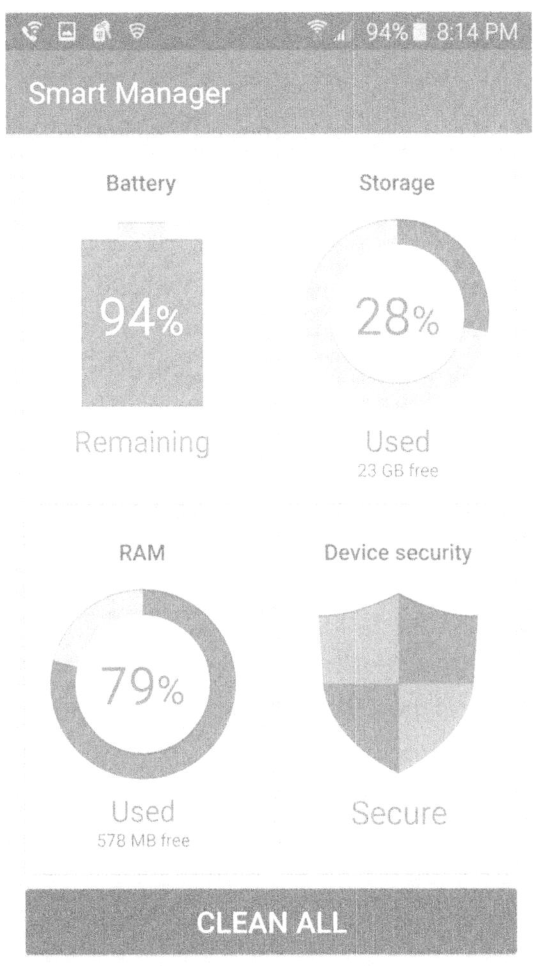

TIP: Smart Manager may not be included on AT&T and Verizon models.

Checking for Over-the-Air (OTA) System Updates

Android system updates, which generally only occur 1-2 times per year, are automatically delivered to you over the air. When one is available, you'll receive a notification with upgrade instructions in your notification panel. If you'd like to manually check for updates, just in case, go to system settings → "About device" → "Software update." If an update is available, your Galaxy will detect it and prompt you to download it.

Everything You Need to Know About Backing Up Your Data

One of the most confusing aspects of Android is how to ensure all your data is backed up. For a new Android user, it can be very unclear what's backed up where, and how to restore data if needed.

The truth is, there is no good one-stop, centralized backup solution. I think this will be a focus for Google in the next few years, but until then, you have to use a piecemeal approach, combining multiple methods. Here's what you need to know:

- **Apps:** There is no need to back up apps downloaded from the Google Play Store. You can always re-download your apps from the Google Play Store at any time. Switching to a new Android device, or accidentally wiped your device? Just log into your Google account and follow the prompts to automatically restore all your apps.
- **App data:** Some apps automatically back up data to your Google account. For these apps, your data will be restored when the apps are reinstalled. Unfortunately, not all apps do this, and there's no easy way to know which ones do. To make sure all of your app data is backed up, use Helium Backup from the Google Play Store, or Titanium Backup (p. 284) if you root (p. 281) your device.
- **SMS and MMS messages:** Back these up using your Samsung account. Go to system settings → "Backup and reset" → "Back up my data." Make sure "Message" is selected, and tap "Back Up Now." To restore at any time, go to system settings --. "Backup and reset" → "Restore." Note that this only saves the last backup. If you want to save multiple backups to file, try SMS Backup & Restore (p. 317).
- **Gallery Photos and Videos:** The best way to back up your camera images and videos is by using the auto-backup feature in Google's Photos app. When this feature is enabled, your Galaxy will automatically upload all photos and videos you capture to your Google account, where they will be safely stored. You can view all uploaded photos and videos at any time by visiting https://photos.google.com/ on your desktop computer. To enable auto-backup, open the Photos app in your app drawer and swipe through the intro screens. Tap ≡ → "Settings" → "Back up & sync." Make sure the teal slider is turned on, and choose whether you want to back up on Wi-Fi networks only, or also on your cellular data connection. You also have a decision to make about photo quality; Google allows you to store an unlimited number of photos that are 16 MP or less, but any photos larger than 16 MP will count toward your Google account's storage quota. Fortunately, if your Galaxy is your main camera, this is an easy decision, because its maximum resolution is

exactly 16 MP. Therefore, you can choose the unlimited "High quality" storage option without sacrificing any quality at all. After you've configured auto-backup, your Galaxy will upload your camera media every time you take a new photo or video!

- **Gmail, Contacts, Calendar:** These are always automatically synced with your Google account—no manual steps necessary. If you lose or reset your device, the next time you log into a Google account on an Android, your Gmail, Contacts, and Calendar data will be automatically restored. You'll also see options to back up Contacts and Calendar data in the Samsung account backup screen, but there's no need to do this—it's already in your Google account.
- **Documents:** If you have other files on your device like Microsoft Office documents, make sure you have a cloud storage app like Google Drive (p. 265) or OneDrive (p. 301) and that you're saving all your files on your cloud drive instead of on your device's internal storage.
- **Call History:** You can back up your call logs using your Samsung account, using the same procedure described for SMS and MMS messages. Select "Phone" in addition to "Messages."
- **Other media (purchased songs, eBooks, etc.):** For songs, movies, eBooks, and so on, there is generally no need to backup this data. You can always re-download it from the app you bought it from (Google Play, Amazon Kindle, etc.).

Create a KNOX Device-Within-a-Device to Separate Work and Play

Want to use your Galaxy for both personal and work use, but create a clear barrier between the two? Download the Samsung KNOX app from the Google Play Store. This app lets you create a completely separate "virtual" environment for work use. You can access all your essential applications and features, but they won't have access to any of your personal data. It's like carrying two Galaxies in your pocket. For example, inside the KNOX app you'll find the apps you're used to like Google Chrome, Gmail, Contacts, and so on, but they'll all be fresh and ready to set up with your work information—there will be no overlap with the same apps outside of KNOX. Pretty handy.

Chapter 9: Advanced Functions

By now, we've discussed nearly everything there is to discuss about your Galaxy, at least as it comes in the box. In this chapter, you'll learn how to extend the functionality of your Galaxy and become a bona fide power user yourself.

Connecting Your Galaxy to Your PC or Mac

Installing USB Drivers

Some Android devices support USB Mass Storage Mode out of the box, meaning that computers will automatically mount them as flash drives when connected over USB. Unfortunately, the Note 5 / S6 Edge+ are not among these devices. If you connect your Galaxy to your Windows or Mac computer via USB without first installing the proper drivers, the connection will fail.

To remedy this situation on Windows, you need to install Samsung's USB drivers. Go to the following link and scroll down to "Manuals & Downloads." Click "Download (EXE)" to download and install the necessary USB drivers on your computer. The drivers found at the link below work for both the Note 5 and the S6 Edge+.

http://www.samsung.com/us/support/owners/product/SM-G928TZKATMB

(Short URL: http://goo.gl/4rLXt9)

On Mac OS, you don't need any Samsung-specific drivers, but you do need the official Android File Transfer tool

http://www.android.com/filetransfer/

Accessing Files

On Windows, once you have properly installed the Samsung USB drivers, you can access your Galaxy as you would a USB flash drive. If AutoPlay opens, click "Open device to view files."

If AutoPlay does not open, open Windows Explorer and go to Computer → name of your device.

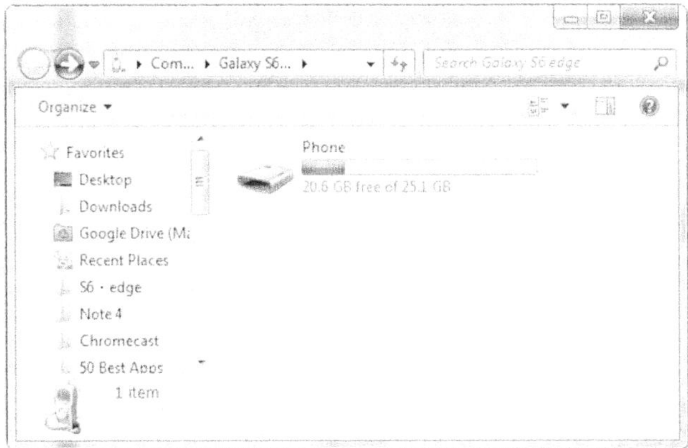

Once you have accessed your device, open the "Phone" subdirectory to view its internal storage (remember it has no external microSD storage option). You can copy, paste, and move files just as you would elsewhere on your PC.

TIP: Be very careful about deleting or moving system or app files—only do so if you have a specific reason to and you know what you're doing.

On Mac OS, Android File Transfer will open as soon as you plug in your USB cable. You can drag files in and out of this window as if it were a Finder window.

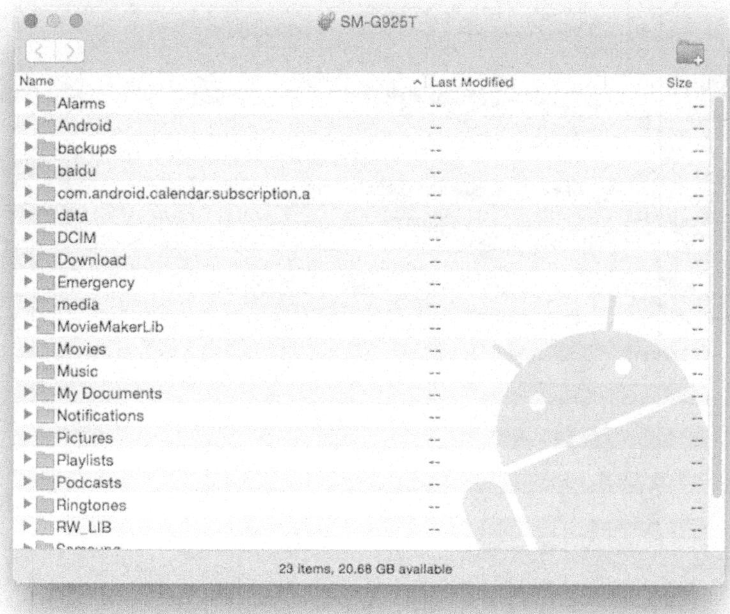

TIP: If your Galaxy is having trouble connecting to your computer via USB, make sure USB debugging is switched off in system settings *→ "Developer Options (p. 252)."*

Remote Controlling Your Galaxy with AirDroid

AirDroid is a free third-party app that lets you control your Galaxy using a web browser on your desktop computer. You can transfer files via Wi-Fi, view photos, edit contacts, manage music, view notifications, send text messages, and more. It's a very interesting and useful tool to complement basic USB connections, because it lets you go way beyond simply copying files.

Download AirDroid from the Google Play Store. Install it and make sure your device is connected to the same Wi-Fi network as your computer. Start AirDroid and your device will guide you through the setup process. You can create an account with AirDroid if you wish, which will let you control your device even if it's not on the same Wi-Fi network as your computer.

I suggest you experiment with AirDroid to see how it's most useful for you. Also, consider downloading the new dedicated desktop client, which sits in your computer's system tray to provide notification monitoring and text messaging even when you don't have an AirDroid browser window open.

https://www.airdroid.com/en/get.html

Rooting Your Galaxy to Unlock More Power

If you've read about Android online, you've probably seen people talking about "rooting" their phones. What does this mean, and why would you want to do it?

Android is based on Linux, and in Linux (and all Unix-like systems) the most privileged administrator account is called the "root" account. With root privileges, it's possible to execute any code you wish—code that is not normally possible to run. So, rooting your device lets you do cool stuff that's not otherwise possible.

Here are some things you can do after rooting your device:

- Block all advertisements in web browsers and apps
- Share your cellular connection over Wi-Fi even if you don't pay for your carrier's hot spot option
- Back up your apps and app data with Titanium Backup
- Back up your entire system state with Nandroid backups
- Permanently delete bloatware
- Use Greenify to freeze background apps and save battery power
- Install custom ROMs (versions of the Android OS that enthusiasts have modified, de-bloated, or otherwise improved.)
- … and much more.

In this chapter, I will show you how to do all of these things.

Note that the rooting process really comprises three separate steps:

1. **Gaining root access itself:** This lets you do everything in the above list except install custom ROMs.
2. **Installing a custom recovery:** A custom recovery is necessary to install custom ROMs, as well as to perform Nandroid backups (p. 284). This is optional; if you are satisfied with the stock ROM and do not need Nandroid backups, it's perfectly fine to root your device but not install a custom recovery.
3. **Install a custom ROM:** If you want to go all the way, the ultimate step in the rooting process is to install a streamlined custom ROM. Most custom ROMs are based on the stock ROM that your Galaxy ships with, but have carrier bloatware removed and additional features added. For example, many custom ROMs have call recording, battery optimizations, and so on. You may also be able to find more

exotic ROMs, such as one based on the "pure" Android OS that ships with Nexus devices.

Root Warnings—Read this first!

Before we continue further, I want to give you a word of warning. The Note 5 and S6 Edge+ have a built-in security layer called Samsung KNOX, a group of features that's targeted toward commercial and enterprise companies. To make a long story short, KNOX helps Samsung sell devices to corporate customers who need superior data security. However, if you root your device, you will trip the KNOX security flag and permanently lose KNOX features. Even if you're not a corporate user, this can affect you in several ways.

- First, tripping the KNOX flag voids the manufacturer warranty. If you void your warranty in this way, Samsung has the right to withhold support from you in the future.
- Second, tripping the KNOX flag permanently disables Private Mode (p. 229).
- Third, tripping the KNOX flag permanently disables the Knox app (p. 277).
- Fourth, tripping the KNOX flag permanently disables Samsung Pay (p. 248).

TIP: *When I say "permanently," I mean it. Once you've rooted your device and tripped the KNOX flag, there is no way to reset it.*

That said, thousands of users have rooted their Samsung devices and tripped their KNOX flags. Retaining the Samsung warranty is not as important as it sounds because other types of warranties and insurance plans are readily available from cell carriers themselves, and almost none of them care about your KNOX flag. As for losing Private Mode and Samsung Pay, you'll have to make your own judgment about whether you're willing to trade those features for the advantages of root.

If you still want to root your device and/or install a custom ROM, continue reading.

Device Rootability

At the time of publication, not all devices can be rooted. As of August 2015, this is the status of each device's "rootability":

	Note 5	**S6 Edge+**
Sprint	**Yes**	No
T-Mobile	**Yes**	No
AT&T	No	No
Verizon	No	No

If your device is listed as "no," remember that by the time you're reading this book, it may be possible to root your device. I suggest checking the XDA links below for the most up-to-date information.

Note that to root, you will need access to a Windows computer. If you have a Mac, you can complete the process with a Boot Camp installation of Windows or a Parallels virtual machine. Note that VMWare Fusion will not work.

Root Instructions

> **FINAL WARNINGS:** *Rooting voids your warranty, permanently disables Private Mode, permanently disables Samsung Pay, and permanently trips your KNOX flag.*

Check the following links for the most up-to-date information about rooting your device. I do not publish instructions in this book because rooting methods and software change very rapidly and information goes out of date quickly. In general, the rooting process entails downloading a tool called ODIN and using it to re-flash your device's memory, but beyond that, the details vary.

Sprint

Note 5: http://forum.xda-developers.com/sprint-galaxy-note5/development

S6 Edge+: http://forum.xda-developers.com/sprint-galaxy-s6-edge-plus/development

T-Mobile

Note 5: http://forum.xda-developers.com/tmobile-galaxy-note5/development

S6 Edge+: http://forum.xda-developers.com/tmobile-galaxy-s6-edge-plus/development

AT&T

Note 5: http://forum.xda-developers.com/att-galaxy-note5/development

S6 Edge+: http://forum.xda-developers.com/att-galaxy-s6-edge-plus/development

Verizon

Note 5: http://forum.xda-developers.com/verizon-galaxy-note5/development

S6 Edge+: http://forum.xda-developers.com/verizon-galaxy-s6-edge-plus/development

Things to Do After You've Rooted Your Galaxy

Imaging your Device with Nandroid Backups

Nandroid backups are a special and powerful type of backup, and are only possible when you've rooted *and* installed a custom recovery. A Nandroid backup creates an exact image of your device's internal memory and compresses it into a single folder. This lets you freely tinker and experiment with your device, because you can always quickly and easily revert to a fixed "last known good state" using a Nandroid backup folder.

To create a Nandroid backup (assuming you've already installed a custom recovery), you'll need to boot into recovery by restarting your Galaxy while holding the Volume Up + Home + Power buttons. Use the "backup" and "restore" options of your custom recovery to back up your data. If you want to store your Nandroid backups for safekeeping, you can copy them to your computer's hard disk via USB.

Backing Up Apps and App Data with Titanium Backup

Titanium Backup lets you backup and restore your apps and app data to a single folder. It's most useful when you're installing a new custom ROM—it's easier to backup and restore your apps using Titanium Backup than to re-download everything from the Play Store, and you are sure to not to lose any app data. (Google's new Tap & Go restore system (p. 34) could eventually give Titanium Backup a run for its money, but not until it properly and reliably backs up ALL app data like Titanium Backup does.)

The free version of Titanium Backup performs basic backups and restores but purchasing a pro key gives you many more options ($5.99 on the Google Play Store).

Before using Titanium Backup for the first time, you'll need to enable USB debugging. To do so, go to system settings → "About device." Double-tap on "Build number" repeatedly and you will get a notification that developer options have been enabled. Go back to system settings, tap "Developer options," switch the slider in the upper-right-hand corner of the screen to "On," and tick the checkbox next to "USB debugging."

> ***TIP:*** *In some cases, enabling USB debugging can prevent a proper USB connection with your computer. If you have trouble connecting over USB after enabling USB debugging, disable it again.*

To perform a backup with Titanium Backup, tap → "Run" next to "Backup all user apps." Select the apps you wish to back up and then tap . This will back up all your apps and associated data. By default, you'll find your backed up apps in the

/TitaniumBackup/ folder when you connect to your Galaxy via USB. Remember to copy this folder to your computer for safekeeping, if desired.

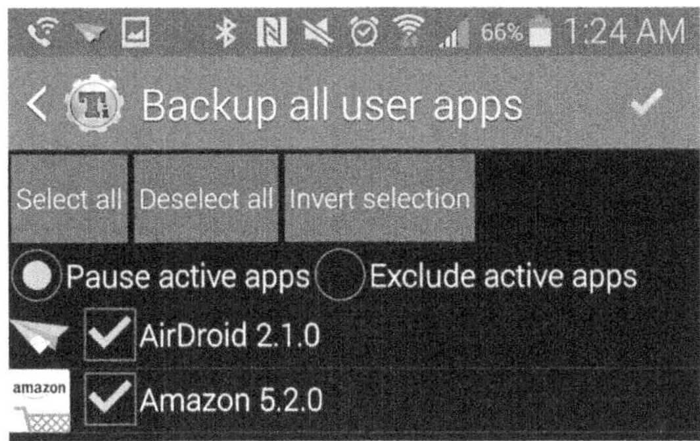

To restore a backup, use the "Restore missing apps with data" option. Here, you can select whether to restore apps with data, apps only, or data only.

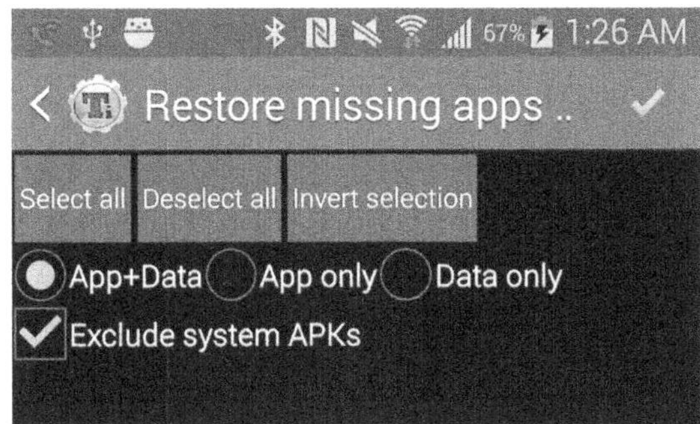

WARNING: *It's okay to restore apps and app data when moving to a new custom ROM, but you should never restore system data on a new custom ROM, or you will cause a multitude of errors and have to start over from scratch.*

That's all there is to it—unless you want to use any of Titanium Backup's other features, which are numerous. If so, I suggest consulting the official documentation here:

http://www.titaniumtrack.com/kb/titanium-backup-kb

Blocking Ads with AdAway

Blocking ads is one of the best things you can do after you've rooted. There are several apps designed for this purpose, but I have found AdAway to be the best. It blocks advertisements everywhere on your device—in the stock browser, in Chrome, and in apps.

AdAway is not on the Google Play Store; it is on an alternative platform called F-Droid. Download F-Droid at the link below and install it to your Galaxy. Search for "AdAway" in F-Droid and install it by tapping the latest version number at the bottom of the screen. Open AdAway, tap the button entitled "Download files and apply ad blocking." Reboot your device when the process is done, and it will be ad-free!

https://f-droid.org/

Tethering Your Internet Connection for Free

Another advantage of rooting is that you can use Wi-Fi tethering without paying your carrier's hot spot fees.

> ★ ***WARNING:*** *Although your carrier has no way of knowing with certainty that you are tethering, you will set off alarms if you use a massive amount of bandwidth. I advise against using this method to stream video or download large files. Use it for regular web browsing and you will be fine. Of course, I take no responsibility for your actions if you choose to violate the terms of your contract.*

The best way to do this is to install a custom ROM that features "unrestricted native tethering." A ROM like this will let you use the built-in tethering feature in system settings → "Mobile HotSpot and Tethering." You can download custom ROMs from the XDA links provided above.

If you cannot find a suitable custom ROM, or you want to have unlimited tethering on a rooted stock ROM, the next best option is to use the third-party tethering app called **WiFi Tether Router**, available for $2.50 from the Google Play Store. This app can generally be made to work, although sometimes it is finicky, which is why it is not my preferred solution. Purchase and install this app. Open it and tap "Configure WiFi Router." You may see a message about "Scan always available." If so, tap OK, uncheck "Always allow scanning," and then tap ⮌ to return to the app.

Enter the following settings:

- **Network Name SSID:** *Your choice*
- **Encryption Type:** wpa2-psk
- **WiFi Password:** *Your choice*
- **WiFi Channel:** 1
- **Interface:** wlan0

- **Method:** 3- HostApd
- **No Firmware Reload:** Unchecked
- **Drivers:** nl80211
- **WiFi Mode:** G
- **Keep Screen ON:** Unchecked
- **Prevents Stand-By:** Checked

Tap ⮌ to save these settings.

If you have T-Mobile, go to system settings → "Mobile networks" → "Access Point Names" → ADD. Enter the following settings:

- **Name:** T-Mobile Tethering
- **APN:** fast.t-mobile.com
- **Proxy:** Not set
- **Port:** Not set
- **Username:** Not set
- **Password:** Not set
- **Server:** Not set
- **MMSC:** http://mms.msg.eng.t-mobile.com/mms/wapenc
- **Multimedia message proxy:** Not set
- **Multimedia message port:** Not set
- **MCC:** 310
- **MNC:** 260
- **Authentication type:** Not set
- **APN type:** default,supl,mms
- **APN protocol:** IPv4
- **APN roaming protocol:** IPv4

Tap ⮌ to save these settings, then change the radio button to select the new APN.

Next, go to system settings → "Wi-Fi." Tap any known networks and "Forget" them. Make sure your Wi-Fi is on, but you're not connected to any networks. Now, go back to WiFi Tether Router and tap "Enable WiFi Router." If all settings are correct, your Galaxy will create a new network with the specified SSID.

Finally, download a user agent spoofer for your desktop browser of choice, and set it to an Android device. This step is very important, because without it, your carrier can still detect you're using a desktop browser. If you use Chrome, this is a good spoofer:

> https://chrome.google.com/webstore/detail/user-agent-switcher/ffhkkpnppgnfaobgihpdblnhmmbodake/related?hl=en
>
> *(Short URL: http://goo.gl/bfMhPR)*

Freezing Background Apps with Greenify to Save Battery Power

One longstanding problem with the Android OS is the way it handles apps running in the background. It tends to be too permissive, allowing apps to send and receive data and keep your device's processor working, draining valuable battery power. (Android 5.0 Lollipop has made some improvements but has not completely addressed the problem.) Greenify solves these problems. Once installed and configured, it periodically freezes apps in the background so they cannot affect your battery life. You can still launch and use frozen apps—but they'll be automatically frozen within minutes of exiting them. I notice a dramatic difference in my device's battery life when I enable Greenify, and it's one of my favorite apps.

To use Greenify, first download and install it from the Google Play Store. Open it and tap . Select apps that you do not want to let run in the background. Any apps you select will be *completely* frozen while operating in the background and will not be able to send you any notifications or transmit data. For this reason, be careful which apps you select.

Once you have selected the apps you want to freeze, tap .

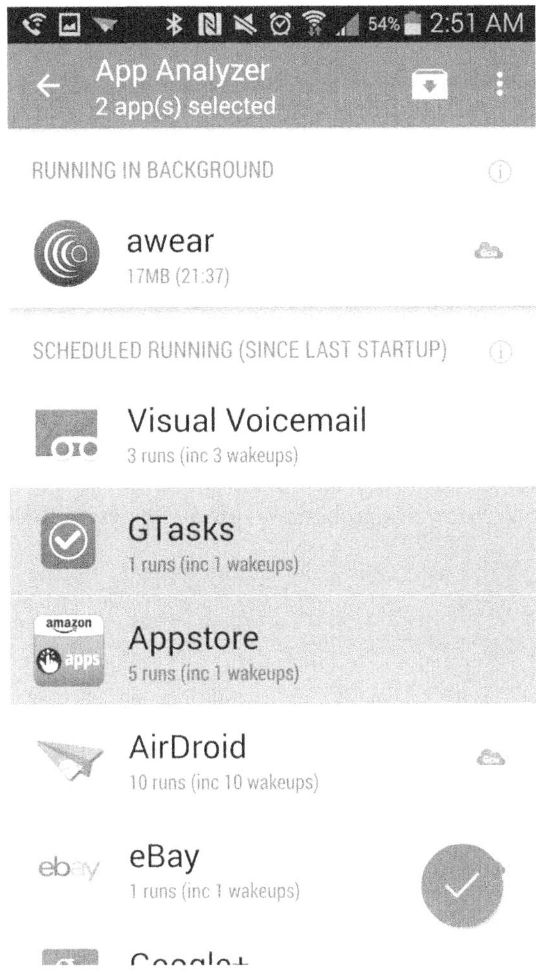

After you have done so, the ✓ will turn into zzz. You can tap this button to manually freeze all the apps you've Greenified, but this automatically occurs every few minutes even without your involvement, so it is not necessary to manually tap zzz during normal usage.

That's it! Greenify will work in the background, freezing inactive apps so they can't consume your CPU and battery power. You should experience significant improvement in your Galaxy's battery life. Remember to update Greenify periodically with the + button as you install new apps on your Galaxy.

Automating Tasks with Tasker

Tasker is one of the most powerful and unique Android apps available. It lets you program your Android to do almost any automated task you can imagine. Want your Galaxy to disable Wi-Fi and start playing music when you get in your car? No problem. Want it to automatically download and apply a new wallpaper every day? You can make it happen. Tasker has almost unlimited power but the learning curve is steep.

If you want to learn how to use Tasker, I suggest starting with this YouTube channel:

> https://www.youtube.com/playlist?list=PLjV3HijScGMynGvjJrvNNd5Q9pPy255dL
>
> (Short URL: http://goo.gl/RZdj7S)

Overclocking Your Galaxy with Custom Kernels

Want to overclock (or underclock) your Galaxy's CPU? You can do this with a custom kernel. Once you have rooted and installed a custom recovery, download a custom kernel from your carrier's page on XDA (look in the "Original Android Development" sub-forum). Make sure you do your research first—don't fry your Galaxy by changing settings you don't understand.

Getting Inverted Apps and Other Mods

If you have rooted and installed a custom recovery, you can install "flashable ZIP" mods. Flashing a ZIP mod is basically flashing a single feature you might find on a custom ROM. For example, in your device's sub-forum on XDA, you might find a flashable ZIP to enable call recording. Another popular one is inverted stock apps—a mod that turns light-colored app backgrounds to black. This is easier on the eyes and on your device's battery. To find flashable ZIP mods, look for posts tagged "[MOD]" in the "Themes and Apps" sub-section of your device's XDA forum. Note that only a few such mods were available at the time of writing; more will become available in the coming months.

DON'T Accept Over-the-Air Updates

If you root your Galaxy without installing a custom ROM, you will still receive notifications of new over-the-air updates from Samsung or your carrier. You must not install these updates, or you'll likely lose root. Furthermore, if the update patches the root exploit, you may not be able to get root back until a new exploit is developed. Take care not to sabotage your efforts by applying an OTA update to your rooted Galaxy.

Unrooting

Unrooting is easy: just download a stock ROM from your carrier's sub-forum on XDA and flash it using ODIN. Note that this will NOT reset your KNOX flag—there is no way to reset a tripped KNOX flag.

Using NFC Tags to Quickly Perform Tasks

One cool and little-known feature of the Note 5 / S6 Edge+ is their compatibility with Samsung's TecTiles 2 tags. These are tiny 1x1" stickers with embedded RFID chips. You can place them around your home, car, or office and program them to do different tasks when you tap your phone on them. For example, you might stick one on your car's dashboard and program it to toggle GPS, open the Maps app, and start playing music.

You can buy TecTiles 2 from Samsung.com, Amazon.com, or similar online retailers.

To use TecTiles 2, download and install the Samsung TecTiles app from the Google Play Store. Follow its instructions to program your TecTiles 2. Make sure NFC is turned on or your device will not detect TecTiles 2 tags when you tap it against them.

Personally, my most-used TecTile 2 is one on the wall next to my bed. I have a night and a normal profile, and my TecTile 2 switches between them. At night, I tap my Galaxy to decrease the brightness, silence it, and open the Clock app so I can set an alarm. In the morning, I tap my Galaxy on the same TecTile 2 to turn up the brightness, and turn my ringer on again.

TIP: Make sure you purchase TecTiles 2, not the original TecTiles. The originals are incompatible with the Note 5 / S6 Edge+.

Using a USB OTG Cable to Connect USB Devices

USB OTG (On-The-Go) is another little-known feature of Android and is fully supported on the Note 5 and S6 Edge+. Purchase a USB OTG adapter like the one linked below, and you'll be able to connect USB flash drives, mice, keyboards, game controllers, and other USB devices to your Galaxy. It is even possible to use USB OTG in conjunction with a USB hub to connect multiple devices at the same time. USB OTG is a great feature to know about as a Note 5 / S6 Edge+ owner, since they lack microSD card slots. USB OTG is the next best thing.

http://www.amazon.com/dp/B00871Q5PI

If connecting a USB flash drive, use a file browser like ES File Explorer (p. 310) to view and copy files.

Saving Battery Power

At various points in this book, I have made suggestions about how to conserve battery power. Here, I have consolidated them all for you and added some additional information.

In general, the greatest source of power consumption on Android devices is the screen. On the Note 5 / S6 Edge+, you will notice a massive difference in battery life depending on the brightness setting you use. If you're having battery life woes, this is the first thing to check. I find that on my Galaxy, even 20% brightness is more than enough for comfortable usage except in bright sunlight.

> ***TIP:** The Note 5 and S6 Edge+ have Super AMOLED screens, which do not have a backlight. Rather, the brightness of each individual pixel is individually controlled. This means that it takes less power to display darker colors. One trick to reduce your screen's power consumption is to use dark wallpaper and set apps to use dark themes when possible.*

The second greatest source of battery drain is apps themselves. In general, you will notice your battery life decline as you install more apps—and to some degree, this is normal. If you are installing apps that perform background services, which many do, they will use power.

However, many apps are poorly coded and drain much more than their fair share of battery power. Try to only install reputable apps (p. 167), and if your battery is draining faster than it should, uninstall or disable apps you're not using. If you root your Galaxy, install Greenify (p. 288) to completely freeze background apps. Greenify is amazing for improving your battery life.

You can view estimates of battery usage by app in system settings → "Battery." Pay particular attention to any apps listed under "Abnormal battery usage." If you're having a serious problem and can't seem to find the culprit, your only option may be to factory reset your Galaxy and install apps a couple at a time until you identify the offender.

Here are some additional ways to reclaim battery life:

- Use Power Saving Mode and Ultra Power Saving Mode (p. 254) when possible.
- Use Wi-Fi instead of cellular networks when possible; the Wi-Fi radio requires much less power. Some people think that turning Wi-Fi off saves battery life throughout the day. This is not true. If you are connected to a Wi-Fi network, your Galaxy will consume less power than if you were connected to a 4G LTE network.
- As mentioned above, use dark wallpaper for your home screen and lock screen.

- Delete unused widgets from your home screens and disable unused features in system settings.
- Enable Music Auto Off in the Music app (if you use it).
- Disable "Location" in the notification panel when you don't need GPS or other location detection.
- Disable Bluetooth in the notification panel when you don't need it.
- For apps that regularly connect to the Internet, check their settings menus to see if you can reduce the frequency with which they check for updates.
- Buy a high-capacity aftermarket battery pack from a site like Amazon.com. Read about these in Chapter 12 (p. 322).
- Avoid "task killer" apps like Juice Defender. These apps don't actually save battery power, and sometimes they even consume more. Use Greenify (p. 288) instead.
- Install a third-party launcher like Nova Launcher (p. 314) to disable the battery-draining parallax motion effect that occurs when you tilt your Galaxy on the home screen or app drawer. Unfortunately, there's no way to disable this effect in the stock launcher.
- In really tight situations, press and hold the power button, and then tap "Emergency mode (p. 273)." The functionality of your device will be greatly reduced, but your battery life will be extended as much as possible.

TIP: Advanced users may want to check out BetterBatteryStats ($2.16 on the Google Play Store). It has a steep learning curve beyond the scope of this book, but is a very powerful tool for determining what is draining your battery.

Keeping Your Battery Healthy

To make your battery last as long as possible in the long run, try to run it down to ~10% every couple weeks—but try not to go much lower, and if you must, charge it up as soon as possible thereafter. It's okay to run it down to 10% more often—just don't let it drain all the way and sit idle for an extended period of time, because doing so will eventually ruin your battery. If you treat you battery properly, it should last for as long as you own your Galaxy.

TIP: Use the included charger to charge your Galaxy when possible. Your Galaxy can absorb four hours of juice in just 10 minutes using Adaptive Fast Charging.

Online Resources / Getting Help with Your Galaxy

There are numerous Android-related online communities, but two of my favorites are Android Central and XDA. Android Central is an excellent source of Android news and reviews, while XDA is my preferred source for all things related to rooting and customization. The site has dedicated forums for each of the major carriers:

> *Note 5:* http://forum.xda-developers.com/note5; http://forums.androidcentral.com/samsung-galaxy-note-5/
>
> *Galaxy S6 Edge+:* http://forum.xda-developers.com/s6-edge-plus; http://forums.androidcentral.com/samsung-galaxy-s6-edge-plus/

Either of these websites is a good place to ask for help with your Galaxy—but in my experience, XDA is a better place to seek help with troubleshooting and anything related to rooting.

Chapter 10: Preloaded Apps

Good work. By now, you know more about your Galaxy than 99% of other users—but we're not done yet.

In this chapter, I'll give you a quick rundown of several preloaded apps whose purpose may not be immediately obvious. I tell you what each one does—often it's unclear without experimentation—and provide my commentary on overall usefulness and potential alternatives. The Note 5 and S6 Edge+ include some very good and interesting apps, but they also include some "bloatware," junk apps that Samsung gets paid to include but are not the best options available.

NOTE: Depending on your cell carrier, you may be missing one or two of the apps in this section, or you may have some extra apps not mentioned here. This is completely normal. This chapter contains the core list of stock apps, but each carrier has the final say on what comes preloaded on their phones.

Amazon

Normally, I'd complain about a shopping app being preloaded on my phone, but come on… it's Amazon. I love Amazon. You love Amazon. You probably bought this book on Amazon. Amazon is great. And, the Amazon app is actually one of the best e-commerce apps on Android. It's fast, responsive, and unlike many of its competitors, isn't missing any features. In many ways, it's actually superior to browsing Amazon on the web thanks to its streamlined interface. I frequently use the app when placing orders with Amazon.

Furthermore, the Note 5 / S6 Edge+ come with the full Amazon App, which includes the Amazon Appstore. The full Amazon App isn't available on the Google Play Store—Google only offers the "Amazon Shopping" app which excludes the app store component—because Google prohibits apps on the Play Store from having their own built-in app stores. The Amazon App normally has to be downloaded separately from Amazon's website, so it's a nice bonus that it's included.

Note that the Amazon app is not for reading Kindle books, listening to Amazon Music, or watching Amazon Instant Video. Amazon has separate apps for these services. You can get the Kindle and Prime Music apps from the Google Play Store (p. 166), but you'll need to get the Prime Instant Video app from the Amazon App.

App Source

App Source is a replacement for TouchWiz's app drawer. It offers an alternative way of organizing and categorizing your apps, and recommends other app downloads based on what you already have. In my view, App Source is pure bloatware. It doesn't add any meaningful functionality to your device, and all of the app recommendations are paid product placements. I suggest you disable (p. 267) App Source and don't look back.

Briefing

Briefing is a content aggregator based on the Flipboard app, which is available on the Google Play Store. It combines your news and social media feeds to create a personalized "magazine." By default, it's accessed by swiping left from the main home screen. I'm personally not a fan of its flashy "magazine" interface, and I don't like how easy it is to accidentally open on the home screen. I recommend disabling Briefing (p. 264), and using gReader (p. 311) instead for your RSS needs.

Calculator

A very basic calculator. Works fine, but I recommend RealCalc (p. 316) if you want a scientific calculator.

Calendar

Samsung's Calendar app, discussed at length here (p. 160). This app is sometimes called "S Planner" in Samsung's product documentation. If you don't like the Samsung Calendar for any reason, try downloading the official Google Calendar app from the Google Play Store. However, I personally think the Samsung Calendar is more attractive and intuitive than the Google Calendar.

Camera

For capturing photos and video, and discussed at length here (p. 120). Although there are alternative camera apps available on the Google Play Store, I strongly recommend sticking with the stock app, as it's quite powerful and is optimized for your Galaxy's hardware. It is possible to find alternative camera apps on the Google Play Store, but you'll find that photos taken with them are much lower quality than photos taken with the stock Camera app.

Chrome

The Android version of Google's popular Chrome web browser. Discussed at length here (p. 94). Chrome is my Android web browser of choice, for its speed and ability to sync bookmarks, open tabs, and history with my desktop computer.

Clock

Samsung's stock Clock app, discussed here (p. 143). Includes a timer, stopwatch, world clock, and alarms. If you're looking for a more beautiful and full-featured clock app, try Timely from the Google Play Store.

Contacts

Samsung's stock phone book, discussed here (p. 135).

Drive

Google Drive is a cloud storage app. It lets you upload, back up, and download files to and from an online hard drive, and synchronize your files across multiple devices. Clients are available for multiple operating systems, including Windows, Mac OS, and Android.

In general, I am a huge advocate of cloud storage services. I used to use Dropbox, but I now use Drive because it provides more free storage space and integrates with my Google account. Drive is a critical part of my workflow. I save all of my personal and work files to Google Drive folder while using my computer. This way, they're always available on my Galaxy and on any computer that has Internet access.

In addition to keeping your files backed up and available on the cloud, Drive also saves every single version of your files, so you can revert to previous versions if you accidentally overwrite a file. This has been invaluable for me and many other users.

If you aren't using a cloud storage service, pick one and start now. I suggest Google Drive, but the Note 5 / S6 Edge+ do come with 100 GB free on Microsoft OneDrive, which is also a competent service and a compelling incentive. Read more about Drive here (p. 265).

Email

A generic POP3/IMAP email client; nothing special. The Gmail app (p. 112) actually supports non-Gmail POP3 and IMAP email accounts now, so I suggest using it instead of the Email app if you have a non-Gmail email account you want to set up on your Galaxy.

If you're not satisfied with this solution, try the TouchDown (p. 320) app from the Google Play Store, which is completely free and a lot more powerful than Email.

Facebook

The official Facebook app for Android. Lets you connect with friends and family who use the Facebook social network.

Galaxy Apps

Galaxy Apps is Samsung's app store. I recommend avoiding Galaxy Apps and getting all your apps from the official Google Play Store or Amazon app store (p. 169) instead. That way, all your Android apps will be available to you in the future, whether or not you have a Samsung phone. Also, apps in Samsung's app store aren't always kept up to date, and the selection of apps is extremely limited compared to the Google Play Store.

That said, there are a couple situations in which you might have to use Galaxy Apps. First, some free software updates (e.g., voice synthesis files, camera modes, themes, etc.) must be downloaded with this app. Second, if you go to the "Exclusives" tab, you can redeem several free gifts (p. 251) from Samsung, some of which are worthwhile.

Gallery

For viewing and editing photos and videos. Discussed at length here (p. 130). If you don't like the stock Gallery app, try downloading Focus from the Google Play Store.

Gmail

Gmail is Google's official Gmail Android app. Used for sending and receiving mail with your Gmail account. The best Gmail client available. Discussed at length here (p. 112).

Google

This app is nothing more than a shortcut to Google Now (p. 174). It does the exact same thing as pressing and holding .

Google Settings

Google Settings consolidates a bunch of miscellaneous Google settings for apps and services like Play Games, Google Now, and Google Fit. Unfortunately, the key word is "miscellaneous." Google could have made this app a full-fledged Google control panel—a central resource to control all your Google-related settings. However, they didn't. The app is really just a hodgepodge of settings that they couldn't fit anywhere else, plus shortcuts to settings pages in some, but not all, of the Google apps on the Note 5 / S6 Edge+. It's a bizarre app. You might want to look through it once to make sure everything is set the way you want it, but you probably won't ever use it again.

Hangouts

Hangouts is the mobile app for Google's chat platform—the same one you see when you're logged into Gmail on your computer. Hangouts is a fine app and Google has improved it a lot since it came out. It does not significantly drain your battery while running and works very well for text or video chatting with your contacts. If you use Gmail chat a lot, Hangouts is the best app to chat on the go.

> ***TIP:*** *Hangouts now also supports SMS (text messaging) and MMS (picture messaging). If you want to use Hangouts instead of Messages for texting, open it and go to ☰ (in upper left corner) → "Settings" → "SMS" and enable SMS.*

Instagram

Instagram is a social media network based on photo sharing. Whereas Facebook and Google+ are designed to let you share links, status updates, photos, and more, Instagram emphasizes photo sharing and de-emphasizes everything else. You can browse other users' photos, and follow users if you particularly like their taste. Other users can browse your photos and follow you as well. The more followers you get, the higher your Instagram "social status" rises.

Internet

The stock Android web browser. I recommend using Chrome (p. 94) instead, which is faster and syncs with the desktop version of Chrome. However, Internet does have some perks, like the ability to save web pages for offline viewing and to auto-fill login information using the fingerprint reader.

Lookout

Lookout does three things: 1) antivirus, 2) backup of your Google contacts and photos, and 3) allows you to locate your phone by GPS if you lose it.

In my opinion, Lookout is the best all-in-one Android security app available… but despite that, it's unnecessary and redundant.

- The anti-virus feature is unnecessary as long as you adhere to my best practices (p. 167) when downloading new apps. I've never used an antivirus app on Android, and I've never gotten a virus. Research apps before you download them, the way I teach you to, and you'll never get a virus either.
- The backup function is redundant because your Google contacts are already automatically backed up with Google, and you should be using Google+'s automatic photo backup (p. 276) to back up your photos directly to your Google account instead of to Lookout's website.
- The device-locating feature is helpful, but you can already locate your device using Android Device Manager (p. 228), or if you want even more powerful features, Cerberus (p. 308) (my personal favorite).

Basically, I consider Lookout to be bloatware because it targets users who are misinformed and/or scared of nonexistent threats. It's designed to suck you in so you'll pay the monthly subscription fee. As long as you know what you're doing—which you do, by now—you don't need Lookout.

Maps

The Android version of Google Maps. An amazing app—the only one you'll ever need to navigate. Discussed at length here (p. 150).

Messages

The stock app for sending text messages (SMS) and multimedia messages (MMS). I personally like it a lot. If you don't, popular alternatives on the Google Play Store include Textra, Chomp SMS, and Go SMS. As I mentioned earlier, you can also now use Hangouts as your SMS client.

Messenger

Messenger is Facebook's chat app, and lets you chat with your Facebook friends for free. This and other chat apps like WhatsApp (p. 320) have become popular because they let you text without burning up your SMS limit. Messenger used to be a part of the Facebook app. Why Facebook decided to split it off into a separate app is anyone's guess.

Don't confuse Messenger with Messages, which is the built-in text messaging app.

Microsoft Office

The Note 5 and S6 Edge+ are preloaded with Microsoft's new, official Office apps, including Word, Excel, and PowerPoint. These apps have near-perfect compatibility with all your Office documents, and are a big improvement over older third-party Android office suites such as Hancom Office and Polaris Office. In my opinion, they are the best office apps available for Android. Read more about them here (p. 182).

Milk

Milk is Samsung's streaming music service. It allows you to listen to dozens of different curated "stations" in multiple genres. It's free to listen, but there are some limitations. You'll have to endure between-song ads, you can't listen offline, and you can only skip a limited number of songs per hour. To remove these restrictions, you can sign up for a subscription for $3.99 per month.

In my opinion, there are much better options on the market than Milk. Pandora and Spotify come to mind. In particular, I think Spotify is the best streaming music value today. It costs more than Milk ($9.99 per month), but it has a huge catalog and lets you stream anything you want, at any time. Read more here (p. 145).

Music

The stock music player. A competent app, but check out Poweramp on the Google Play Store if you want something more powerful. Discussed here (p. 147).

My Files

My Files is a file manager. It lets you access the file system of your Galaxy.

My Files works fine but it is inferior and limited compared to the excellent and free ES File Explorer (p. 310). ES File Explorer has a better interface, allows root (p. 281) access to file directories, and is frequently updated. Ditch My Files and don't look back. The one exception is that you'll need to use My Files to view files you've hidden using Private Mode (p. 229).

OneDrive

Microsoft's cloud storage service. The Note 5 / S6 Edge+ come with 100 GB free on OneDrive. I personally use Google Drive (p. 265) instead, although OneDrive gets the job done as well.

OneNote

The Android version of Microsoft's note-taking app OneNote. Personally, I'm a fan of Evernote (p. 310) for note-taking, but many folks swear by OneNote.

Phone

The stock dialer. It is possible to replace it (check out ExDialer on the Google Play Store), but I usually stick with the stock dialer myself. Discussed here (p. 100).

Photos

The Photos app is essentially Google's version of the Gallery app. It lets you browse and view photos saved on your Galaxy. However, unlike the Gallery app, it also displays photos that are saved to your Google Photos account online, and lets you automatically upload camera photos to your Google account, where they can be safely stored and viewed at https://photos.google.com/.

Personally, I stick to the Gallery app for viewing photos on my phone, but I do take advantage of Photos' automatic backup feature, and I suggest you do, too. Read here (p. 276) for more information on enabling auto-backup.

Play Store

The number one, fully official source for downloading new apps for your Galaxy. Discussed here (p. 166). The second biggest app store is the Amazon app store (p. 169).

Play Movies & TV/Music

These apps let you buy and consume media from Google. Although only Play Movies & TV and Play Music come preloaded on the Note 5 / S6 Edge+, you can download the other Play apps free from the Play Store, including Play Games, Play Books, and Play Newsstand.

The Play apps work well, have reasonable prices, and have a large selection. Whether you use them or not will likely depend on the degree to which you've already bought into other platforms. For example, I read all of my eBooks on my Kindle, so I buy eBooks exclusively from Amazon and never from Play Books. Similarly, if you are already invested in iTunes, you might not want to buy music from Google Music. But if you're not already invested anywhere else, Google Play is not a bad platform on which to start a media collection. The situation you want to avoid is buying a bunch of media on one platform and then switching to another platform later. If you do this, your investment is wasted. Read more here (p. 185).

S Health

S Health offers several tools to track and maintain your fitness, including a pedometer, a GPS tracker for running, a food tracker, a weight diary, and more. See more information on S Health here (p. 258).

S Note (Note 5 only)

S Note is Samsung's memo pad app. It's designed to let you take full advantage of the S Pen and the Wacom digitizer built into the Note 5. S Note is not bloatware—it's actually a very well-designed and useful app. I even prefer it to popular third-party memo pad apps like Papyrus.

S Note is discussed at length here (p. 205).

S Voice

S Voice is Samsung's personal assistant. It offers most of the same features as Google Now (p. 174), but unlike Google Now, doesn't have a card system. Discussed here (p. 181).

Samsung Gear

Samsung Gear is the companion app for Samsung Gear smartwatches. If you buy one, use this app to connect it to your Galaxy. If you don't have a Gear Smartwatch, this app doesn't do anything.

Samsung Pay

Samsung Pay is the configuration app for Samsung's upcoming tap-to-pay service. When Samsung Pay goes live in late September 2015, you'll be able to use your Galaxy to pay at *any* standard credit card terminal. Use the app to add your credit and debit cards. Read more about Samsung Pay here (p. 248).

Samsung+

The Samsung+ app gives you one-touch access to Samsung customer support (including live video chat), app recommendations, Galaxy tips & tricks, and more. While you probably won't use Samsung+ on a daily basis, I would recommend checking it out because it does have some valuable content, especially for first-time Galaxy owners. Note that you'll need to sign into a Samsung account to use this app.

Scrapbook

Scrapbook is a repository for content you clip with the S Pen's Smart Select feature. Read more about using the S Pen and Scrapbook here (p. 195).

Settings

The system settings app. Same as swiping down the notification panel (p. 70) and tapping ⚙. Discussed here (p. 58).

SideSync

A new app from Samsung that lets you mirror your Galaxy's screen on your computer, or on an Android tablet. See a tutorial on SideSync here (p. 237).

Skype

The Android version of the Skype video chat client.

Smart Manager

A utility that lets you monitor battery usage, storage, RAM, and device security. Read more here (p. 274).

Video

Samsung's stock video player app (launched from the Gallery if you tap on a video file). Works for viewing basic videos, but if you need an advanced video player, try MX Player (p. 313) or VLC from the Google Play Store.

Voice Recorder

Samsung's stock application for recording audio.

Voice Search

Voice Search is Google's voice search utility. Opening it does the exact same thing as saying "OK, Google" out loud when Google Now (p. 174) is enabled.

Wallet

Google's tap-to-pay app. Use this to add your credit and debit cards, which you can then use at any credit card terminal that accepts contactless payments. Google Wallet will be mostly obsolete when Samsung Pay (p. 248) goes live in September 2015, because unlike Google Wallet, Samsung Pay taps into the Note 5 / S6 Edge+'s built-in LoopPay chip to let you use your Galaxy to pay at *any* credit card terminal, not just contactless-enabled terminals.

WhatsApp

A chat client that lets you text other WhatsApp users without burning through your SMS limit. WhatsApp is hugely popular among young folks, especially outside of the United States. Whether or not you'll want to use it depends on 1) if you have a limited number of text messages on your plan, and 2) whether any of your family and friends use it. Note that you can only use WhatsApp to message other WhatsApp users.

YouTube

Lets you stream videos from YouTube, the biggest video site on the Internet.

Chapter 11: The 50 All-Time Best Android Apps

Below is a list of my all-time best app recommendations, taken from my book, *The 50 All-Time Best Android Apps*. Some are free and some are paid. I am in no way affiliated with any of the developers, and I stand to gain nothing from your purchases. My recommendations come from my own experience and research. http://www.amazon.com/dp/B00L8ES1L2

1Weather

1Weather is an attractive, functional weather app. It contains all the weather information you need, including hourly, daily, and weekly forecasts. It also offers real-time weather mapping, sunrise/sunset information, and push notifications to keep you informed of changing conditions. Plus, you can easily switch between cities when you travel. In my opinion, no other Android weather app comes close to 1Weather's functionality, style, and simplicity.

Price: Free from the Google Play Store / $1.99 in-app purchase to remove ads

AirDroid

AirDroid offers a unique way to control your Android device—using a web browser on your desktop computer. After you have installed the app on your Android, you just go to http://web.airdroid.com/ in your browser to open the control panel (or install the new system tray utility on your computer). From there, you can view photos and videos, change your ringtone, manage contacts, send and receive text messages, listen to music on your Android device, transfer files, take screenshots, and more.

In this way, AirDroid is good for many purposes—mass updates of your phone book with the convenience of a keyboard, showing photos on a big screen, transferring files wirelessly instead of over a USB cable, texting on your computer, and more. Read more here (p. 280).

Price: Free from the Google Play Store / $1.99 per month for premium

Amazon

The Amazon app has two components: 1) online shopping and 2) Amazon's app store. Prior to 2014, the Amazon Appstore was a separate app, but it's now integrated with the e-commerce component in the Amazon app. This 2-in-1 value means that the Amazon app is one of the all-time best. The shopping experience is bug-free and just as good, if not better, than the desktop experience. And, the app store component makes it easier than ever to check Amazon's free app of the day. The Amazon app is a must-have, and best of all, it's preloaded on the Note 5 and S6 Edge+. Read more here (p. 169).

Price: Free, preloaded

Authenticator

Google Authenticator is a two-factor security solution that works with many websites that require a password login, including Gmail, Dropbox, Lastpass, and Evernote.

What is a two-factor security solution?

With Authenticator, anyone who logs into your (Gmail, Dropbox, Lastpass, Evernote, etc.) account will be required to input a code generated by Authenticator in addition to the password. This way, even if someone steals your password, they will not be able to log into your account without also having physical possession of your Android. Authenticator even works when your device has no Internet connection. The biggest downside is that only a select few websites support it.

Once you're comfortable using Authenticator, consider downloading the "Authy" app from the Play Store. It's like a beefed-up version of Authenticator that backs up all your 2-factor keys online, so if you lose or reset your Galaxy, you won't risk getting locked out of your accounts.

Price: Free from the Google Play Store

Barcode Scanner

Barcode Scanner allows you to scan barcodes and QR codes. I use it to comparison shop at the store, to quickly pull up product reviews, and to scan QR codes. Barcode Scanner also happens to be required for some features in Authenticator.

Price: Free from the Google Play Store

Boson X

Boson X is one of the few Android games that has stood the test of time for me. It is a unique arcade-style game with a fantastic soundtrack. It's easy to pick up and play when you only have a few minutes to kill, but deep enough to keep you occupied for hours if you want. Not many games strike this balance as well as Boson X.

Price: $2.99 from the Google Play Store

Call Recorder by skvalex

Have you ever wanted to record voice calls on your Android phone? Although quite expensive at $9.95, Call Recorder by skvalex is the best call recording app available and is capable of recording to both WAV and MP3. Plus, root access is not required. But before recording any calls, make sure you're aware of the wiretapping laws in your jurisdiction.

Price: Free trial from http://goo.gl/u690rm / $9.95 to buy on the Google Play Store

Cerberus Anti Theft

Most "Best App" lists say that Lookout is the best Android anti-theft app available, but I disagree. Cerberus is my security app of choice. Unlike Lookout and most other phone-locating security apps, Cerberus has absolutely no monthly fee—only a one-time purchase of $4. Better yet, it doesn't slow down your phone, doesn't drain your battery, works reliably, and can even hide itself from the app drawer. Its online control panel is simple and streamlined and works every time. Additionally, unlike with Android Device Manager (p. 228), Cerberus lets you remotely control your Galaxy by sending text messages—which it can receive even when it's outside of data coverage. I trust Cerberus more than any other app to help me retrieve my Galaxy should I ever lose it.

Price: Free trial from the Google Play Store / ~$4 to buy

Chipotle

No, this is not a joke! For a long time, Chipotle only had an iOS app and they did a poor job of announcing the Android app when they finally released it, so I want to spread the word. The app is well-designed, easy to use, and most importantly, allows you to order online and go straight to the register to pick up your order. No more waiting in line. Any app that can save 20-30 minutes of my day is a winner. If you don't eat at Chipotle but you do eat at other quick serve restaurants, see if they have a similar app on the Google Play store that let you skip the line. Many do.

Price: Free from the Google Play Store

Cloud Print

Want to wirelessly print from your Galaxy? Cloud Print is an official Google app that lets you do exactly that. You just install a Chrome extension on your desktop computer, register your printer with Google Cloud Print, install the Android app, and you're set. No printer drivers or complicated wireless settings needed. The Android app lets you print documents, photos, PDFs, and more. You can also print directly from mobile Chrome or any app that supports the Share Via (p. 91) tool. Read more here (p. 262).

Price: Free from the Google Play Store

eBay

eBay's mobile app is free and much better than its slow and buggy mobile website. In the past, the official app was inferior to a third-party app called Pocket Auctions, but it's come a long way since then. It supports all major features, including search filters, best offers, PayPal payments, and so on. If you're a regular eBay user, get it now. You'll also want to grab the free PayPal (p. 315) app for additional PayPal features beyond auction payments.

Price: Free from the Google Play Store

ES File Explorer

ES File Explorer is a full-featured file manager. Although Android does not prominently feature a file and folder storage system like on desktop computers, these things do exist behind the scenes and ES File Explorer lets you access them. It is much more powerful than the "My Files" app that comes with the Note 5 / S6 Edge+, and I recommend it wholeheartedly for copying, moving, renaming, and deleting your files. If you've rooted (p. 281) your Galaxy, ES can also access read-only system partitions.

Price: Free from the Google Play Store

Evernote

Evernote is a cross-platform cloud note-taking app, and supports both Windows and MacOS in addition to Android. How many of us just email notes to ourselves, or scrawl them on the backs of napkins? Evernote is a much easier and more secure way of keeping notes organized and synchronized between devices. Any note you save into Evernote is automatically backed up in the cloud and copied to your other devices, so you'll never lose data or be without your notes. I use Evernote for shopping lists, journaling, organizing notes for my books, brainstorming, and more. And unless you store a ton of images or audio recordings in your notes, you'll be totally fine with the free service.

Price: Free trial from the Google Play Store; desktop version available at https://evernote.com / Premium service $5 per month

Fenix for Twitter

I used to recommend Talon for Twitter, but it's defunct now. With Talon gone, I believe Fenix is the best option. It's stable, well-designed, and functional. Of all the Twitter apps I've tested, it's what I always come back to.

Price: $4.49 from the Google Play Store

Google Drive

Google Drive is so much more than a simple app. Drive gives you cloud storage space, where you can upload and store files from your computer or mobile device. (And if you weren't already aware, you already have a Drive account if you have a Gmail account. Access it at http://drive.google.com.)

The benefits of using Drive are threefold. First, any files saved on your Drive are backed up. If your computer hard drive crashes or you lose your Galaxy, any files saved to your

Drive will survive. Second, since you can access Drive via your computer or the app on your Galaxy, your files are available no matter where you are. Forget to email yourself a file? No problem—as long as your desktop computer has the Drive software installed and you saved the file to your Drive, you can get it with the Android app. Third, Drive saves every version of every file. Accidentally overwrite your thesis? Just log into the web interface and roll back the file.

Personally, I have the Windows/Mac desktop Drive software and the mobile app, and I save all my work files to my Drive folder. This way, I never lose data and I am never without my data.

In the past, I recommended Dropbox instead of Drive. However, Google now offers significantly more free space than Dropbox (15 GB vs. 2 GB), and its software is just as good. If you aren't already using Drive, start today.

Price: Free from the Google Play Store

Google Rewards

Google Rewards is a free download from the Google Play Store that gives you Play Store credit in exchange for filling out market research surveys. When you first install the app, you'll fill out some demographic information, and then whenever you fit the profile for a survey that Google is running, you'll get a notification in your notification tray. It takes a minimal amount of time to respond to these surveys and you can earn $50+ per year doing it—often times enough to cover all of your Google Play purchases. Just be honest with your responses—Google employs a variety of techniques to screen your answers, and if they detect you're trying to game the system, they'll stop sending you surveys.

Price: Free from the Google Play Store

gReader

gReader is an RSS news reader that synchronizes with a Feedly account to bring all your news to your Galaxy. If you aren't familiar with RSS feeds, here's what you need to know: RSS feeds are files that contain recent posts from their respective websites. Most news websites and blogs publish them. When you import them into an RSS reader like Feedly, they let you read news from multiple sources all in one place without visiting many different websites. It's fast and convenient. gReader is simply an app for using your Feedly account on your Galaxy

If you want the best-looking RSS app, you might prefer the official Feedly app or Pulse. But for a functional, no-nonsense RSS reader with plenty of functions like offline reading, gReader is the way to go. There's a free version, but the paid version removes ads and provides extra features like better widgets and voice dictation of articles.

Price: Free trial from the Google Play Store / $4.69 to buy

GTasks

Many Android devices (including the Note 5 and S6 Edge+) don't come with a good to-do app, and where those apps do exist, they generally don't sync with Google Tasks. GTasks is a simple to-do list that solves this problem. If you want a simple to-do list that you can access from both your Galaxy and your Gmail account on your computer, GTasks is the way to go. It has a nice, simple interface, and it has never failed to save and synchronize my tasks.

Price: Free trial from the Google Play Store / $4.99 to buy

Key Ring Reward Cards & Coupon

Key Ring stores all of your loyalty and shopping rewards cards. Don't let those frequent flyer miles go to waste! Better yet, it allows you to easily share cards with other Key Ring users and access weekly fliers and coupons that cashiers can scan right from your phone's screen. The one downside is the in-app ads, and there is no premium version to remove them.

Price: Free from the Google Play Store

Kitchen Timer

Kitchen Timer corrects the one-timer-at-a-time deficiency found in the stock Clock (p. 143) app. Kitchen Timer allows you to set up to three timers at once and doesn't require any unusual installation privileges. It's a great, bare-bones app and is completely free. I use it all the time when I'm cooking multiple dishes at once.

Price: Free from the Google Play Store

Lastpass

Lastpass is a cross-platform password manager. I use it extensively on my desktop to autofill personal information and credit card numbers, generate random passwords, and store my login info for everything. The Android client is a must-have because it makes all your passwords available on the go, and has an excellent helper app that can autofill login information in any app. If you're looking for a password manager, I highly recommend

Lastpass. I used to use Dashlane, but Lastpass has been improved a lot in the last year, and offers a better experience for a lot less money.

Price: Desktop client is free from https://lastpass.com/, Android client is free from the Google Play Store; subscription (which is necessary for cloud syncing to Android) is $12/year

MX Player

MX Player is my favorite video player. The built-in Video app is sufficient if you only watch short clips, but if you watch a lot of movies, TV shows, or files in obscure formats, MX Player will provide a much better experience. It also handles subtitles like a champ. The paid version removes ads.

Price: Free trial from the Google Play Store / $5.99 to buy

Mycelium Bitcoin Wallet

If you don't know what Bitcoin is, you can skip this app. If you do, all you need to know is that Mycelium is the best Bitcoin wallet for Android. It has features that other apps don't, such as full BIP38 paper wallet support, and it's open source so you can be confident it's safe to use. I always keep some bitcoin in my Mycelium wallet in case I stumble upon a store or restaurant that accepts it.

Price: Free from the Google Play Store

Netflix

If you have a Netflix subscription, the Netflix app is a must-have. If you don't have a Netflix subscription, what are you thinking?!? Netflix is one of the best consumer services in today's economy, period. The value is… amazing. Get a subscription so you can watch amazing video like Breaking Bad, House of Cards, Sherlock, Law & Order, and more. Early adopters of the Note 5 / S6 Edge+ on T-Mobile can even get a free year of Netflix (redeem by 10/30/2015):

http://www.samsungpromotions.com/t-mobilenetflix

Price: Free from the Google Play Store (Netflix streaming subscription required)

Nova Launcher

Nova Launcher is a highly customizable home screen replacement. If you're tired of the stock TouchWiz look, then try Nova Launcher. You can customize the number of rows and columns for the apps displayed on each screen, margins, scroll effects, shadows, your app tray, and much more. You can even hide apps from your app drawer.

Price: Free trial from the Google Play Store / $4.00 to buy

Office Suite 8 Pro

Office Suite 8 Pro is an excellent, feature-packed office suite for Android. It's fast, highly compatible, and has a great user interface. If your number one priority is document compatibility, you'll be better off using the official Microsoft Office apps that come preloaded on the Note 5 / S6 Edge+. But, if you value user interface design and ease of use, Office Suite 8 Pro is arguably better than Microsoft's apps. It's not cheap, but if you wait until a major holiday to buy it, you can sometimes get it on sale for $9.99 or less from Google Play and/or the Amazon app store.

Price: Free 7-day trial from the Google Play Store / $14.99 to buy

Pandora

Pandora is a music streaming service. Its library of songs is much smaller than Spotify's and it doesn't let you play specific songs, but it's a great resource for discovering new music similar to what you already like. I don't pull up Pandora when I want to hear a specific song, but rather when I want to hear something new. Pandora is free, but you can only skip 6 songs per hour and you have to endure ads unless you pay for the premium service. I don't really recommend subscribing, though—your money is much better spent with Spotify (p. 145). Take what you get from Pandora's free service and run with it. Read more here (p. 145).

Price: Free from the Google Play Store / subscription service $4.99 per month

PayPal

If you use PayPal for personal payments or business, the Android app is a must-have. It's much faster and easier than using the full PayPal site on a mobile browser and supports most common functions. (Though, it does not have the ability to create a custom invoice, which I would like to see added.) I use it to square up restaurant checks with friends and family, to make online purchases, and to take payments for my business.

Price: Free from the Google Play Store

Play Music

Although Google Play Music is not as powerful as some other third-party MP3 players, the features of the Play Music ecosystem nevertheless make it the best way to listen to your music collection on the go. Why? Google allows you to upload up to 20,000 of your own songs to the cloud—for free—which are then available to stream on your Galaxy via the Play Music app, from your web browser, or from any public computer. This allows you to have your entire MP3 collection available on-demand through your Galaxy, without requiring any storage space. But don't worry—if you want to download music for offline playback, Play Music makes that easy, too. Overall, Play Music is an amazing and free service and is the absolute best way to take your music collection with you. Read more here (p. 146).

Price: Free from the Google Play Store / Download Google Play Music for Chrome from https://support.google.com/googleplay/answer/4627259?hl=en

Pocket Casts

Pocket Casts is, in my opinion, the best podcast app for Android. It does a magnificent job of managing, filtering, downloading, and playing your podcasts, and can even back up your settings to the cloud.

Price: $3.99 on the Google Play Store

Pushbullet

Pushbullet has 2 parts: an Android app and a Chrome desktop browser extension. When both are installed and configured, all notifications on your Galaxy are mirrored on your desktop computer, and you can even browse and reply to texts from your computer. Pushbullet is a must-have, because when you're sitting at your computer, it's far more convenient to see notifications on your monitor and reply to texts with your keyboard than to pick up your phone every time it sounds a notification.

Pushbullet's functionality somewhat overlaps with AirDroid (p. 280), but is a great choice if you don't need all the extra features of AirDroid. Personally, I have both installed on my Galaxy. I use Pushbullet on a daily basis because it's lighter weight and runs transparently in the background, and I start up AirDroid whenever I need device management features beyond just notifications and texting.

Price: Free from the Google Play Store

RealCalc

RealCalc has a nicer interface than the stock Calculator app and offers scientific functions. It also supports RPN mode and allows for a great deal of customization. The paid version adds more features such as fraction conversions, landscape mode, and support for degrees and minutes. It's my preferred Android calculator app.

Price: Free trial from the Google Play Store / $3.49 to buy

Reddit is Fun

If you read Reddit, I highly recommend Reddit is Fun. It's a much better way to browse Reddit than using a mobile browser and has all the features you could possibly want. There are a few other Reddit readers on the Google Play Store, but in my experience Reddit is Fun is the best of them.

Price: Free trial from the Google Play Store / $1.99 to buy

Ringtone Maker

Ringtone Maker does exactly what it sounds like: it lets you edit MP3s and other audio files to create custom ringtones and easily assign them to contacts on your phone. It's much easier to use Ringtone Maker's all-in-one package than to try to use a separate music editor and figure out how to set the resulting file as a ringtone in OS settings. Ringtone Maker is absolutely free and adds a feature that should be, but rarely is, included by default on Android smartphones. Read more here (p. 141).

Price: Free from the Google Play Store

Scanner Radio

This app is awesome. It allows you to live stream police and emergency services radio frequencies to your Android. If you are in close proximity to an emergency response, you often can tune into the local frequencies and find out what's going on first-hand. Sometimes, you can even hear foot chases and other criminal pursuits as they happen.

Price: Free trial from the Google Play Store / $2.99 to buy

Screen Adjuster

Screen Adjuster is a small, free app that allows you to set your screen's brightness below the normal minimum level. It's very useful in dark environments to avoid losing your night vision or to avoid distracting other people in public venues like movie theaters. I use it before bed to minimize the impact of my Android's screen on my melatonin levels. Science!

Price: Free trial from the Google Play Store / $0.99 to buy

SMS Backup & Restore

This app allows you to backup and restore your SMS and MMS messages to your Galaxy's internal storage or Dropbox. It works seamlessly and quickly unlike many other text message backup apps. I highly recommend using it to back up your messages or to transfer them to a new phone. (Note: you can also use your Samsung account to back up text messages (p. 276).)

Price: Free trial from the Google Play Store / $3.49 to buy

Snes9xEX+

This app is an excellent and free Super Nintendo emulator. After you have downloaded ROM game files from the Internet, you can load them into SNES9xEX+ and play them exactly as they were on the original console. (Legal caveat: you must own the original cartridges to legally download ROM files.) Remember Super Mario World, Zelda, and Final Fantasy II/III? Great games—play them with Snes9xEX+.

The author of Snes9xEX+, Robert Broglia, sells emulators for most other classic gaming consoles as well. Snes9xEX+ is the free one that hooks you. The rest cost money, but they're all excellent apps.

Price: Free from the Google Play Store

Speedtest

Speedtest is a free app that tests the speed of your Internet connection, be it Wi-Fi or cellular. It's useful to help diagnose connectivity problems, or just to show your friends how much faster your 4G LTE cell connection is than their home cable connection.

Price: Free from the Google Play Store

Spotify

Spotify is a streaming music app that competes with Pandora. Unlike Pandora, however, it allows you to select one artist and listen exclusively to them for free on shuffle mode. (For the smartphone app, that is; the desktop and tablet apps actually allow you to pick any song you want at any time—even without a subscription—but with advertisements.) If you want to select songs individually on the Android smartphone app, you have to pay for the premium service. Spotify is a great complement to Pandora and has a huge library of songs (there's not much you won't find on it). If you subscribe to one streaming service, Spotify gets my vote. I have a subscription to it. Read more here (p. 145).

Price: Free from the Google Play Store / subscription service $9.99 per month

SuperBeam

SuperBeam is the best way to perform blazing-fast wireless file transfers between Android devices. SuperBeam uses Wi-Fi Direct but implements it a lot more effectively than the Android OS does. When two Android phones have SuperBeam installed, they are on the same page—end of story. There's no messing around with complicated device settings like Android Beam or Wi-Fi Direct. I strongly recommend you use SuperBeam to transfer large files between Android devices.

Price: Free trial from the Google Play Store / $1.99 to buy

Tapatalk

If you read or participate in any online discussion forums, Tapatalk is an absolute must-have app. It condenses forum interfaces into a mobile-friendly format and makes it much easier to read and post from your Android device. It's kind of like an RSS reader, but for forums. Tapatalk is probably one of my most-used apps—in fact, I would even use a desktop version if they made it. Nearly all major online discussion forums support Tapatalk as of 2015.

UPDATE: The most recent versions of Tapatalk are going downhill—I suspect the company has been bought out or is being influenced by some financial interest. I suggest downloading Tapatalk 4.9.5, the last good version of the app, instead of getting the latest from the Google Play Store.

http://www.apkmirror.com/apk/tapatalk-inc/tapatalk/tapatalk-4-9-5-android-apk-download/

(Short URL: http://goo.gl/XgK7bS)

Install it using the .APK installation method (p. 170).

Price: Free trial from the Google Play Store / $2.99 to buy

TeamViewer

TeamViewer is a cross-platform screen-sharing program. You set up the client on your desktop computer and then access and control it from your Android phone. Yes, this means you can control your computer's screen right from your Android device! It works very well, even over slower connections. TeamViewer is incredibly cool and useful, and best of all it's completely free for personal use.

Price: Free from the Google Play Store; desktop client available at http://www.teamviewer.com/

TeslaLED

TeslaLED is a free flashlight program that's brighter than the built-in Flashlight (p. 267) toggle. It includes several handy widgets for quickly turning your camera flash LED into a flashlight. I also really like that it doesn't request any unusual permissions at installation.

Price: Free from the Google Play Store / $1.00 optional donation

TouchDown For Smartphones

TouchDown is the best Microsoft Outlook replacement, bar none. It has all the built-in features of Outlook including Mail, Calendar, Tasks, and so on. If your work uses Exchange, TouchDown is simply an excellent way to keep up with your work on the go. Moreover, because it consolidates all the functions of Outlook into a single app, it creates a very nice barrier between your work life and your personal life. It's not cheap, but if you use Outlook it's well worth it.

Price: Free trial from the Google Play Store / $19.99 to buy

TuneIn Radio

This app allows you to stream local and national AM/FM radio stations over the Internet. It's very useful for listening to radio stations in other parts of the country, for example while traveling. It can also be useful for tuning in to local stations when your regular radio reception is poor but you have a good Internet connection.

Price: Free trial from the Google Play Store / $9.99 to buy

Uber

Unless you've been living under a rock for the last year, you've probably heard about Uber. It's a new taxi/private car/rideshare service that competes with traditional taxi cabs (and has been the target of a lot of lawsuits from taxi unions). Instead of flagging down a taxi on a city street or calling a dispatcher, you just launch the Uber app and request a ride. The wait is usually short and the drivers professional. Payment is made through the app, and no tip is required or expected, making Uber cheaper than most regular taxis. Uber operates in medium-to-large cities in 57 countries.

Price: Free from the Google Play Store

WhatsApp Messenger

Don't have unlimited texts? No problem. Get WhatsApp and get your friends to do the same. It uses a proprietary network to send and receives text-based messages without burning through your SMS quota. There are a lot of services like WhatsApp, but it has my recommendation because it is the most popular one and your friends and family are more likely to already have it. WhatsApp comes preloaded on the Note 5 / S6 Edge+.

Price: Free from the Google Play Store

Wikipedia

The Wikipedia app is a fast and lightweight way to read Wikipedia articles on your Galaxy. For me, there's one key reason it's better than accessing the mobile website through a browser: its ability to invert colors so you can read white text on a black background. Not only is this easier on the eyes, it's also easier on battery life.

Price: Free from the Google Play Store

ZArchiver

ZArchiver is an archive manager compatible with a huge array of file types, including .zip, .rar, .7z, and many, many more. It is very fast, lightweight, and completely free.

Price: Free from the Google Play Store / $1.30 optional donation

Chapter 12: Accessory Shopping Guide

There is a wide range of accessories available for the Note 5 and S6 Edge+. In this chapter, I provide examples of both official and third party accessories to give you an idea of what's available. I also recommend specific accessories that I have experience with.

Please note that there are hundreds, if not thousands of accessories already available for the Note 5 and S6 Edge+, and it would be impossible to cover them all here. If you're interested in any of the accessories I discuss in this chapter, you should do your own research to compare prices and brands. For example, many of the official Samsung accessories I discuss have off-brand alternatives that may be just as good and/or cheaper. And, the products I link to may be cheaper from other vendors. This chapter is only a starting point.

TIP: *Register your Galaxy on Samsung's website to receive a coupon good for 30% off any mobile accessory $59.99 or less.*

http://www.samsung.com/us/support/register/product

After registering, you'll receive an email entitled "Your gift for registering your Galaxy," containing your coupon code for the Samsung store, linked below.

http://www.samsung.com/us/mobile/cell-phones-accessories

Cases

There are several categories of cases for the Note 5 and S6 Edge+. The most general and widely appealing type is the **TPU case**. TPU cases are flexible but firm plastic. They hold their shape extremely well and resist stretching over time. TPU cases only became popular in the last few years, but they're a huge step up from the old cheap rubber cases that caught on fabric and were easily stretched.

I've been using Cush's S-Line TPU case with my Note 5 ($8 street price) and I like it a lot for its slim profile and affordable price. For the S6 Edge+, the Spigen Rugged Armor TPU case ($10 street price) provides a similar experience.

Note 5: http://www.amazon.com/dp/B0112ZPXXA

S6 Edge+: http://www.amazon.com/dp/B010MWEOCU

These cases offer a great balance of slimness, grip in the hand, price, and protection. They easily slip in and out of a pocket but aren't slippery in the hand. They also have great volume and power buttons that never fail to make contact with the buttons on the Galaxy.

Similar TPU cases are available from most carriers' retail stores, although you'll likely pay 2-3 times what you would pay for an online brand like Spigen or Cush.

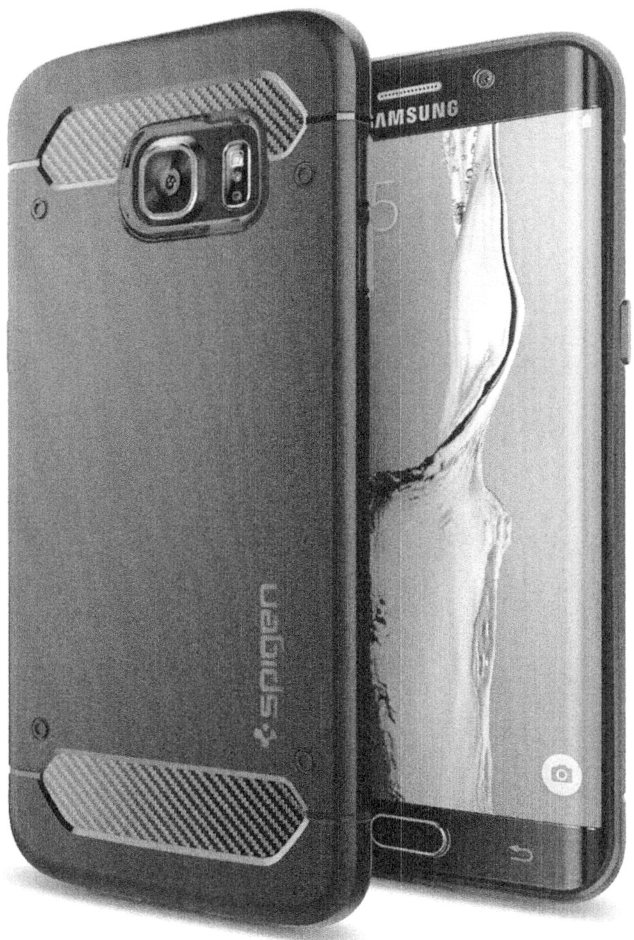

Sometimes you can find cases shaped like the Spigen but made of **hard plastic**. These are common on eBay and usually sell directly from Asia for 3-4 dollars shipped. However, I recommend TPU instead because of its grippy texture and because it won't crack.

Another alternative is the **S-View Flip Cover** ($55 street price), which provides more functionality but less protection. It flips open and closed like a book cover, and while closed, lets the Galaxy display information such as the time and date through the case.

Note 5: http://www.samsung.com/us/mobile/cell-phones-accessories/EF-ZN920CBEGUS

S6 Edge+: http://www.samsung.com/us/mobile/cell-phones-accessories/EF-CG928PWEGUS

If you want something really heavy duty, the **OtterBox Defender** ($50 street price) is a good solution. It provides *excellent* protection including a built-in screen protector. However, it's big—really big. It makes the Galaxy seem absolutely massive, actually. But the protection it offers is second-to-none. Plus, the word is that OtterBox is using a new formulation for the outer shell, making it tougher and more stretch-proof than ever before.

At the time of writing, the Defender is only available for the Note 5, but there is a slimmer OtterBox called the **Symmetry** ($50 street price) that provides tough protection for the S6 Edge+ while also showcasing its design.

Note 5 Defender: http://www.amazon.com/dp/B00Z7S0ZPU/

S6 Edge+ Symmetry: http://goo.gl/f1BEUL

Other types of cases are available but less common, such as belt holsters, pouches, kickstand cases, and even wooden cases. Amazon and eBay are good starting points to find something more unusual.

TIP: *The Note 5 and S6 Edge+ have different dimensions than previous Galaxy devices, so if you have cases for the Note 4, S6 Edge, etc., you won't be able to use them with your new Galaxy unless they're loose-fitting.*

Cables & Connectivity

Audio/Video Connectivity

To stream music, photos, and video from your Galaxy to your TV, you should purchase a Google Chromecast. It works amazingly well for wirelessly streaming all kinds of content—music, videos, and photos—and is only $35.

http://www.amazon.com/dp/B00DR0PDNE

Be aware that the Note 5 and S6 Edge+ are not compatible with common MHL-to-HDMI adapters, or older Samsung AllShare Cast devices.

TIP: *If you buy a Chromecast, make sure to pick up a copy of my book, Unlock the Power of Your Chromecast!*

http://www.amazon.com/dp/1494820609

Data Cables

The Galaxy S5 had a Micro USB 3 port, but the Note 5 and S6 Edge+ are back to the regular Micro USB 2 port that's found on almost all modern smartphones. I suggest using the included cable whenever possible, but any decent quality micro USB data cable will work. If you find that a micro USB cable is not making a data connection, it's possible that it's a cheap, charging-only cable. If you ever encounter this situation, just try another cable.

Also, consider picking up an inexpensive USB OTG cable to connect your Galaxy to flash drives, mice, keyboards, and more ($1.20 street price).

http://www.amazon.com/dp/B005GI2VMG/

Read more about USB OTG here (p. 291).

Headsets

The Note 5 / S6 Edge+ support both wired and Bluetooth wireless headsets. (Most carriers include a basic wired headset in the box.) Samsung sells a variety of both, although Amazon has a larger selection and lower prices. Learn how to pair a Bluetooth headset here (p. 234).

If you're looking for a basic Bluetooth headset, I recommend the Plantronics M50 ($50 street price).

http://www.amazon.com/dp/B005IMB5NG/

Batteries & Chargers

The Note 5 and S6 Edge+ are very power-hungry devices, yet at the same time their battery life is considerable. To accomplish this, they use power-efficient architecture with 3,000-mAh batteries, charged by a 2.0 amp charger with Adaptive Fast Charging technology. The included power brick is much more powerful than typical smartphone chargers and outputs far more current than any computer's USB port. For optimal charging times, you should always charge with the provided charger through a wall outlet. Note that generic 2.0 amp chargers from other devices will *not* charge as quickly as the stock charger with the Adaptive Fast Charging capability.

TIP: *The generic brand name for "Adaptive Fast Charging" is Quick Charge 2.0. Any charger labeled as Quick Charge 2.0 will charge your Galaxy as fast as the original Samsung charger.*

One downside of the Note 5 and S6 Edge+ is that they don't have removable batteries, so you can't pick up a spare like you could for previous Galaxy models. However, you can pick up a USB battery pack like this Choetech, which supports Quick Charge 2.0 and will recharge your Galaxy multiple times. I keep one in my backpack and it often comes in handy.

http://www.amazon.com/dp/B00ZCGLBT6/

Wireless Chargers

The Note 5 and S6 Edge+ have built-in support for industry standard Qi- and PMA-compatible wireless charging pads. Wireless charging isn't nearly as fast as wired Adaptive Fast Charging, but it's a lot more convenient on a desk. I have the following Anker charger ($20) and it works great:

http://www.amazon.com/dp/B00HIZ3ZI4/

If you're willing to shell out a little more ($70), you can pick up Samsung's new Fast Charge wireless pad, which is compatible with both the Note 5 and S6 Edge+. It charges your Galaxy about 40% faster than a standard charging pad.

http://goo.gl/iXZQoQ

Car Chargers

Any standard car charger with a micro USB connector will charge your Galaxy, but low-current chargers won't provide much juice. Go for a Quick Charge 2.0-compatible unit like this Powermod ($16 street price):

http://www.amazon.com/dp/B00P9UILUM/

Bluetooth Speakers

There is a new grade of cheap but effective standalone Bluetooth speakers that pair nicely with the Note 5 / S6 Edge+. Examples include the Oontz Angle Plus ($35 street price) and the DKnight Magicbox ($35 street price).

Oontz: http://www.amazon.com/dp/B00NC3SU6I/

DKnight: http://www.amazon.com/dp/B00F5NE2KG/

These units are about the size of a smartphone, but thicker. They're much more powerful you're your Galaxy's internal speaker, and have a battery life in the 10 hour range. These little speakers are great for when you need a little (or a lot of) extra volume. More expensive variants exist, like the Bose SoundLink Mini ($199 street price), but the price-to-performance ratio of the cheaper units is impressive.

Screen Protectors

There are countless brands of screen protectors, some of which are only a couple dollars per pack. However, I suggest springing for more than the bare minimum quality. The Note 5 and S6 Edge+ have some of the best screens of all time—why would you cover them up with a hazy screen protector?

My favorite protectors for the Note 5 are Spigen's Full HD PET ($10 street price). These are crystal clear and are a great value for the money.

Note 5: http://www.amazon.com/dp/B010MWD59I

For the S6 Edge+, try these curved Skinomi protectors. Note that some S6 Edge+ screen protectors do not cover the edges at all, so be careful if you purchase an alternate brand:

S6 Edge+: http://www.amazon.com/dp/B011M7ZTUA/

Vehicle Docks

Samsung sells a Universal Vehicle Navigation Mount for the Galaxy series ($30 street price), which is compatible with both the Note 5 and S6 Edge+. It's useful both improving hands-free access, and/or using your phone as your main GPS.

http://www.amazon.com/dp/B0089VO7HE

Another popular and cheaper option is the iOttie dashboard mount ($20 street price):

http://www.amazon.com/dp/B007FH716W/

Home Lighting

Have you heard of Philips Hue or LIFX bulbs? They're the two most popular Wi-Fi home LED lighting systems, and they're smartphone-controlled. Both systems' apps are compatible with the Note 5 / S6 Edge+, so there has never been a better time to get some fancy new lighting for your place. Both systems offer millions of colors including a full white spectrum, programmability and timers, and more. Find them on Amazon and read reviews on Google to determine which system is best for you.

Smartwatches

Smartwatches are becoming a big business. The Note 5 and S6 Edge+ is compatible with most of the major types, including Android Wear, Galaxy Gear with Tizen OS, Pebble, Sony, and more. You'll have to do your own research if you want to get the best watch for your purposes, but I personally own a Pebble, Android Wear, and a Sony Smartwatch 2 and I prefer the Pebble for its long battery life and to-the-point functionality.

Other Accessories

Other accessories include, but are not limited to:

NFC TecTiles 2: These are programmable RFID stickers. You can place them around your home, car, and office, and execute custom actions when you tap your Galaxy against them. The Note 5 and S6 Edge+ are only compatible with TecTiles 2. Read more about TecTiles here (p. 291).

Various Other Peripherals: Bluetooth keyboards, etc.

My Other Books

If you enjoyed this book, you might be interested in purchasing some of my other recent books.

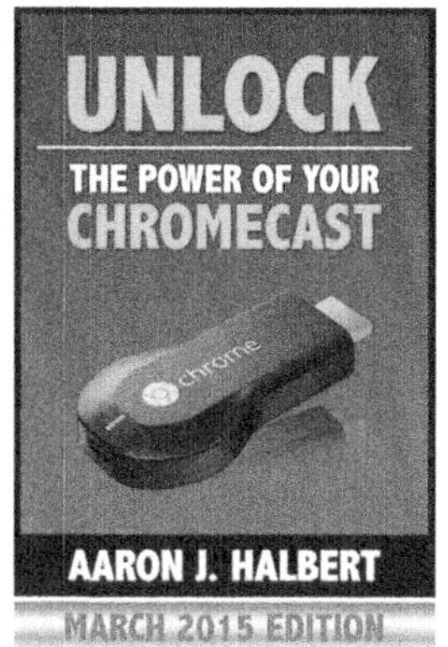

Unlock the Power of Your Chromecast

http://www.amazon.com/dp/1494820609/

Samsung Galaxy S6 and S6 Edge: The 100% Unofficial User Guide

http://www.amazon.com/dp/1511935421/

Samsung Galaxy Note 4: The 100% Unofficial User Guide

http://www.amazon.com/dp/1505391385/

Made in the USA
Coppell, TX
08 June 2021

57044614R10184